PENGUIN BOOKS

The Case of the Pope

Geoffrey Robertson QC is founder and head of Doughty Street
Chambers, the UK's largest human rights practice. He has appeared
in the courts of many countries as counsel in leading cases in
constitutional, criminal and international law and served as the first
President of the UN War Crimes Court in Sierra Leone, where he
authored landmark decisions on the illegality of recruiting child
soldiers, the legal limits of amnesties and the right of journalists
to protect their sources. He has led missions for Amnesty International and acted for Human Rights Watch in the Pinochet case.
His successful argument in the Privy Council case of *Pratt v
Jamaica* has secured the lives of hundreds of death-row prisoners.
He defended in the last two cases brought for blasphemy in Britain
(against Salman Rushdie and *Gay News*), represented Catholic
lawyers and youth workers detained without trial by Lee Kwan Yew
in Singapore and was counsel in *R v Ahluwalia* which established a
defence for provoked women and in *Bowman v United Kingdom,* which
struck down the electoral law inhibiting campaigns by Catholic
pressure groups.

He sits as a recorder and is a master of the Middle Temple and a
visiting professor of human rights law at Queen Mary College.
In 2008 he was elected by UN staff and then appointed by the UN
Secretary-General as a distinguished jurist member of the UN
Justice Council.

His books include *Crimes Against Humanity: The Struggle for Global
Justice* (Penguin), a memoir, *The Justice Game* (Vintage), and *The
Tyrannicide Brief* (Vintage), an award-winning study of the trial of
Charles I. The Report of his recent *Inquiry into the Massacre of Political
Prisoners in Iran* is available at http://www.iranrights.org/english/
document-1380.php.

By the same author

Reluctant Judas
Obscenity
People Against the Press
Geoffrey Robertson's Hypotheticals (Vols. I and II)
Media Law
Does Dracula Have Aids?
Freedom, the Individual and the Law
The Justice Game
Crimes Against Humanity
The Tyrannicide Brief
The Levellers: The Putney Debates
The Statute of Liberty

A PENGUIN SPECIAL

The Case of the Pope

Vatican Accountability for Human Rights Abuse

GEOFFREY ROBERTSON QC

PENGUIN BOOKS

PENGUIN BOOKS

Published by the Penguin Group
Penguin Books Ltd, 80 Strand, London WC2R ORL, England
Penguin Group (USA) Inc., 375 Hudson Street, New York, New York 10014, USA
Penguin Group (Canada), 90 Eglinton Avenue East, Suite 700, Toronto, Ontario, Canada M4P 2Y3
(a division of Pearson Penguin Canada Inc.)
Penguin Ireland, 25 St Stephen's Green, Dublin 2, Ireland (a division of Penguin Books Ltd)
Penguin Group (Australia), 250 Camberwell Road, Camberwell, Victoria 3124, Australia
(a division of Pearson Australia Group Pty Ltd)
Penguin Books India Pvt Ltd, 11 Community Centre, Panchsheel Park, New Delhi – 110 017, India
Penguin Group (NZ), 67 Apollo Drive, Rosedale, North Shore 0632, New Zealand
(a division of Pearson New Zealand Ltd)
Penguin Books (South Africa) (Pty) Ltd, 24 Sturdee Avenue, Rosebank, Johannesburg 2196, South Africa

Penguin Books Ltd, Registered Offices: 80 Strand, London WC2R ORL, England

www.penguin.com

First published 2010
1

Mussolini, painted by Diego Rivera, 1933, copyright © 2010 Banco de México Diego Rivera Frida Kahlo
Museums Trust, Mexico, D.F. / DACS

Set in 11/13 Bembo Book MT Std
Typeset by TexTech International
Printed in Canada by Webcom Inc.

ISBN: 978-0-241-95384-6

www.greenpenguin.co.uk

For my father

Preface

I wrote a short comment for the *Guardian* and the *Daily Beast* at Easter 2010, when Pope Benedict XVI was expected to (but did not) address the crisis in his church caused by revelations of worldwide clerical sex abuse. I pointed out that the rape and molestation of children, committed on a widespread and systematic scale, could amount to a crime against humanity, and that the leader of any organization that protects its perpetrators from justice might bear 'command responsibility' under international law. I further opined that the Pope's claim to impunity because he was head of a state, namely the Holy See – a claim recently made on his behalf by the Bush administration in US courts – was open to serious question: it relied on a squalid deal with Mussolini back in 1929 which bore no comparison to the grant of sovereignty to independent people. The UN had been wrong to accord to the Catholic Church a portentous status that is denied to all other religions and NGOs.

My views would doubtless have gone unremarked had not an enterprising sub-editor chosen to publish them under the headline 'Put the Pope in the Dock', a novel idea which immediately became an international news story. Soon Christopher Hitchens, an old friend who had sparked my interest in the subject, and Richard Dawkins and Sam Harris who supported it were dragged into what became, in an absurd tabloid splash, 'Plot to Have Pope Arrested'. So my original point was lost in sensation. It was that Popes are not immune from legal action and that unless the Vatican confronts its history of protecting paedophile priests and abandons its claim to deal with them under Canon Law, then its leader might well be sued for damages or end up as the subject of investigation by the prosecutor at an international court.

The fact is that tens of thousands of children throughout the world have been sexually abused by priests who have mostly been secretly dealt with by an ecclesiastical law that provides no real punishment and gives them ample opportunity to re-offend. Astoundingly, this has not been recognized as a human rights horror by the UN's ineffectual Committee charged with oversight of the Convention on the Rights of the Child, or by states like the US and UK that issue reports tracking serious human rights violations, or even by organizations like Amnesty International and Human Rights Watch. This may, in part, be a result of the good works done by so many Catholics and by Catholic aid organizations like Caritas and CAFOD, which I admire and to which I pay tribute at the outset. But it is also a consequence of the mistaken recognition of this religious organization as a state, with powerful diplomatic connections to governments and a beatific head to whom political leaders make pilgrimages in order to be blessed. The notion that this man of peace and moral principle could turn a blind eye to an international crime defies their belief.

But there is no doubt that the scale of the sex abuse scandal came about because of directives from the Vatican – specifically from the Congregation for the Doctrine of the Faith (CDF) – which required all sex abuse complaints to be processed in utter secrecy and withheld from local police and courts, under a Canon Law that was obsolete and ineffective and non-punitive. The Holy See claims the right to operate the system as one of its 'statehood' privileges, along with the exclusive right to speak and lobby at the UN to promote its theological agenda: homosexuality is 'evil', and so is divorce; women have no right to choose, even to avoid pregnancies that result from rape or incest; IVF is wrong because it begins with masturbation; condom use, even to avoid AIDS within marriage, must never be countenanced. The political power associated with statehood has proved beguiling for a Pope who, as Joseph Cardinal Ratzinger, was the Prefect (head) of the CDF from 1981 to 2005 and it was on his watch that a vast amount of the sex abuse took place. How much he knew of its extent, and how offenders were moved around parishes and trafficked to other countries and hidden from local criminal justice, will not be clear until the CDF is required to open its files, although enough evidence has emerged to make his moral responsibility – and that of John Paul II – a matter for anxious debate. His legal responsibility is complicated by his claim to sovereign immunity, but it is surely worth asking, at a time when Benedict XVI has set his face against essential reform, whether the Pope should be the one man left in the world who is above the law.

I am grateful, as ever, to my friend Mark Stephens for his encouragement and to the outstanding research and insight of Jen Robinson. My thanks for additional material to Matthew Albert, Lionel Nichols, Stephen Powles and Angela Giannotti, and to my PA Judy Rollinson. I am also grateful to Tina Brown for encouragment and to Caroline Michel, my agent, who inspired me to write the book, whilst Stefan McGrath and Will Goodlad at Penguin deftly arranged for its publication in record time and agreed to keep the numbered paragraphs in which, as a lawyer, I think and write. It is a great honour, in Penguin's seventy-fifth anniversary year, to be published as a *Penguin Special* – the first since 1989. Finally, my thanks to my wife, Kathy Lette, once a Catholic.

Doughty Street Chambers
9 August 2010

Diego Rivera captures a truth about the Lateran Treaty. The pro-Fascist Pope Pius XI blesses (with fingers crossed) the demagogue Mussolini, having stayed silent when his death squad murdered the courageous democrat MP Matteotti (below right).

Contents

1. Suffer the Little Children

Now that I have been in the Catholic Church nineteen years, I cannot recollect hearing of a single instance in England of an infidel priest . . . I am speaking of cases when a man keeps a fair outside to the world and is a hollow hypocrite in his heart.

John Henry Newman, Apologia Pro Vita Sua *(1865)*[1]

1. Every person is entitled to claim the right to religion, and to manifest it in community with others by 'teaching, practice, worship and observance'.[2] The corollary of this right – expressed in these words in the Universal Declaration and every Convention on human rights – is that churches must be free to propound the tenets of their respective faiths but always (and this is a condition explicitly imposed by all such Conventions) subject to laws necessary in a democracy to protect public interests and the rights and freedoms of others. Church leaders and personnel are not only subject, like everyone else, to the laws of the nation where they live, for breaches of which they can be prosecuted or sued for damages, but to international criminal law – a law under which some political and military leaders and several priests and nuns have been convicted and severely sentenced for crimes against humanity. The psychological influence over their followers that is entrusted to any priest is both potent and capable of abuse (dramatically illustrated in the video of Orthodox priests blessing Serb soldiers before they executed their innocent victims at Srebrenica). So spiritual office can provide no immunity: 'benefit of clergy' has long been abolished in Britain, where the first principle of the rule of law is that formulated by Dr Thomas Fuller in 1733: 'be you ever so high, the law is above you'. As Lord Bingham explains it, 'if you maltreat a penguin in the London

zoo, you do not escape prosecution because you are the Archbishop of Canterbury'.[3] How, then, can one religious leader be above all laws, whether national or international and whether civil or criminal? His Holiness the Pope, it is asserted by his followers and diplomats, is unaccountable as well as infallible, whether he were to maltreat a penguin on a visit to London Zoo or engage in hate-preach against homosexuals or to allow the Catholic Church to operate a worldwide sanctuary for child abusers.

2. This issue has arisen in the context of the evidence of clerical sex abuse which has emerged in court cases in the US (where court settlements so far exceed $1.6 billion); in official reports in the Republic of Ireland that sexual abuse of children by priests was widespread (one judicial report described it as 'endemic' in Catholic boys' institutes); and in similar patterns lately emerging in Europe and Australia and Canada. The facts, as church leaders admit with apologies that are now profuse, are shameful and scandalous. But they have consequences far beyond the reputational damage to the church. The evidence establishes that at the direction of the Vatican, wrongdoers were dealt with in a manner that protected them from exposure, silenced their victims, aided and abetted some to move on to commit further offences, and withheld evidence of their serious crimes from law enforcement authorities. In effect, the church has in many countries been running a parallel system of criminal justice, unbeknownst to and deliberately hidden from the public, police and parliaments, in which the guilty went unpunished and the lips of their victims were sealed – by forced oaths and confidential legal settlements. This alternative system of 'justice' was overseen for almost a quarter of a century by Cardinal Ratzinger (who in 2005 became Pope Benedict XVI); that so much wrongdoing happened on his watch raises serious questions about his competence as an administrator and a leader. Now he is the commander of the Vatican – in law, its absolute monarch – and he is head of the Holy See, which purports to be a sovereign state. Any grossly negligent leader can be fixed in international law with 'command responsibility' for crimes against humanity; most national crim-

inal laws make it an offence to conceal evidence of serious crime, and civil law has vicarious liability for those whose negligence has caused or contributed to human suffering. On what basis can it be said that the Pope and the Holy See can avoid investigation for these different forms of legal accountability?

3. The sexual abuse of children is an outrage – bad enough in ordinary cases of 'stranger danger' paedophilia, and worse when teachers or scout-masters or baby sitters or parents abuse the trust placed in them and molest their charges. But worst of all are priest offenders, who groom their victims in confessional or on retreats or otherwise through the spiritual power vested in them (often absolving the child after they have satiated their lust). Victims describe their assault as, quite literally, soul destroying – damaging their capacity for faith as well as the equilibrium of their future lives.[4] The evidence suggests that victims of clerical abuse take longer to heal, and are more likely not to heal at all, than others subjected to abuse as children, and the damage is aggravated when they are sworn by the church to 'pontifical secrecy' but know that their betrayer is forgiven and free to attack again. This is why the Vatican's responses to the child abuse scandal, from the time of its first major exposure by the *Boston Globe* in 2002, has been woeful, first in pretending that it was an entirely 'American' problem and then that its incidence in the church is no different from that in other organizations, then blaming 'gay culture' or media malice, and never – even today – facing up to the central fact that the church, for many years under the guidance of Cardinal Ratzinger at the CDF, had become a law unto itself, providing a concurrent system of secret proceedings under which abusive priests found forgiveness, victims were silenced and national law enforcement was frustrated.

4. The church's response, still echoed by those like Alan Dershowitz who defend the present Pope, is that hierarchical sex abuse occurs in all religious institutions and in secular schools, and it is wrong to 'stereotype' the Roman Catholic priesthood. But the evidence does reliably show a remarkedly higher level of abuse in Catholic

institutions (see Chapter 2), and in any event the defence misses the point, namely that this church, through its pretensions to be a state, with its own non-punitive Canon Law, has actually covered up the abuse and harboured the abusers. Moreover, this particular religion endows its priests with god-like powers in the eyes of children, who are put into their spiritual embrace from the time when they first develop the faculty of reasoning. By the age of 7, very often, Catholic children are taking communion – an awesome experience for them in which the priest performs before their eyes the trans-substantiation miracle of changing the bread and wine into the body and blood of Christ, through the authority given him by the sacrament of holy orders. Then, at the same age, the impressionable and nervous child is made to confess his sins – the priest, God-like, dispenses forgiveness. Father Tom Doyle explains the phenomenon of child obedience to a priest's sexual requests as induced by 'reverential fear': the victims have such emotional and psychological respect for the abuser that they cannot deny their requests. 'Catholics are indoctrinated from their childhood that priests take the place of Jesus Christ and are to be obeyed at all costs, and never questioned or criticized.' A church that puts its children from this early age under the spiritual control of its priests, representatives of God to whom they are unflinchingly obedient, has the most stringent of duties to guard against the exploitation of that obedience to do them harm. That duty includes the duty of handing over those reasonably suspected of child sex abuse to the secular authorities for trial and, if convicted, for punishment. It is this duty that Joseph Cardinal Ratzinger, a.k.a. Benedict XVI, has for the past thirty years adamantly refused to accept.

5. Everyone knows that subjecting a child to an act of sexual molestation is a crime deserving of punishment, irrespective of whether it is also a sin requiring penitence. Marooned on a deserted island in the middle of the Pacific Ocean, the mutineers of HMS *Bounty* and their descendants lived for almost two centuries without the benefit of a law book, yet the Privy Council (the highest court in the Commonwealth) had no doubt that the Pit-

cairn Islanders knew these acts were wrong: 'conduct of that kind cannot be regarded as other than criminal and deserving of punishment'.[5] Unless, that is, it was conduct committed by a Catholic priest, which the church has treated as a sin deserving only of penance, and has done its best to hide malefactors from the arrest, public trial and sentences of imprisonment that befell the Pitcairn Islanders and most other child molesters who are subject to public justice. What moral blindness has made a church renowned for its benevolence so reluctant to root out and punish all the child abusers in its midst, and even willing – as the evidence clearly shows – to move them on to greener pastures with unsuspecting flocks?

6. At a sociological level, these questions have only tentative answers, and it is not my purpose (or expertise) to explore them. Certainly, the commitment to celibacy and the church's condemnation of masturbation as a mortal sin sets up an unendurable tension for many priests, and senior churchmen have accepted that up to half are in some way 'sexually active'. This does not explain why so many – on some estimates, from 6–9 per cent – are sexually active with children.[6] The priesthood offers incomparable opportunity and spiritual power for paedophiles, and some have deviously infiltrated it, but most offenders appear to be psycho-sexually immature, often in denial about their condition and hoping that the rigours of the priesthood will protect them from themselves. Instead, they find a brotherhood, a sodality that closes ranks to protect them not from themselves but from the consequences of their actions, because the overriding philosophy of their superiors has been to avoid scandal to the church. This translates into a culture of ready forgiveness for sexual sins. Richard Sipe, a former priest turned psychiatrist, argues that the prevalence of masturbation in seminaries, and the ready forgiveness in confession, 'forms a cycle of guilt that binds clerics and confessors together wherein secret sexual transgressions become minimalized and trivialized – *even sex with minors becomes just another sin to be forgiven*'.[7] He reports that transgressing priests see themselves as privileged, and for their pains and their

poverty (many are genuinely kind and hard-working) feel 'entitled' to use children for their sexual release. He describes this culture as 'altruism in the service of narcissism': the good they do has a *quid pro quo*: self-gratification and self-aggrandizement. The eminent Catholic historian Gary Wills is inclined to agree: 'The infantilism of priests, the combined sexual inexperience and prurience resulting from celibacy, the belief that a celibate male is more attuned to spiritual reality than a married man – all this created a framework where sins, when they occurred, had to be denied, the victims had to be blamed, the solution to the problem was simply one of praying harder. Where therapy failed, the confessional would take the sinner with spiritual force beyond the worldly wisdom of psychiatrists.'[8]

7. However this may be, the plain facts that are now emerging show that sexual abuse of children by priests in the Catholic Church has been at a level considerably above that in any other organization, and that it has been covered up by many bishops with the support and at the direction of the Vatican. The cover-up has included an almost visceral refusal to call in the police, the swearing of complainants and witnesses to utter secrecy, and proceedings under a clandestine Canon Law biased towards the accused priest and in any event threatening no real punishment for the guilty. Transgressors likely to re-offend have been moved to parishes where their record is not known, or to different countries: some 60 per cent of US priests were 're-assigned' in this way after the first report that they were child abusers.[9] The 'traffic' of paedophile priests to and from the US, especially to Ireland, Mexico and Rome, is well authenticated, and there is emerging evidence of transferring them to parishes in Africa and Latin America where they have come under little or no scrutiny. No explanation has been forthcoming for why this was tolerated at the highest levels of the church, especially during the Papacy of John Paul II and the prefecture of Cardinal Ratzinger at the Congregation for the Defence of the Faith. Negligence, certainly, in turning a blind eye to the mounting crisis, and naïve prejudice in seeking to blame it on 'gay culture' or malicious

journalists, but something else seems to have been at work in 2001, when the Pope and his top cardinals agreed to congratulate a French bishop for hiding a paedophile priest from the police and then re-assigning him to offend again, and again in 2004 when the Pope brought to Rome and personally blessed a notorious sex offender who had founded a misogynistic religious order. These and other incidents demonstrate a certain arrogance in the exercise of the power of the statehood that has been vouchsafed to the Holy See – a power to live above the law and to flaunt the impunity that is associated with sovereignty. Whether one religious order alone is entitled to that power is a question that requires close examination.

8. Then, of course, there is the question of forgiveness or, more specifically, who should do the forgiving, and when? The sexual abuse of children is a serious crime, and whether or not it is a sin (as most serious crimes are) does not matter, on earth in any event. Forgiveness is generally reckoned to be the prerogative of victims, not of those who employed and tolerated their abusers. At the very least it is a right that belongs to the state, after the abuser has served the punishment that its courts have imposed. But the Catholic Church insists on forgiving its criminal priests when they have confessed and claimed to be repentant and said prayers or done a few charitable works, and that forgiveness has come with a determination to protect them from arrest and trial. The problem was highlighted by the Pope's apology to his Irish faithful in March 2010: while condemning the sin he could not bring himself to damn the sinners – thrice he told the perpetrators that forgiveness was theirs for the asking and praying and repenting. This is hardly a deterrent to weak men tempted to abuse children. A church which believes in the possibility of redemption for the worst of criminals, even those with a propensity to re-offend, is morally praiseworthy, but not when it protects them from trial and punishment under their national law and provides them with fresh opportunities to rape those who in law and fact are not capable of giving consent. The error of treating perpetrators of child sex abuse as sinners in need of

fatherly counsel, rather than as criminals deserving of punishment, compounded by the motive of protecting the church's reputation at any cost, has been buoyed by the belief that because the Holy See and its immune leader can do no wrong in the eyes of diplomatic law, they can do no wrong.

9.   There are few recorded instances of attempts to hold the Vatican itself, or its Pontiff, liable for the church practices of hiding paedophile priests, or covering up their crimes, or for moving them on to different parishes despite knowing of their predisposition to re-offend. In some countries there have been civil actions for damages against the direct employers of the offending priests, i.e. the bishops and their dioceses. These have mainly been settled by insurers, usually on 'hush money' terms which enjoin victims to perpetual silence in return for compensation. The payments have been considerable and in some cases massive (especially in the US with its class action suits), made by insurers for fear of the angry reaction of jurors not only to evidence of the abuse but also to the negligence and connivance of the church authorities. These settlements are unsatisfactory for many victims, because they do not provide the closure that comes from catching the 'big fish', i.e. holding the Vatican accountable for designing and directing the perpetrators' escape route through the parallel justice system of Canon Law. Moreover, some uninsured US dioceses have put themselves into bankruptcy so as to avoid paying heavy damages, hence victims have no option but to look to Rome for compensation. It is in this context that the Pope and the state-cum-church he heads (the Holy See) have been proposed as defendants in civil actions. But the US State Department has intervened, issuing a 'suggestion of immunity' (which is not a 'suggestion' at all, but a direction that American judges are bound to accept). Since the Holy See is a state, says this certificate, the Pope has 'head of state immunity': he can never be sued, nor prosecuted, and the Holy See has state immunity, which (with certain exceptions) removes its liability for civil wrongs.

10. This 'statehood' is attributed to the Holy See on the strength of its ownership of a block of land in Rome. It gives the Roman Catholic Church all sorts of advantages denied to other religions and to NGOs. Most significantly, the Holy See's status at the UN as the only 'non-member state' means it can do pretty much all that a state member can do, except vote. And its army of diplomats exploits this privileged status relentlessly, in UN conferences and agencies, to promote its dogmas – to the diminishment of women and divorced couples and the demonization of homosexuals. Statehood enables it to obstruct efforts to combat HIV/AIDS by promoting the use of condoms, and to condemn any family planning measures that smack of toleration of abortion (even to save the life of the mother) or IVF or artificial insemination or surrogate motherhood or embryo transfer or even pre-natal scans. The Catholic Church is fully entitled to advance these views, which accord with those of some Middle Eastern states (the Holy See is frequently in alliance at the UN with Libya and Iran), but it has no right to preferential treatment in doing so if it is not a state. That issue should be decided objectively, and not simply by the actions of nations which have, usually for domestic political reasons, sent diplomatic representatives to the Holy See and received papal *nuncios* in return. The Catholic Church must be answerable for the way it has sheltered paedophile priests: its pretensions to statehood should not give it immunity in international law nor in international affairs more than its due as one of a number of respected world religions.

11. The clerical sex abuse scandal has most visibly raised these issues, but there are other laws and other problems for political prelates who, for whatever theological reason, encourage viciousness or violence or discrimination within the community. Freedom of religion does not protect hate-preach, as some extremist mullahs have found when convicted at the Old Bailey. In 2009, a number of American evangelists and a Texas talkback host were barred from Britain for fear that they would stir up homophobia, and this year a religious eccentric was arrested in a city centre for

expressing the view to a passing policeman that homosexuality was wrong. Sensibly, the authorities decided not to pursue a prosecution: this was one oddball shouting 'fire' in an empty theatre. But Pope Benedict XVI is no voice in the wilderness. Were he to repeat in a public sermon his oft-stated view that homosexuality is 'evil' and gays are all people with defective personalities,[10] he would be using the full force of his spiritual office to vilify a section of the population protected by equality legislation and public order law. There is of course a line which should normally be drawn in favour of free speech, although the power of papal denunciation is far greater than that of banned Islamic and American evangelists even (in fact, especially) when expressed in decent language to religious congregations. If Pope Benedict XVI were to threaten to unleash the full force of views that have been accused of inciting 'macho muggings' of gays in Brazil and other Catholic countries, the Home Office could not, consistently with its decisions in other cases, permit his entry. But it would be inconceivable for the UK government to ban the Pope: on the contrary, they have invited him on a 'state visit', for which UK taxpayers must pick up half of the bill, currently estimated at £20 million – an imposition that could not be exacted were he not recognized as the head of a state. He will, it is said, emerge at Edinburgh from the papal plane resplendent in his 'head of state' robes ('a red satin manalatta trimmed with fur on top of a rochet, and wearing the embroidered Papal stole') for his meeting with a fellow head of state – Queen Elizabeth II (who must wear black – only Catholic queens can meet the Pope in white) and will reappear the next day in his more modest 'head of church' white robe to conduct a public mass. In the latter case, his vestments deserve respect, but in the former, it is time to point out that the emperor has no legal clothes.

12. The examination in this book has been triggered by recent revelations about the scale of the abuse of children by Catholic priests and the way in which complaints have been handled by the church, in light of Vatican instructions calculated to keep these crimes from the purview of civil law enforcement. I begin

with a summary of such facts as have been ascertained to date (August 2010) predominantly as a result of civil actions in the US and judicial inquiries in the Republic of Ireland, but with further information about church dealings with offenders in Australia, Canada and Europe. I then turn to the Vatican's claim to be immune from accountability for these offences in civil, criminal and international law, a claim which is heavily dependent upon its demand to be treated as a state with its own Canon Law rather than as the headquarters of a religion with no power other than to discipline its priests. Its immunity in respect to the legal actions over clerical child abuse turns on this issue. So does its extraordinary influence over international social policy by virtue of its unique position as a non-member state of the UN and hence enabled, unlike other religions and human rights organizations, to promote its dogmas at conferences and conventions and in countries where they are alleged to encourage discrimination against women and homosexuals and to handicap the fight against HIV/AIDS. Necessarily, the question of whether the Holy See is a 'Santa Claus state' (no matter how many believe in it, it does not really exist) requires some analysis of international law, a complex subject which I have tried to keep simple without becoming simplistic. I note that many Catholic NGOs support the denial of statehood to the Holy See, both as a matter of principle (the church should not involve itself in politics) and because of the practical results of inflicting its religious tenets on the organization of humanitarian aid. It goes without saying – although it needs to be said – that disbelief in the statehood of the Vatican does not imply any disbelief in God.

A Note on Terminology

13. Thus far I have used 'the Vatican' and 'the Holy See' (and sometimes 'the Pope') interchangeably. As will become clear when I turn to the statehood debate, they denote different legal entities. The Vatican is a territory of some 108.7 acres (1.2 square miles) in the

city of Rome, comprising little more than a palace with muse-ums, a big basilica and a large garden, which is 'home' only to the Pope and a shifting population of several hundred Catholic bureaucrats. It was given its special status in Italian law under the Lateran Treaty negotiated by Mussolini in 1929. The Holy See (from '*sedes*' – a seat, usually of bishops) is a much older, some-what metaphysical entity denoting the government of the Roman Catholic Church – by the Pope, the Curia and the body of cardinals and its own Canon Law, which provides rules for the administration of the church and its spiritual offices, and for tri-als of sins against the faith (heresy) and morals (sex abuses, including sex with minors). In past centuries the Holy See pos-sessed large European territories, fought wars and entered into diplomatic alliances, but the 'papal states' in central Italy were extinguished when the Italian army of the *Risorgimento* took Rome in 1870.

14. The Pope is a supreme commander – absolute ruler of the Vati-can and head of the Holy See, which has a 'secretary of state' – Cardinal Bertone – and before him Cardinal Sodano, currently Dean of the College of Cardinals – and a set of ministers and institutes which deal with subjects ranging from political ques-tions and diplomacy to liturgy and the appointment of bishops. The Holy See conducts diplomatic relations of some kind with 178 countries, although only one third of this number actually sends ambassadors to Rome. The Holy See maintains a network of diplomatic posts (*nunciatures*) and dispatches papal *nuncios* as ambassadors to countries with significant Catholic populations. The Pope is regarded as the last absolute monarch, serving until death, when the Curia meets in the Sistine Chapel to elect his successor (signalled by puffs of white smoke and the cry '*Habemus papam!*').

15. On its official website the Vatican describes itself as an 'absolute monarchy' in which the 'Head of State is the Pope, who holds full legislative, executive and judicial powers'.[11] He delegates the daily running of the Vatican to a Pontifical Commission of

Cardinals whom he appoints. Benedict XVI succeeded Pope John Paul II on 19 April 2005 – he was the well-known German conservative theologian Joseph Ratzinger, who worked as a priest for less than a year before taking up an academic career. He served as Bishop of Munich before coming to the Vatican in 1981, on his appointment as Prefect (i.e. head) of the Sacred Congregation for the Doctrine of the Faith (CDF). This office, of great significance in the child abuse scandal, was the successor to the Inquisition and is charged with the duty of disciplining the clergy: under Cardinal Ratzinger it excommunicated several supporters of 'liberation theology' and of the ordination of women. It is regarded as the single most powerful institution in the Vatican, operating as a Star Chamber without due process and since 2005 has been headed by Cardinal William Levada.[12] As well as dealing with heresy it oversees priests who sin against the 6th Commandment of the Decalogue ('You shall not commit adultery'), which under Canon Law includes the sexual abuse of persons under 18.

2. Sins of the Fathers

But if anyone causes one of these little ones who believe in me to sin, it would be better for him to have a large millstone hung aroung his neck and be drowned in the depths of the sea.

Matthew 18.6 (New International Version 1984)

16. All institutions which teach or guide young people must be alert to the danger that adults might abuse their trust. A religious organization which imposes celibacy upon its priests, and endows them with power of spiritual guidance and provides them with ample opportunities to influence young children, must be particularly alert. The leaders of the Roman Catholic Church have long been aware of the danger to children from clerics who were paedophiles, or unable to resist temptation as a result of lust or loneliness, drugs or personality disorder. The church suffered its first child sex scandal as long ago as 153 AD; its first law against abuse of boys by its clergy was passed at the Council of Elvira in 306 AD.[1] When Canon Law was codified in 1917 the abuse of children under 16 (the age is now 18) was specifically outlawed as a sin and five years later the church issued its first instruction on the Canon Law procedures and penalties for this offence. It was re-issued to all bishops in 1962 in the papal instruction *Crimen Sollicitationis* ('*Crimen*'). *Crimen* was revised in a Declaration promulgated by Cardinal Ratzinger, as Prefect of the CDF in 2001, and again in the 'New Norms' for grave offences – *de gravioribus delictus* – he published in 2010 as Benedict XVI.

17. Before, and certainly after, the Reformation the church had suffered endless ribald stories about the licentiousness of priests and nuns, a staple of both continental pornography and anti-clerical

Protestant propaganda. This did not focus particularly on child sex abuse (the age of consent had not been fixed), although England's first anti-buggery laws were directed by Henry VIII against Catholic priests. Centuries later, the Nazi regime in Germany kept the Catholic church in line by threatening prosecutions of clerical child molesters and cartoons about paedophile priests would feature in 'Hitler Youth' magazines. But after the war the problem seemed to vanish: very few cases of clerical sex abuse were dealt with in public courts around the world for the next half century, in what we now know were times and places where it was widespread. A warning – delivered personally to Pope Paul and by correspondence to various Vatican officials and bishops in the 1950s and 1960s – came from Reverend Gerald Fitzgerald, founder of 'the Servants of the Paraclete' which treated erring priests under the rubric 'priests help priests'. He told the Pope that sex abuse was on the increase ('several seminaries have been deeply affected'), that it was incurable and that it would become 'devastating to the standing of the priesthood'. His recommendations (that novices should be carefully screened for sexual problems; that some priests should be permitted to marry, that there should be a strict rule that abusers must be defrocked and instructions issued to all priests that 'mutual masturbation is a mortal sin') were ignored, and his letters only emerged in 2007, in a law suit in New Mexico where he had founded the Paraclete order. It was typical of the time that the Bishop of Manchester could write secretly to the Order about a 'problem priest' involved in 'a series of scandal-causing episodes with young girls' and conclude that 'the solution to his problem seems to be a fresh start in some diocese where he is not known'.[2] In desperation Fitzgerald suggested that the Vatican acquire a Caribbean island to which its paedophile priests might be exiled, but the growing tourist trade in the selected sanctuary (Caricou) made this proposal unrealistic as well as unwanted. The Vatican and its bishops turned a deaf ear to Fitzgerald, ignoring his warnings (delivered as early as 1952) that 'leaving them [paedophile priests] on duty or wandering from diocese to diocese' would mean 'the proximate danger of scandal'.

The US Cases

18. That scandal welled up for half a century, behind a wall of 'pontifical secrecy' which protected clerical sex criminals from exposure and arrest, until the dam burst in Boston in 2002. It began with a banner headline in the *Boston Globe* of 6 January 2002:

   CHURCH ALLOWED ABUSE BY PRIEST FOR YEARS
   Since the mid 1990s, more than 130 people have come forward with horrific childhood tales about how former priest John Jay Geoghan allegedly fondled or raped them during a three decade spree through half a dozen Boston parishes. Almost always, his victims were grammar school boys. One was just four years old.

19. In a series of exposés, the *Boston Globe* reported (and church documents later confirmed) that Cardinal Bernard Law and his senior churchmen had been well aware that a number of their priests were molesting young boys, and had done nothing about the complaints of their victims other than to transfer the priests to different parishes where their propensity was unknown. Law himself was transferred to the Vatican so he would be safe from public anger and police investigations, and made pastor of a large Basilica – a position of honour instead of shame – and was further honoured by being chosen to preside at a mourning mass for John Paul II. Meanwhile, his church back in Boston had to pay over $100 million in damages for the negligence and callousness that had characterized his reign. Throughout the nation, victims of sex abuse who had stayed silent for years, often decades, plucked up the courage to tell journalists and lawyers, and civil actions for negligence against bishops and their dioceses proliferated, culminating in a massive $660 million settlement of a class action by the Archdiocese of Los Angeles, where police inquiries are continuing.[3] The incredible insouciance of senior churchmen is captured in Appendix A, which provides just one example of how a known paedophile was given every opportunity (which he took) to molest young boys in Californian parishes for

15 years after he had told Cardinal Mahony that he had abused young boys.

20. It also emerged that William Levada – appointed by Pope Benedict in 2005 to succeed him as Prefect Cardinal of the CDF – had been made aware by church lawyers of the danger of paedophile priests as early as 1985, but had done nothing. As Bishop of Portland, he had so mishandled abuse cases that his archdiocese was plunged into bankruptcy from which it could only emerge when it raised the money to pay a $75 million settlement. Other dioceses – including Spokane, Washington, Tucson and Arizona – have resorted to bankruptcy to shield themselves from child abuse lawsuits, thus providing an incentive for victims to sue the Holy See instead, the entity to which the bishops had paid contributions and from which they have received instructions as to how they should deal with 'problem' priests.[4] The total bill for sex abuse is spiralling towards $2 billion (not including legal fees) and continues (given the protracted nature of negligence claims in the US) to rise – to an eventual $5 billion, so *Forbes* magazine predicts. Although most law suits settled, the depositions taken on video from senior churchmen in some cases survived, and were used to devastating effect by Amy Berg in her 2007 Oscar-nominated documentary, *Deliver us from Evil*. It featured one paedophile priest, Father Oliver O'Grady, telling how he had been moved through five Californian parishes in a career of raping children; their testimony was harrowing and was juxtaposed with his, amoral and entirely lacking in insight. The most moving scenes (because they moved to anger) were clips from the depositions of senior churchmen, arrogantly excusing their own conduct.

21. The American media has exposed sex abuse scandals in almost every state of the Union.[5] There was a pattern of turning a blind eye to complaints against priests unless or until public scandal threatened. Then, the priest would be withdrawn, sent for counselling or therapy, then re-assigned to a different parish where no-one was told of his offence and so no close watch was kept on him lest he re-offend. Often the priests were assigned as hospital

chaplains (even in children's hospitals) and those with academic ability were enrolled in universities to study Canon Law, so they could return and participate in canonical trials where they would be responsible for investigating allegations of sex abuse against other priests. Bishops had a predilection for naively accepting far-fetched defences: when a witness (a fellow priest) observed a colleague 'straddling a kneeling 15-year-old altar boy in a dark rectory room', Archbishop (now Cardinal) Levada accepted that this was 'horseplay and wrestling'. He suspended the witness instead of the 'wrestler', whose later confession to the truth cost the archdiocese $750,000 in damages. Another priest who spread-eagled boys and photographed them naked convinced his bishop that he was helping them learn 'how Christ felt through humiliation and physical pain'. A cardinal in Chicago dismissed complaints as 'horseplay that could have been misinterpreted', whilst a priest caught tightly embracing a young boy in a beach house might have been 'merely hugging'. Bishops later blamed their own ignorance about paedophiles to explain why they looked the other way ('you send them on a retreat, they come back, you send them on another assignment'). Reasons for not reporting abusers to police ranged from 'at the time, I didn't even think to report them', to 'the gospel teaches reconciliation. We believe in forgiveness', or to the more honest 'with our shortage of priests, I can't risk not ordaining him'. In Idaho, a bishop urged a colleague in England to hire a priest who had molested an 8-year-old boy, because the child's brother had threatened to go to the police and the priest 'is in jeopardy of arrest and possible imprisonment if he remains here'.

22. In New York, bishops sent confessed molesters to Africa instead of to gaol. Recent investigations have indicated a traffick in paedophile priests to and from the US with Ireland, Rome, Mexico and Africa. (In May 2010, Associated Press published thirty such examples and they continue to mount as cases of paedophiles trafficked from Europe to Africa come to light.) All this was done – or was meant to be done – with the approval of the CDF, which under *Crimen* had to be informed of all these cases,

and sometimes with the connivance of the *nuncio*, sent by the Vatican to keep an eye on local bishops and priests. In Cleveland, a bishop who was also a lawyer has been accused of advising other church lawyers to remove documents from the personal files of suspected priests when he told a meeting of bishops: 'If there's something you really don't want people to see, you might send it off to the apostolic delegate [the *nuncio* at the Holy See's Embassy in Washington] because they have immunity.' This is an important issue: diplomatic immunity can sometimes be a cover for crimes by diplomats – but by priests?

23. Early in the mounting scandal, the Catholic Bishops Conference in America proposed a 'zero tolerance' strategy, which would include reference of accusations to the police, and greater use of laicization (defrocking) for guilty priests. This was vetoed by the Vatican, on the grounds that it was unfair on priests who were entitled to all the defence rights afforded by a full Canon Law trial. Its cardinals were scathing about the idea that bishops should report suspects to the police. 'If a priest cannot confide in his bishop for fear of being denounced then it would mean that there is no more liberty of conscience,' said Tarcisio Bertone, the second in command at the CDF and now second in command (Secretary of State) to Benedict XVI. He rejected, hyperbolically, 'the demand that a bishop be obligated to contact police to denounce a priest who had admitted paedophilia'. Cardinal Castrillon Hoyos defended the church's preference for 'keeping things in the family'. Archbishop Hemanz announced that such a rule would 'damage the presumption of innocence' (how, he did not explain) and Cardinal Rodríguez expostulated that it was akin to Stalinist persecution, before moving his metaphor Westwards – 'we are pastors, not agents of the FBI or CIA . . . I'd be prepared to go to gaol rather than harm one of my priests'. Cardinal Bravo of Nicaragua, quite staggeringly, likened victims to Potiphar's wife – driven to lie by pleasure, spite, and unrequited love – 'we are dealing with presumed victims who want to gain large pay offs on the basis of calumnious accusations'.[6] These voices from the Vatican in 2002 – Cardinal Ratzinger's too was

raised against the 'manipulated' and 'planned' campaign in the US press ('less than one per cent of priests are guilty') – show the extent to which arrogance and ignorance alike had affected members of the Curia. They regarded the scandal as 'an American problem', caused not by paedophile priests or the negligent indulgence of bishops and the CDF in Rome, but by sensational US journalism, American tort law and tort lawyers, and 'gay culture' within the church. The Holy See did however sponsor an expert conference on paedophilia in 2003, which reported (to the surprise and disbelief of some of its officials) that there was no causal link between a priest being a homosexual and being a sexual abuser.[7] (This finding has been ignored: as recently as Easter 2010, Bertone was publicly blaming the child sex scandal on homosexual infiltration of his clergy.)

24. Faced with this unfolding crisis, it is to the credit of the US Catholic Bishops Conference that in 2002 it decided to commission an objective study of the problem. It retained a group of respected criminologists from the John Jay College of Criminal Justice in New York to conduct a comprehensive review, and their report, published in 2004, drew some very disturbing conclusions. It recorded that since 1950, no fewer than 10,667 individuals had made plausible allegations against 4,392 priests – 4.3 per cent of those active in the period.[8] These bare figures are almost certain to be an underestimate (the church now accepts 5.3 per cent and others claim the true figure could be 6–9 per cent): the study had no compulsive powers or even confidential access to parish records and was reliant upon information made available to it voluntarily by church authorities – some not competent at record keeping. But on any view, the falsity of Ratzinger's claim of 'less than one per cent' had been conclusively demonstrated.

25. The report notes the 'time bomb' nature of child sex abuse – many of its victims are so damaged that it takes them years – even decades – to come to terms with it sufficiently to speak out.[9] Only 13 per cent of allegations were made in the year of the crime and 25 per cent were not made until thirty years afterwards. This

means the church will face allegations for many years to come. It also means – and this is an important matter in providing justice for victims – that the time limits on prosecution which exist in many countries will enable many abusers, when belatedly exposed, to evade criminal trial. Virtually all countries have time limits for actions in tort (that branch of civil law which allows victims injured by assaults or through negligence to sue for damages) and these deadlines – six years in most common law jurisdictions – are apt to bar many victims from obtaining compensation. It means that the Canon Law time limits for taking action against paedophile priests (ten years from the victim's eighteenth birthday) have also been unrealistic and unfair – a point partly conceded by the Pope in July 2010, when they were extended to twenty years, but not – as justice requires – abandoned altogether.

26. The study showed that the vast majority of the Catholic Church's abusive priests were ordained before the late 1970s (thus putting paid to Benedict's claim that 'the gay culture' of the 1980s and 1990s was to blame) and many had multiple victims or had abused victims over a long period of time. Most victims were between the ages of 11 and 14 (16 per cent were 8 to 10 and 6 per cent were under 7) and the great majority – 81 per cent – were boys. Sex acts ranged from masturbation to oral sex practices and buggery, and were usually committed at the parish residence or in the church or the church school. Grooming tactics included emotional intimidation and 'spiritual manipulation' (for example promises of absolution) and even blackmail (threats of damnation and hellfire if 'our secret' is revealed can be a potent threat to young children when made by a priest – although for most youngsters trained to see him as the agent of God, 'you can trust me, you won't go to hell because I'm a priest' – procures a nervous obedience). Abusive clerics generally had a personality disorder, and some were paedophiles, others ephebophiles (who harbour a predatory sexual attraction to teenagers). The John Jay College in a later study concluded that homosexuality of itself was not a factor in their offending, and other studies associate the character disorder with mandatory celibacy, which can lead to loneliness,

depression, low self-esteem, alcoholism and frustrated sex drive. (This conclusion has been resisted by the Vatican ever since 1139, when the Lateran Council voted to impose a vow of chastity, despite the prescient warning from one of its bishops that 'when celibacy is imposed, priests will commit sins far worse than fornication. They will seek sexual release wherever they can find it.'[10])

27. The truly shocking finding was that 76 per cent of child sex abuse allegations made against priests had never been reported to law enforcement authorities.[11] Only 6 per cent of accused priests had been convicted, and a mere 2 per cent had received prison sentences (a non-custodial sentence for child abuse usually reflects 'good character' evidence provided by the church). The minimal number of priests convicted may in part be attributable to victim delays in reporting offences: in many US states charges could not be laid because of time bars erected by statutes of limitation. There was evidence of church 'transfer' of some re-offenders – 143 priests had been accused in more than one diocese. Incredibly, only 6 per cent of priests were defrocked by the Canon Law process called 'laicization' – the conversion from an ecclesiastical to a lay condition – and a further 21 per cent simply had their ministry restricted (for example they were barred from saying mass for a period, or from supervising altar boys). Some resigned or retired with their reputations unblemished but most of those credibly accused had been 'referred for evaluation' or sent on a spiritual retreat, often to the Paracletes in New Mexico, although this order has never claimed that its treatment 'worked' for paedophiles. In cases (1,872 of them) where the plausible allegation had been fully substantiated, only 1 per cent were excommunicated and only 6 per cent were laicized: 29 per cent were allowed to resign or retire, 10 per cent were merely reprimanded and 53 per cent were 'sent for treatment'. It is not clear what the treatment entailed: according to the Archbishop of Los Angeles, in this period it was widely believed that counselling would be sufficient. Chemical castration (MPH or Deprovira) was available but rarely used. Behavioural therapy, which seeks to make the offender recognize the shamefulness of his conduct

and empathize with victims, can be helpful, but it was well known that in many cases it fails to prevent recidivism.

28. The John Jay study was important in establishing the scale of child abuse, all the more because its statistics probably underestimate the problem, and in refuting the public claim made by Cardinal Ratzinger in 2002 that less than 1 per cent of the priesthood was involved, and the confident assertion of Cardinal Castrillon Hoyos, Prefect of the Congregation of the Clergy, that the problem was 'statistically minor . . . less than 0.3 per cent of priests are paedophiles'.[12] It named no names, although the newspapers soon did, identifying leading figures in the US church as having turned a blind eye and pointing at the Vatican as the source of their authority for so doing. The worst case involved the rape and buggery of 200 deaf boys in Wisconsin over a period of twenty years by Father Lawrence Murphy. His bishop refused to act on victim complaints until eventually – many victims later – the church began a secret canonical process and in 1996 notified the CDF – the relevant Vatican office, headed by Cardinal Ratzinger. He took no action (he was worried about the risk of 'increasing scandal' and so emphasized 'the need for secrecy') until the priest became terminally ill, whereupon Ratzinger ordered the Canon Law trial to end so that the priest, whom he knew to be guilty, could die as a respected member of his brotherhood. Another shocking case occurred in 1981 when the Bishop of Oakland urgently recommended Father Stephen Kiesle to the CDF for defrocking after he had actually been convicted in a criminal court for tying up and molesting two young boys in a San Francisco monastery. Ratzinger, by then its Prefect, procrastinated for four years, despite anxious and repeated requests, for fear of provoking what he described as 'detriment within the community of Christ's faithful'. Because of the priest's 'youth' – he was 38 – he was allowed to continue to work with children. He was convicted again in 2004 for molesting a young girl, after earlier prosecutions for his abuse as a priest had been debarred by a statute of limitation.[13] Ratzinger's signature on a 1985 letter, in which he placed 'the good of the universal church'

above the need to remove this incorrigible child rapist, was published by the press in 2010 and implicated the Pope in covering up the sexual abuse of children while he was head of the Vatican office responsible for dealing with it.

29. It may be that throughout this period (and until very recently) the Vatican perceived or chose to perceive clerical sex abuse as only 'an American problem' – so Pope John Paul II had previously described it to *Time Magazine*.[14] His spokesman queried whether 'the real culprit is a society that is irresponsibly permissive, hyper-inflated with sexuality that can induce even people who have received a solid moral formation to commit grave immoral acts'.[15] In time, this defence would morph into a different kind of blame shift, to another aspect of American society – its sensational press reporting and its ambulance-chasing tort lawyers. As late as April 2010, Cardinal Levada was appearing on PBS *Newshour* to pin the blame on unfair reporters from the *New York Times*, fed with information by plaintiffs' attorneys.[16]

The Republic of Ireland

30. But this defensive reaction – to blame terrible sex abuse by Catholic priests on permissive America and its newspapers and attorneys – could not survive the evidence from three judicial inquiries into the church in the Republic of Ireland, where it turns out that molestation in Catholic Boys' Institutions, Reformatories and Orphanages has been 'endemic'. That was the conclusion of a High Court Judge, Justice Sean Ryan, when he delivered a massive five-volume report after nine years of interviews with thousands of victims, teachers and officials. The Ryan report established that these institutions, mainly run by the Christian Brothers, had policies which actually encouraged the abuse of thousands of children. When confronted with evidence against paedophile priests, bishops simply transferred them to other parishes, where many re-offended. Victims who complained

were silenced by being forced to take secrecy oaths. Police (the *guardai*) were not interested in investigating priests, whom they automatically trusted. Even Canon Law (which provides a church trial for sex abuse allegations) was ignored by the church authorities. This was despite the point made by an earlier judicial inquiry into abuse in the Diocese of Ferns, which accused the church of 'failing to appreciate the horrendous damage which the sexual abuse of children can and does cause. The Inquiry was struck by the hurt still borne by mature and fair-minded victims who gave evidence before it'.[17]

31. The Ryan report established that sexual abuse, ranging from erotic fondling to violent rape, was systemic in boys' institutions and occasional in girls' schools.[18] These cases were 'arranged with a view to minimizing the risk of public disclosure and consequent damage to the institution and the congregation. This policy resulted in the protection of the perpetrator.' It was clear that the bishops were aware of the propensity of abusers to re-offend, but they were concerned about 'the potential for scandal and bad publicity should the abuse be disclosed. A danger to children was not taken into account.'[19] There was a 'culture of silence'. Some abusers were released to work in state schools where they continued to molest children. The police were not told.[20] Children with learning disabilities, orphans and those with physical or mental impairment were particularly vulnerable to vicious or lecherous priests, and their suffering makes for harrowing reading. What became almost unendurable to many Catholics in Ireland was the revelation that church leaders had participated in silencing the victims – sometimes by going so far as to extract oaths of secrecy from small children in what must have been intimidating ceremonies. Cardinal Brady, Catholic Primate of Ireland, swore two teenagers to secrecy in 1975 after they had made true accusations against Father Brendan Smyth, who abused over 100 children in the course of his career: Brady is considered by some to have acted dishonourably by refusing to resign when his conduct, albeit as a church official many years before, came to light.[21] (Although in August 2001 the Pope refused to accept the resignations of two

Irish auxiliary bishops, signalling the Vatican's truculence – and perhaps its contempt for meaningful apologies.)

32. A second report, later in 2009, was even more devastating, especially in respect of Vatican responsibility. A tribunal chaired by Judge Murphy analysed the cases of forty-six paedophile priests who had, between them, abused thousands of children. It examined the secret church files relating to these men and established that the Archbishop did not report them to police, preferring to avoid public scandal by moving them to other parishes. The Commission concluded that, as early as 1987, church leaders were well aware of the risk to children, because in that year they cynically took out insurance policies to cover the legal costs of defending future compensation claims. In 2009, the Irish government issued a public statement: the Murphy report 'shows how clearly a systematic, calculated perversion of power and trust was visited on helpless and innocent children'. (As we shall see, an attack which includes rape and sexual slavery directed against innocent children on a widespread scale through abuse of power can amount to a crime against humanity.) Judge Murphy concluded:

> The Dublin Archdiocese's preoccupations in dealing with cases of child sexual abuse, at least until the mid-1990s, were the maintenance of secrecy, the avoidance of scandal, the protection of the reputation of the church, and the preservation of its assets. All other considerations, including the welfare of children and justice for victims, were subordinated to these priorities. The Archdiocese did not implement its own Canon Law rules and did its best to avoid any application of the law of the state.[22]

33. The importance of the Murphy report was not only that it found that clerical child abuse was covered up, but 'the structures and rules of the Catholic Church facilitated that cover up'.[23] It partly blamed the state, for 'allowing the church institutions to be beyond the reach of normal law enforcement process' but recognized that the church itself, as controlled by the Canon Law of the Vatican, had protected its most important members (i.e. its priests) from prosecution, to avoid scandal and to protect its assets should it be sued. It had no regard for victims, whose

complaints were met 'with denial, arrogance and cover up and with incompetence and incomprehension in some cases'.[24] The Irish bishops and their senior advisors were culpably irresponsible in refusing to report priests to the police, even when they knew they were guilty of serious crime, although that was part of a mindset (that confidentiality should be preserved at all costs) and this mindset had derived from the Vatican's Canon Law rules. The Commission wrote repeatedly to the CDF in Rome seeking information about these rules. The Vatican did not reply, but arrogantly complained to the Irish Foreign Ministry that, since the Holy See was a sovereign state, it should only receive communications from states, and not from judicial commissions (this is a good example of the pettiness which 'statehood' can induce). The Commission then wrote – repeatedly – to the papal *nuncio*, Giuseppi Lazzarotto, who quite disgracefully refused to extend even the courtesy of a reply. (He was severely criticized in the Murphy Report and then in the Press and parliament, but by then he had moved to become the papal *nuncio* to Australia.) One Irish cardinal (Connell) who had served on the CDF under Ratzinger for twelve years also refused to give the Commission any assistance, because he had taken an oath of secrecy never to reveal its workings.

34. Notwithstanding this truculence, which denied the Commission any access to Vatican files or any information about its dealings with sex abuse in Ireland, Judge Murphy was able to examine the statutes and rules that had been laid down by Rome in the form of Canon Law (which only the Pope can change) and Papal Decrees. The Commission established that the procedures for dealing with child sex abuse were first promulgated (in Latin) in 1922 and reaffirmed to all bishops in 1962 in the decree *Crimen Sollicitationis* (also in Latin), a decree so secret that it was kept from the church's lawyers and was not published until 2003, after it had been leaked to a plaintiff's lawyer in America. It provided the rules for the inquisitorial system under Canon Law, and it ensured that everyone in the process (including the accuser) was sworn to secrecy and that nothing – even cases which resulted in conviction at trial – could be made public or even made known

confidentially to the police. A further instruction from the Vatican under Cardinal Ratzinger's hand, entitled *Sacramentorum sanctitatus tutela* was issued in May 2001, requiring that all credible allegations of sex abuse (having 'a semblance of truth' – i.e. there was a *prima facie* case) must be referred to the CDF's office in Rome. There Cardinal Ratzinger, as its Prefect, would advise the bishop on how to deal with the case, or alternatively could decide to deal with the matter himself. This was said to be intended to provide uniformity in dealing with such allegations throughout the Catholic world, but since they were still dealt with in utter secrecy neither the Catholic nor the rest of the world was much the wiser, and there were of course lengthy delays taking many cases beyond the time limits of national laws.

35. Astonishingly (and the Murphy Commission was duly astonished) it transpired that under Canon Law, the fact that an accused priest was a paedophile actually amounted to a defence, since paedophilia might produce uncontrollable impulses which were not blameable under ecclesiastical law. Murphy found that two priests 'convicted' by church courts for serial abuse of children had been successful in their appeal to Ratzinger, probably because the CDF had applied this Canon Law defence. It was, the Commission reported, a matter of 'grave concern' that Canon Law should stray so dramatically from the law of the land, which expects paedophiles to control their urges to molest small children and provides no defence when they fail. Moreover the law in Ireland, as in the UK, has no time bars for serious offences. Until 2001 Canon Law barred proceedings more than five years after the alleged offence (this was extended to ten years by Ratzinger's 2001 decree, to run from the eighteenth birthday of the victim, and is now twenty years). In consequence of these differences, abusive priests who would have been gaoled under common law were not even investigated under the law that the church, as instructed by the Vatican, operated exclusively in a parallel system of secret justice. This parallel law, unlike most national laws, is additionally defective because it places no duty upon those aware of abusive priests – and many fellow priests

and Catholic lay officials do become aware of them – to report them to police. This obstruction of criminal justice is furthered by the fact that Canon Law penalties (for example orders to pray or do penance or to minister only to adults) were 'virtually unenforceable' and that the pastoral approach of ordering treatment for paedophiles was 'wholly ineffective'. The penalty of removing priests from their ministry, even when it was applied, still allowed them to meet and molest youths in social or secular circumstances. In consequence, Murphy concluded that 'the abuse of children in Dublin is a scandal. The failure of the archdiocesan authorities to penalize the perpetrators is also a scandal.'[25]

Other Countries: The Pattern

36. These scandals in Ireland in 2009, after the scandals in the US since 2002, were followed in 2010 by scandals throughout Europe. In Germany an inquiry into a Jesuit order discovered that fifty priests had abused over 200 children in their school care.[26] It turned out that Pope Benedict himself, when Bishop of Munich, had approved the transfer of a known paedophile priest, Peter Hullermann, to another parish without reporting him to police even after he continued to molest boys – his subsequent offences in his new parish would probably not have been committed had Bishop Ratzinger reported him to the authorities.[27] The Bishop of Bruges suddenly resigned after admitting having molested a youth in a way which had 'marked the victim forever'. (The bishop had saved himself from being marked forever by the law: he waited to confess his crime until after the ten-year limitation period had elapsed, and then only after his victim had began to tell other people.) Meanwhile in Norway, Archbishop Mueller had been allowed by Pope Benedict to resign, after admitting to abusing a 12-year-old altar boy in the early 1990s – a crime that had been hushed up by a confidential compensation payment and had not been reported to the police until (yet again) the statute of limitation had expired. An even worse case was that of Austrian

Cardinal Groer, who had molested an estimated 2,000 boys in his twenty-year passage to a bishopric, during which time he was protected by John Paul II, who even permitted him to retire without punishment and to be hidden for his last years in a nunnery, after his criminal behaviour became public. Some of his victims were paid 'compensation' in return for keeping quiet about this massive scandal, which had taken place on Ratzinger's watch at the CDF in the 1980s and 1990s. The Prefect and the Pope were also told in 2000 that Polish Archbishop Julius Z. Paetz was abusing trainee priests: they ignored this information at the time and did not ask Paetz to resign until the truthful allegations became public, several years later.

37. European scandals may in time pale by comparison to eventual revelation of the liberties priests have taken with children in the developing world, especially in countries in Latin America and Africa, where no official investigations have yet been conducted and where many abusive priests have been sent to operate with little or no supervision. In May 2010 the first reports were published of intensive trafficking of child-molesting priests from Germany, Italy, Ireland and the US to Nigeria, South Africa, Mozambique and the Congo. The head of the South African Bishops Conference admitted that 'the misbehaviour of priests in Africa has not been explored in the same glare of the media as in other parts of the world', and complained that the continent had been sent priests who were 'wolves wearing sheepskin'. Meanwhile Pope Benedict was meeting African bishops in the Vatican and preaching to them about the evils of divorce.[28]

38. In Latin America too, the scandals began to emerge, none worse than the dreadful case of Father Marcial Maciel Degollado ('Father Maciel'), a Mexican priest who had founded a reactionary clerical order. He was a good friend of Pope John Paul, who blessed him in the Vatican in 2004 despite his long and notorious history of child sex abuse and his fathering of several children (whom he also abused). The following year, Pope Benedict invited him to lead 'a reserved life of prayer and penance' – an invitation

presented, in the twisted logic of the Vatican, as a 'punishment', although it did not amount to defrocking, let alone to a criminal penalty (see also para 184).[29]

39.   Commenting on these and other high profile cases exposed by the media in 2010, Benedict's supporters blamed Pope John Paul II, notwithstanding that he is due to be beatified shortly, but the fact remains that Cardinal Ratzinger, as head of the CDF and the Pope's potential successor throughout the period, shares responsibility for the cover up. In April 2010 Benedict made one symbolic gesture – on a visit to Malta he met privately with victims of abusive priests, of whom fifty had been identified out of the 850 clergy on the island. One victim told the press he had been abused since the age of 10 by a priest who 'woke me with a kiss often with his tongue in my mouth and then masturbated me' and then conducted an early morning mass giving the boy the Host with the hand that had just fondled him. This priest, like other clerical abusers in Malta, has now been banned from saying mass but is being harboured in a local monastery, safe from criminal prosecution. 'I asked the Pope why the priest had abused me. He said he did not know,' another victim recalled. The church has been fighting their claims for compensation on tactical legal grounds for seven years.[30]

40.   The same pattern of child sex abuse has emerged in other countries: a comparatively high incidence of commission of the crime by priests; the church's determination to deal with complaints in utter secrecy, without informing outside law enforcement; a process involving obstacles for victims and complainants and forgiveness for priests, often moved to new parishes where they offend again, or merely ordered to undergo treatment programmes (usually unsuccessful) or to do spiritual penance. The worst that can happen – the direst ecclesiastical penalty – being laicization, which is rarely imposed and in any event leaves the ex-priest free to find re-employment with children in state schools or institutions. Victims who are offered compensation can only receive it if they bind themselves to life-long confidentiality

agreements. This process has been conducted according to the rules laid down by the Vatican and overseen by Cardinal Ratzinger as head of the CDF between 1981 to 2005, and then as Pope.

41. In Australia the church has suffered many scandals resulting from frequently violent sex abuse: 90 priests have been convicted, but many more have been protected from the criminal justice process because the church has kept allegations secret and made confidential settlements. The Archbishop of Melbourne responded early to the problem, in 1996, by appointing a so-called 'Independent Commissioner' – an elderly Catholic lawyer – who receives complaints and investigates them (although he is powerless to requisition evidence) and may award compensation of up to AUD$75,000 (but only if the victim agrees to confidentiality). In 2010, the media revealed that he had ordered payments in respect of the sexual molestation of children by 300 priests, only one of whom had been defrocked.[31] This 'Melbourne Response' has been severely criticized by police for tipping off their targets, because the Commissioner has taken the view that accused priests have a right to know the details of any accusation as soon as it is made: if complainants also chose to involve the police, the latter can find their investigations compromised. The police claim that several covert investigations have had to be aborted after the target was told by the church that he was under surveillance. The Commissioner must tell victims of their right to go to the police, although his letter to one boy who complained that a priest had groped his penis read: 'without seeking to dissuade you from reporting the matter to police if you so desire, I must say that the conduct you describe is unlikely to be held by the court as criminal conduct'. An 'independent commissioner' on this model is no substitute for police investigation and public trial of credible allegations.

42. Victims who have brought their cases to court in Australia have encountered difficulties in proving that the church – an unincorporated association – can be held vicariously liable for the conduct of priests with whom it has no master–servant relationship. (The

position differs from that in America, where each diocese is a corporate entity and may be sued as such.) This has turned Australian attention to the Vatican, which has overall control of disciplining priests. In one reported case it intervened at the request of a priest from a family that had contributed heavily to the church after he was suspended for assaulting six women, one under 16. The Vatican, through its Congregation of Priests, pardoned him and directed that he be sent to another parish which was not told of his transgressions – and he transgressed again.[32] The Vatican also approved the transfer back to Australia of a priest working in Boston, who had confessed there to sex with an underage boy but was shielded from prosecution by the foreign transfer. In the city of Wollongong a courageous priest, Father Maurie Crocker, actually 'blew the whistle' on well-connected brother priests who were passing their victims around a paedophile 'ring'. He went to a local newspaper after his superiors had declined to act. But after their conviction he was ostracized, became depressed and then committed suicide.[33] There is no evidence that any Catholic Church in any country has acted to protect those very few of its priests who informed on paedophiles and, as we shall see (in Chapter 3) whistle-blowing is severely discouraged, on pain of ex-communication, by Canon Law.

43. Canada, too, has had its share of recent scandals, although was fortunate that the first – in 1990, when nine Christian Brothers were gaoled for repeated sexual assaults on boys in an orphanage – was followed by a proper inquiry, which made some useful recommendations.[34] Not all were adopted, however, and in 2001 it was revealed that a Montreal Catholic school had become a den for sexual abuse, hushed up repeatedly by compensation payments for the crimes of priests who were never reported to police by Catholic officials who knew of their guilt. In 2003 police discovered that a bishop had hidden handwritten confessions from one priest whom he had transferred to another parish which was not told about him; the man was eventually convicted of abusing forty-seven girls. The country has been rocked by revelations about sexual, physical and emotional abuse in its

residential schools for aboriginal children, which were government funded and predominantly run by the Catholic Church.[35] A national compensation agreement required the church to pay $80 million dollars (the government had to pay $2.2 billion) and led to the establishment of a Truth and Reconciliation Commission.[36] The Pope has expressed his 'sorrow' for the abuse,[37] but there have been concerns that the church is not fully cooperating with the Commission.[38]

44. One interesting piece of evidence to come out in Canada is a document implicating the papal *nuncio* in a plot to transfer a guilty paedophile out of the jurisdiction before his crimes were discovered by police. The Bishop of Pembroke in Ontario wrote to the papal *nuncio* about transferring a child-molesting priest to Rome ('I would not object to giving him another chance since it would remove him from the Canadian scene'). The problem was that some of his victims were talking, which could be 'extremely embarrassing to the Holy See in Pembroke, not to mention the possibility of criminal charges . . .' However, there was a bright side: 'the victims involved are of Polish descent and their respect for the priesthood and the church has made them refrain from laying charges. Had this happened elsewhere there would be every danger that charges would have been laid long ago with all the resulting scandal . . . it is a situation we wish to avoid at all costs.' Even, it seems, at the cost of harbouring a felon and using the Vatican diplomat's immunity to help him escape justice. This was in 1993: the bishops and fellow priests managed to keep the Polish victims quiet until 2005, when police were informed and began an investigation: in 2008 this particular priest was found guilty of molesting thirteen boys and in 2009 he was finally defrocked – fifteen years after the Vatican was told conclusively of his guilt.

45. Insofar as the church has a success story in dealing with paedophile priests, this is in the UK where in 2001 Lord Nolan, a former Law Lord, condemned the church's failure to recognize the extent and prevalence of child abuse and to report priestly misconduct, which he put down to 'a desire to protect the church

and its faithful from scandal and a Christian instinct to forgive the sinner'. He recommended a set of 'best practice' rules and standards, including a vetting process for novices, the involvement of police at an early stage, a 'paramountcy principle' that the interests of the child should always come first. However, a review committee reporting in 2007 found that implementation of Nolan's recommendations had been 'seriously flawed' and there had been powerful resistance to its implementation from a 'strong and vocal lobby' of priests, who believed that this would destroy their 'legitimate right' to be dealt with exclusively under Canon Law. They have no such rights, of course, because Canon Law protects child molesters from any form of real punishment (see Chapter 3). But undoubtedly church seminaries – probably in all countries – inculcate in priests the belief that one of their entitlements, in return for poverty, chastity and obedience, is a 'right' if accused of a sexual offence, to have a secret and favourable ecclesiastical process rather than a public trial under national criminal law. The review committee acknowledged that there was a direct conflict between the Nolan recommendations (which it supported) and the church's commitment to Canon Law. It therefore recommended that the Catholic bishops should petition the Holy See for a dispensation from Canon Law so that the Nolan recommendations could become part of church law in England and Wales.[39] Regrettably, no such dispensation has been forthcoming.

46. The incomplete implementation of the Nolan recommendations and the fatal influence of Vatican rules and insistence upon secrecy have conduced to a series of scandals. Cardinal Cormack Murphy-O'Connor was responsible as Bishop of Brighton for moving a paedophile priest to a post where he was able to abuse a boy with learning difficulties, despite warnings of his propensity to re-offend.[40] Then there was a cover up of the crimes of a former headmaster of a leading Catholic school in London, St. Benedict's, who had repeatedly abused 10-year-old boys (who knew him as 'Gay Dave') and was eventually sued successfully by a victim in 2006. Notwithstanding this dramatic proof of his paedophilia (a High Court award of £43,000) the church permitted

him to stay and work at nearby Ealing Abbey, where he took the opportunity to groom and molest another boy. Archbishop Murphy-O'Connor had known and approved of his transfer and his successor, Vincent Nichols, was throughout this period the Head of the Office for the Protection of Children and Vulnerable Adults, although he said he had not been told about the case or been asked to advise on it because he did not have any authority over religious orders such as Benedictines (which leaves a large loophole for monks and nuns and other 'religious' who are not priests). That an abuser could remain in the fold for thirty years (he was eventually gaoled in 2009 for offences dating back to 1972) despite a propensity that was known at the school and the Abbey, was castigated by the Independent Schools Inspectorate, which discovered five more abusers at the Abbey and said that 'its policies placed the welfare of monks before that of children'.[41] The Vatican still insists on secrecy and is reluctant to defrock any priest, however vile his crimes. A recent example is provided by the case of one priest, convicted of indecently assaulting vulnerable boys as young as 11 whilst a chaplain at a school for the deaf in West Yorkshire, whence he had been moved after a previous assault on a 9-year-old boy on the Isle of Man. When his bishop, in compliance with the 2001 Ratzinger directive, asked the CDF for advice, he was not told to defrock the convict.[42]

47. It should, however, be acknowledged that a new body, the National Catholic Safeguarding Commission, has made impressive efforts to tackle the problem, with a policy of referring complaints to police and social care agencies: identifying and monitoring several hundred individual priests who are considered to be possible paedophiles, and producing a manual which gives expert and up-to-date guidance on how to detect and deal with suspected child abuse. The Commission struggles, however, to be free from the toils of the Holy See, which must be informed about all its actions and which has so far delivered no dispensation from Canon Law, with which the guidance in the manual frequently conflicts. (There is a somewhat circular instruction that where clergy or 'religious' disagree with actions taken in

compliance with the manual, 'this should be raised with the bishop who will deal with the matter in accordance with Canon Law and the National Safeguarding policies', overlooking the fact that disagreements will probably have arisen in the first place because the two are in conflict.[43]) There is a welcome acknowledgement that confidentiality cannot be absolute, and that the 'paramouncy principle' overrides it whenever a child is at risk. The exception, of course, is the realm of the confessional, where the manual abandons paramouncy principles in favour of pontifical secrecy. At least the confessor is instructed to make it clear to victims that it is not they who have sinned, and to encourage them to seek help and to make disclosures to police or welfare services. But the secret guilt of the priest who confesses it is safe, even when his confessor believes he will re-offend. The manual does not point out that there can be no duty to give absolution to a 'penitent' paedophile, and the church should insist that no absolution be given unless or until the priest confesses to the police (see later, paras 179–181). The National Safeguarding Committee's work shows that the English authorities are taking their responsibility seriously, but have a long way to go: essential reform comes up against the brick wall of the Vatican.

The Vatican's Response

48. In May 2010, archbishops in Britain and Germany asked their congregations for forgiveness for 'terrible crimes and cover ups' and offered prayers for 'those who mishandled these matters and added to the suffering of those affected'.[44] But the man who mishandled so many of these matters was less critical of himself. Faced with three judicial reports evidencing widespread sexual abuse in Ireland, the Pope delivered on 19 March 2010 a 'Letter to the Catholics of Ireland'. It was notable for his refusal to accept that the Vatican itself was in any way to blame for encouraging Bishops to protect child molesters – its insistence on celibacy, secrecy and forgiveness for all or any sins was not addressed. Instead, the abuse was caused by the 'rapid secularization of Irish society',

and 'neglect of – daily prayers, frequent confessions and . . . retreats' and the modern tendency of priests 'to adopt ways of thinking in secular realities without reference to the gospel'.[45] There was a determined refusal to insist on reporting child abuse to police: victims were told that it was essential to cooperate with their religious superiors ('those in authority') so that their response would be 'truly evangelical'. His repeated admonitions to apply Canon Law implied that secrecy should continue and that national law was irrelevant. The only passage referring to law enforcement was ambiguous: 'besides fully implementing the norms of Canon Law and addressing cases of child abuse, continue to cooperate with the civil authorities in their area of competence'. This was an evasive statement, given that past 'co-operation' had been minimal, Canon Law did not require it, and it would only arise 'in their area of competence' if they (i.e. the police) were already taking action – in other words there was still no requirement on the church to take the initiative and call the police. Even after the Easter 2010 scandals, Benedict has not required bishops to report child sex abuse, and his Canon Law decree of 'New Norms' in July 2010 deliberately omitted any mandatory reporting obligation, providing more evidence that he has become a 'problem Pope'.

49. The most telling paragraph of the papal letter addressed the errant priests, whose criminality had brought such shame on their church. Given the seriousness of their offences – often the rape of very young boys – it might be thought that the Pope would have told them bluntly of the peril in which it put their souls, that crimes of this kind could not be forgiven, and that those who committed them were very likely to burn in hell. On the contrary, he assured them repeatedly that their sins could be forgiven and that they could 'bring forth good from even the most terrible evil'. His message was reassuring rather than threatening:

I urge you to examine your conscience, take responsibility for the sins you have committed, and humbly express your sorrow. Sincere repentance opens the door to God's forgiveness and the grace of true amendment. By offering prayers and penances for those you have wronged, you should seek to atone personally for your actions. Christ's redeeming sacrifice has the power to forgive even the gravest of sins, and to bring forth good from even the most terrible evil. At the same time, God's justice summons us to give an account of our actions and to conceal nothing. Openly acknowledge your guilt, submit yourselves to the demands of justice, but do not despair of God's mercy.[46]

50. For priests guilty of 'soul murder' (studies show that those whose faith they betray tend to lose it, and to lose their way in life) this Papal condemnation could be read as a blessing in disguise. It must have been comforting for them to read the repeated proffer of forgiveness and grace, in return for 'God's justice' – i.e. Canon Law – which required a penance (for example some work for charity or extensive prayers) that would not have to be served in gaol, and would not necessarily require the humiliation of defrocking. There could be no better example of the difference between spiritual admonition and criminal punishment, between Canon Law and national law. Criminal law punishment serves a deterrent purpose, emphasizing the risk to be run by would-be offenders. Punishment should also serve the purpose of retribution, to give the victim some sense of justice and of closure – and there is scant comfort for victims in learning that their sexual assailants remain free, but are saying prayers for them. Reform is a third objective, but that is only possible once the offender has paid his dues to society: child molestation in most cases warrants custodial punishment. Benedict's proffer of 'God's justice' to the paedophile priests of Ireland was no substitute for the human justice of arrest and public trial. Canon Law 'punishments' of prayer and penance are not effective sanctions, as Benedict must realize. Yet not once did he direct the Irish bishops to call in the police when they knew or suspected that children were being molested. It is Benedict's most glaring mistake to refuse to use his prerogative powers and to order his bishops, unequivocally and on pain of dismissal, to report those whom they know to be child sex offenders to the police.

51. At Easter 2010 it was anticipated that the Pope would muster the
     courage to confront the mounting scandal head-on. But his cour-
     age was of a different kind: it was, he said, 'the courage to ignore
     the petty gossip of dominant opinion' and to remain silent – to the
     frustration, it should be said, of many of his churchmen. His
     henchmen in the Vatican, however, did speak out. His personal
     preacher, one Father Cantalamessa, told him publicly that media
     treatment of church leaders was comparable to Hitler's treatment
     of the Jews – a statement stupid in its terms and massively insensi-
     tive to Jews and abuse victims. It has not been withdrawn. Then a
     retired bishop, Giacomo Babini, made headlines by blaming it all
     on the Jews (in particular, Jewish journalists working on the *New
     York Times*), who were 'deicides' (god killers) and the 'natural
     enemies' of Catholics. The Dean of the College of Cardinals,
     Angelo Sodano, praised the Pope to his face for standing up to
     chiacchiericco ('petty gossip') and, almost blasphemously, likened his
     travails to that of Christ when He was repeatedly reviled.[47] (When
     Austrian Cardinal Schönborn, one of the Curia's few reformers,
     criticized the 'massive harm' that Sodano's comments had done to
     victims, Benedict had the reformer publicly reprimanded.[48]) The
     'Secretary of State' for the Holy See, Cardinal Bertone, blamed
     the crisis on homosexuality, which he said was connected to
     paedophilia – the incidence of sexual abuse therefore had nothing
     to do with priestly celibacy.[49] For Bertone to blame homosexual-
     ity was too much for the French Foreign Minister, who described
     the linkage as 'unacceptable', and for the Catholic Bishops Confer-
     ence, representing the thirty-two Catholic bishops in England,
     which issued a statement pointing out that sexual abuse of chil-
     dren had nothing to do with homosexuality but with 'a disordered
     attractional fixation' which prevented abusers of children from
     developing the capacity for mature adult relationships. That the
     Secretary of a 'state' should issue statements on sexual psychology,
     and get them so wrong, invites the question to which I later turn,
     namely whether the Holy See should be regarded as a state at all.

52. The Vatican is in denial and its attempts to blame gay culture,
     Jewish journalists, journalists in general, secularism, progress,

'modernity' and (of course) the Devil, has embarrassed many intelligent Catholic leaders – especially in Britain and Germany where they had the decency to make fulsome apologies at their Easter services. It was not for several weeks that reluctant and forced apologies were wrung from Benedict, who said 'now, under attack from the world, which is talking about our sins, we see that being able to do penance is grace and we see how it is necessary to do penance to prepare for pardon'.[50] For this Pope, whose belief in original sin means that 'man has a wounded nature inclined to evil', the darkest of clouds must always have a silver spiritual lining:[51] for negligent churchmen the good news was that doing penance for their sins would procure grace – pardon was theirs for the asking. Benedict himself was more concerned with gay marriage and abortion, which he went to Portugal to denounce as 'among the most insidious and dangerous challenges to society'.[52] He seemed unable to comprehend that the most dangerous challenge to the Holy See was its canonical practice of protecting criminals.

3. Canon Law

Render therefore unto Caesar the things which are Caesar's; and unto God the things that are God's.

Matthew 22:21 (King James version)

53. In 2001, the Vatican actually congratulated Bishop Pierre Pican of Bayeux for refusing to inform police about a paedophile priest and for giving him parish work despite his confession of guilt. 'I congratulate you for not denouncing a priest to the civil administration,' wrote Cardinal Castrillon Hojos, with the personal approval of John Paul II and other senior cardinals, including the Head of the CDF, Cardinal Ratzinger. This came to light after the priest had been sentenced to eighteen years for repeated rapes and assaults on ten boys, and the bishop received a three-month suspended sentence for not reporting the abuse, contrary to French law.[1] The Papal commendation had been copied to all bishops, to serve as an encouragement to them to defy such laws. There could be no clearer example of the Holy See deciding that its own law should trump the criminal law of another nation, or at least requiring its spiritual adherents – nationals of that other nation – to breach the law of their land. Castrillon Hojos, then the Vatican cardinal responsible for the priesthood, was applauded by senior churchmen – in March 2010 – when he said at a conference that 'after consulting the Pope . . . I wrote a letter to the bishop congratulating him as a model Father who does not hand over his own sons . . . the Holy Father authorized me to send this letter to all bishops . . .' The 'model father' had not received the paedophile priest's admission of guilt under the seal of the confessional (a defence under French law to non-disclosure) but in a private conversation, so he could have no possible claim

to any privilege. The Pope's action in approving the commendation and in directing it to be copied to all bishops was a flagrant assertion of the church's claim to deal with criminal priests without interference from local law.

54. There can be no objection to any organization, national or international, laying down rules and procedures for investigating misconduct of members or employees. But when that 'misconduct' amounts to serious crime, the duty to involve law enforcement agencies at an early stage arises either from specific laws (many countries impose statutory duties to report sex abuse on, for example, doctors, teachers and those dealing professionally with children) or from general 'misprision of felony' laws requiring that knowledge or suspicion of serious crime must be passed on to police. On any view there is a moral duty to disclose, unless (and then only arguably) a confession of guilt has been received within a confidential relationship such as that in the confessional between priest and penitent. (For the argument, see paras 179–81.) Mere disciplinary procedures cannot supplant, or provide an acceptable alternative to, the normal process of law enforcement. What appears to have happened in the Catholic Church throughout the last century is that bishops were instructed by the Vatican to regard Canon Law as the only law applicable to priests accused of child sex abuse, and priests were educated in seminaries to believe that they were subject to it, exclusively, when accused of sexual sins with parishioners. But Canon Law in this respect is not 'law' in any real sense (i.e. a rule backed by a temporal enforcement power) but rather a disciplinary process relating to sins for which the only punishment is spiritual – for example an order to pray or do penance, or at very worst, an order for laicization. Canon Law has no public hearings, no DNA test facilities, no enforcement mechanism, and the most severe punishments, excommunication or an order to return to the laity (without entry on a sex offenders' register), bears no comparison with the sentences of imprisonment or community service that can be expected under criminal law. Moreover, the procedures for investigation and proof under

Canon Law are archaic and over-reliant upon admission of guilt. Since the trial proceeds entirely in writing, and is lacking in forensic techniques or even cross-examination as a test for truth, many guilty priests have slipped through the gaping holes in its net.

55. Canon Law was not codified until 1917, and then was revised in 1983, when the most notable change was the lifting of the long-time ban on freemasonry, probably for reasons connected with the Vatican Bank (para 134). It is something of a mish-mash of divine law (dogmatic moral truths); ecclesiastical law (internal church rules, for example about priestly celibacy) and civil law. The apostolic constitution of the Vatican City (*Pastor Bonus*) makes Canon Law the only law in town, but it is the law – with its hundreds of 'norms' (i.e. rules) filtered through Vatican departments (dicasteries) – that binds all Catholics. As the leading commentary on the Canon Law code explains (or not):

The *place* of law is in the Church of Christ where the drama of our redemption is enacted; the *code* of law is to assist the people in the reception of God's saving mysteries.[2]

56. This is all very well for worshippers, who may want their church to act against heresy, schism and apostasy and to make it a serious sin to challenge the infallibility of the Pope or publicly to excite animosity against the Holy See.[3] This is what might be expected of the rules of a religion, but what do 'God's saving mysteries' have to do with priests who have sodomized small children? A great deal, it appears, because

the Church's salvific purpose gives its penal order a unique character which must constantly be remembered . . . a non-penal pastoral approach may lead an offender to a fuller life in Christ more effectively than penalties. Fullness of life in Christ is the ultimate rationale . . .[4]

57. This may be, but it does not explain why the rapist priest should not find a full life in Christ in a prison cell, rather than in the gentle remonstrances of his bishop or the kindly counselling of the Paracletes in their New Mexico retreat. But this is the fundamental philosophy of Canon Law Book VI: 'the salvific character

of church law underlines the code's forceful emphasis on penalties only as a last resort when all other legal-pastoral methods have failed to deal with problematic behaviour'.[5] Given that 'penalties' are usually extra prayers, and that the worst a priest can suffer is reduction to the laity, this means that criminals, who would be unmasked and publically tried and sentenced under secular law, are under Canon Law merely counselled or warned or rebuked – privately shamed but never publicly named. (Canon 1339 insists that the document evidencing the warning or rebuke 'is to be kept in the secret archive of the Curia' to avoid any publicity – even within the church itself). Those who re-offend or are insufficiently remorseful may be ordered to do penance (defined by Canon 1340 as 'the performance of some work of religion, piety or charity,' such as 'prayers, fasting, alms giving, a retreat or community service.') Violations of the celibacy rule can 'be punished gradually by privations and even dismissal from the clerical state' which is as bad as it can get for the priest caught masturbating as for the priest caught molesting: both breach the rule that requires 'non-use of the sexual faculty'. Canon 1395 punishes a cleric 'who lives in concubinage' and who may incur dismissal from the clerical state if he does not give up his girlfriend. Sex with a minor, however, is to be punished under the lesser standard of 'just penalties': as the commentary drily notes, 'somewhat surprisingly, the code does not seem to view such delicts as seriously as other violations of clerical continence.'[6]

58. On what basis does Canon Law claim jurisdiction over a serious criminal offence? Canon 1311 offers the only explanation:

> The Church has the innate and proper right to coerce offending members of the Christian faithful with penal sanctions.

59. This is no explanation at all. The church may have, like any organization, the right to discipline and expel its members, but neither God nor man has ever given it the 'innate and proper right' to protect child molesters from human justice. There is no 'right', innate or otherwise, for a church to establish a parallel justice system for sex crimes by priests and other 'religious', all

the more so since that system operates to remove offenders from receiving what the community – and the law – regards as justice. It amounts, at a political level, to secret intervention in the laws of a friendly state – a breach of the non-intervention rule in the UN Charter. Hiding a child molester, and reassigning him to other parishes where he may molest again, has nothing to do with 'the Church's salvific purpose'. Requiring a paedophile priest to say more 'hail marys' will not stop him re-offending: it may save his soul, but it will not save his future victims.

60. Canon Law in these cases has two very striking features. The first is spelled out repeatedly – it is the need for complete secrecy, not to protect the victim but to avoid scandalizing the community or lowering the reputation of the church. Canon 1352(2) even requires a penalty to be suspended or removed 'if the offender cannot observe it without danger of grave scandal or infamy'. The second, more shocking, fact about the Canon Law code for sexual offences is that absolutely nowhere does it require sympathetic treatment or counselling or support for traumatized victims.

61. Canon Law procedures favour the defendant, under a penal code that before what its commentary calls 'certain tragic ecclesiastical developments' (by which it means public awareness of sex abuse cases) had been mainly used in marriage tribunals.[7] Its provisions relating to child abuse are brief and generalized: the cleric who abuses a child under 18 '*is to be punished with just penalties not excluding dismissal from the clerical state if the case so warrants*'.[8] It lays all responsibility on the bishop, when a complaint which has '*the semblance of truth*' is made, to begin an inquiry, usually undertaken by a senior priest ('the delegate'). Canon 1717.2 requires that '*care is to be taken that this investigation does not call into question anyone's good name*' – and the only way that can be achieved is by proceeding in utter secrecy, without making enquiries of the suspect's friends, neighbours or from children who have in the past come under his care. The priest has 'the right of silence' (now abolished in the UK) and cannot be questioned unless he

waives that right, and no adverse inference can be drawn against him for exercising it.

62. At the end of the preliminary investigation, Canon 1341 enjoins the bishop to proceed to a trial that could lead to a penalty '*only when he perceives that neither by fraternal correction or reproof, nor by any methods of pastoral care*' can scandal be repaired or the offender reformed. This means that where the investigation implicates the priest, his bishop must not proceed to any formal trial or punishment if he thinks that a fatherly word of advice or reproof, or sending the priest for treatment, or to another parish, or limiting his movements, will suffice. Given that this Canon Law presumption against any formal penalty is to be applied for the benefit of those who have admitted or been implicated in the sexual abuse of children, it exhibits a breathtaking disregard for the seriousness of the offence and the danger of re-offending. Canon Law is so deficient that it makes no provision whatsoever for the compensation of victims.

63. Canon Law provisions would be ridiculed if the consequences were not so serious. Under Canons 1395 and 1321, no one can be punished for an offence unless it is 'gravely inputable by reason of malice or culpability'. Since paedophiles are subject to urges and impulses that are difficult to control, the Murphy Commission was told that proof of paedophilia could be a complete defence to a charge of sexually abusing or raping children. The Commission found this a matter of grave concern: 'this is a major point of difference between church and state law. In the former it appears that paedophilia may be an actual defence to a claim of child sexual abuse'. It uncovered several cases where the CDF had intervened to protect priests who had been convicted but diagnosed as paedophiles; on their appeal, Cardinal Ratzinger had prevented them from being defrocked.[9]

64. A bishop might restrict paedophile priests from teaching children, saying mass, training altar boys etc – but there are endless examples of priests under such restrictions nonetheless finding

the opportunity to violate more children (See Appendix A). Abusers who are not paedophiles can be 'laicized': the process is swathed in secrecy and they do not end up on any sex offender register and many re-offend after finding jobs in state schools or child welfare organizations. Canon Law does not provide any kind of workable system for investigating or punishing abusive priests.

65. The difficulties of Canon Law are heightened by its procedural rules, issued as 'a secret of the Holy Office' in 1922 and repeated in 1962 under the hand of Cardinal Ottaviani, the CDF Pro-Prefect before Cardinal Ratzinger, with the title *Crimen Sollicitationis* (Appendix B). Absurdly for any kind of 'rule', the penalty for revealing its existence is excommunication: it is couched in Latin and seems to have been issued only to bishops, who placed it in secret archives. Many of their congregations were totally unaware of it until 2003 when it was leaked to lawyers for US victims interested in bringing action against the Vatican. As its title suggests, it laid down the manner of proceeding in cases of the 'unspeakable crime', namely sexual solicitations by priests of their penitents in the confession box, or in circumstances closely related to taking the sacrament. This crime was not specific to the grooming of children, but the penultimate paragraph applied it to *'any external obscene act, gravely sinful, perpetrated or attempted by a cleric in any way with pre-adolescent children of either sex or with brute animals'*.[10] This was conjoined with 'the foulest crime', namely an obscene act attempted by a cleric *'in any manner whatsoever with a person of his own sex'* – an indication of the Vatican's abomination of homosexuality, even between consenting adults.

66. The *Crimen* procedure is entirely lacking in investigative efficacy. There is obviously no provision for DNA testing, which has become routine in the contemporary prosecution of sexual offenders. The process is conducted entirely in writing – there is no provision for interviewing witnesses, let alone for cross-examination. It is conducted entirely by fellow priests, and if the priest who prosecutes ('the promoter of Justice') considers the complaint unfounded, the bishop must destroy all traces of the

investigation.[11] If the evidence is weighty (for example if there are a number of accusers or accusations, or other forms of corroboration) the bishop even then need not proceed to trial, but can decide merely to give the priest a first oral warning, and even a second oral warning if he offends again. These warnings, depending on the seriousness of the case, are *paternal* (i.e. fatherly advice), *grave* (presumably, 'watch your step') or *most grave* (i.e. 'if you are caught again, you will have to go to Canonical trial').[12] These warnings are to be given in total confidence and copies are to be kept in the secret archives of the Curia in Rome. Again, it must be noted that these admonitions are regarded as appropriate punishment, within the church, for offences that would often receive – and deservedly receive – prison sentences under criminal law. There is no public proceeding, and no equivalent of a sex offenders register – merely a reference in a secret archive in the Vatican, unreviewable to successor bishops if the priest re-offends, and entirely inaccessible to local law enforcement authorities.

67. The investigation under *Crimen* hardly deserves that name: there is no surveillance of the suspect, or power to seize his property or clothing or inspect private homes or possessions. There is no provision at all for one absolutely crucial form of corroboration, namely a medical examination of the victim. All anonymous denunciations are to be disregarded (in practical police work, anonymous accusations are treated with some seriousness). Two persons, preferably priests, who know the complainant (usually a young child, with unformed character and no reputation to speak of), and two who know the priest complained against (and he will have no shortage of 'brothers', and old friends from his seminary) are placed under oath, sworn to secrecy and then asked to testify about their friend's character and reputation. The defendant must never be required to take an oath to tell the truth, and if he agrees to be questioned he cannot breach the seal of the confessional: '*If the defendant, speaking heatedly, lets slip something which might suggest a direct or indirect violation of the seal, the judge is not to allow it to be recorded by the notary*' – even when it amounts to an admission of guilt (see p. 194).[13] All official participants in canonical

courts – the judge, the promoter and the notary – must be priests, and the proceedings must be conducted in complete secrecy, with excommunication the punishment even for the child victim if he were later to tell lawyers or police (see Appendix B, paras 11–13). The rules are silent on the burden and standard of proof and the admissibility of evidence, other than the inadmissibility of any evidence about what was said in the confessional, so the process lacks the basic rules of any real court. The procedures are sclerotic and bureaucratic and it must be doubted whether they can produce convictions other than in open-and-shut cases, usually where the priest has confessed (but if the priest confesses to another priest in the confession box, that can never be revealed to the court).

68. It will be immediately apparent that Canon Law fails the first test of proper legal process, namely that it does not provide an independent and impartial court. The sodality of the priesthood is intimate and self-supporting, and prosecuting and defending priest-counsel will have a close empathy with their colleague, the defendant. As judge, the bishop is trained to have a father–son relationship with his priest. (The right of ordination involves the new priest pledging loyalty to his bishop, who in turn anoints the priest's hands with oil – symbolizing 'a sacred bond of reciprocal obligation and support'.[14]) The bishop obviously cannot judge impartially a man whose welfare is his sacred duty – quite apart from concerns about his own reputation and that of his diocese. A Canon Law trial, for these reasons, cannot be fair to the victim, nor to the public interest in achieving justice. Its very secrecy means that justice will not be seen to be done. All the cases which have established the open justice principle in civil and criminal law point out that publicity deters perjury and encourages witnesses to come forward and, as Jeremy Bentham put it, is the surest guard against improbity: 'it keeps the judge, while trying, under trial'.[15]

69. There are other problems with the bishop (the 'Ordinary') as adjudicator, untrained to analyse evidence and draw inferences, especially in cases concerning sexual abuse. They have been trained under *Persona Humana* (1975) which (notwithstanding

the Kinsey Report) embraced the sexual views of St Paul that 'every genital act must be within the framework of marriage' and that 'masturbation is an intrinsically and seriously disordered act' because 'the deliberate use of the sexual faculty outside moral conjugal relations essentially contradicts the finality of the faculty'. The sexual ignorance of the church's *magisterium* deepened when Karol Wojtyla became Pope John Paul II in 1979; he had helped to compose *Humanae Vitae* and *Persona Humana* and took such a hard line on sexuality that his follow-up encyclical, *The Splendour of Truth* (1988), put contraception alongside genocide as amongst the acts that are 'intrinsically evil'. He forbade further discussion of contraception and instructed his *nuncios* to spy on up-and-coming clerics and to recommend for promotion to bishop only those who unquestioningly supported the prohibition.[16] This led to appointments of men who in many cases lacked street wisdom and insight into human sexual behaviour, and who were to prove astonishingly naïve in accepting the excuses of paedophile priests and in believing that they might be cured by prayer and penitence or by counselling.

70. As for those found guilty of molesting children, the Canon Law penalties are derisory – '*chiefly spiritual exercises to be made for a certain number of days in some religious house, with suspension from the celebration of mass during that period*'.[17] If the bishop apprehends relapse or recidivism, he may subject the priest to 'special supervision' – for example suspension from saying mass or working with children. In the case of grave crimes, like sexual seduction in the confessional, the priest may be suspended from taking confession and '*in more grievous cases he is even to be subjected to reduction to the lay state* (degradatio)'.[18] What is described as 'the extreme penalty' is to be visited only upon those priests whose ministry has caused such '*great scandal to the faithful . . . that there seems to be no hope, humanly speaking, or almost no hope, of his amendment*'.[19] Some CDF decisions that have leaked out show that even serial abusers have had the bishops' orders for laicization quashed by Cardinal Ratzinger because they are old, or their offences are old, or they are young, or ill (see para 28).

71. The terms of *Crimen* are no substitute for police investigation and criminal punishment. They are appropriate, if at all, for a small Masonic society that needs rules to discipline members and, at last resort, to remove them from the club. There is simply no comprehension of child abuse as a serious criminal offence, and no mention of any duty on a bishop or 'promoter of justice' to call in the police. One of the current US cases, *O'Bryan v Holy See*, turns on the question of whether *Crimen* mandates non-cooperation with law enforcement. The Vatican has filed a brief which asserts that 'nothing within *Crimen* could be interpreted to prevent reporting to law enforcement prior to the initiative of the Canonical process'.[20] Although *Crimen* does not specifically prohibit this, its whole tenor and effect belie the Vatican's argument. Canon Law itself enjoins secrecy from the outset, and as a 'secret of the Holy Office', excommunication is the punishment for breach – a more severe penalty, be it noted, than could be suffered by a rapist priest under Canon Law, who might be defrocked but could not be excluded from the church. *Crimen* imposes 'utmost confidentiality' and 'permanent silence' on all persons involved in the process including complainants and their witnesses, who are bound 'under pain of incurring automatic excommunication' (see p. 190).

72. The Holy See's argument (para 223), that *Crimen* cannot be interpreted as disallowing contact with police before the formal canonical process begins, is incompatible with para 23 of *Crimen* itself, which requires the accuser to commence by making a formal denunciation under oath: after he signs it, *'he is to be administered the oath to maintain confidentiality, of necessity under pain of excommunication'* (see Appendix B). So *Crimen* requires the accusation to be shrouded in enforced secrecy: a child or teenager, brought up as a Catholic, is not going to risk excommunication by taking his story subsequently to the police, let alone to the press. The Murphy Commission correctly concluded that such an obligation, as part of a Canonical process, 'could undoubtedly constitute an inhibition on the reporting of child sexual abuse to the civil authorities or others'.[21] There is an almost obsessional

concern for secrecy throughout the paragraphs of *Crimen*: it emphasizes that communications 'shall always be made *under the secret of the Holy Office*' and the document is endorsed by Pope John XXIII, who ordered on 16 March 1962 that it be 'observed in every detail'. It seems plainly intended to exclude any communication to an outside agency once an accusation had been made and to back up that prohibition with the direst threats of spiritual punishment – threats of a kind that child victims would be incapable of withstanding because they are generally brought up in Catholic families, where excommunication would involve unendurable shame and hellfire is taken literally. The congratulations sent to Bishop Pican, with the approval of Pope John Paul II and Cardinal Ratzinger, for refusing to report his paedophile priest to the police, were congratulations circulated to bishops to encourage them to do likewise (see para 53 above). This really disposes of the fallacious argument that the Vatican would be quite content for law enforcers to arrest its guilty priests.

73. Ironically, the Vatican's alternative defence in *O'Bryan v Holy See* is that *Crimen* was so obscure and secret that many US bishops had no idea of its existence and its prescribed norms were frequently not followed. Bishops simply handled child abuse accusations informally, so were not bound by its confidentiality provisions (although they always in fact observed confidentiality). This may well have been true in respect of the complaints in that case and others, although it hardly shows the Vatican in a favourable light. Its Canon Law was clear, yet it took no steps until 2001 to draw its procedures for dealing with child abuse – defective though they were – to the attention of all of its bishops in the US. The same ignorance was displayed by bishops in Ireland – one told the Murphy Commission that he was unaware of *Crimen* until a bishop in Australia discovered in the late 1990s that it was still valid. Murphy commented acidly on 'an unusual situation whereby a document setting out the procedure for dealing with clerical child sexual abuse was in existence but virtually no one knew about it or used it'.[22] Allowing bishops to deal with accusations of serious crime 'informally' – by having

paedophile priests treated or transferred out of the country without any investigation – was on any view grossly negligent, and it was a negligence for which the CDF was responsible throughout the period when it was headed by Cardinal Ratzinger.

74. On 18 May 2001, Ratzinger brought *Crimen* to the attention of all bishops by an apostolic letter which this time was widely published (Appendix C). It had been issued with the Pope's approval, and assumed that *Crimen* had been in full force since 1962. This new apostolic letter, *Sacramentorum sanctitatis tutela*, defined some 'grave delicts', which henceforth were reserved to the apostolic tribunal of the CDF, including 'a delict against morals with a minor below the age of 18 years'. This, like the other ecclesiastical offences, was subject to a time bar after ten years, a period which in sex abuse cases would commence after the minor had reached 18 (so the victim could not complain at all after he turned 29). There were no other changes in procedure and no requirement or even suggestion that the police must at some point be contacted. Once again, it stated emphatically, cases of this kind are subject to the 'pontifical secret'. In Canon Law, in relation to solicitation cases, the pontifical secret is defined in the *Instruction of the Congregation of the Holy Office,* current since 1866:

> In handling these cases, either by Apostolic commission or the appropriate ruling of the bishops, the greatest care and vigilance must be exercised so that these procedures, inasmuch as they pertain to [matters of] faith, are to be completed in absolute secrecy, and after they have been settled and given over to sentencing, are to be completely suppressed by perpetual silence. All the ecclesiastic ministers of the Curia, and whoever else is summoned to the proceedings, including counsels for the defense, must submit oaths of maintaining secrecy, and even the bishops themselves are obligated to keep the secret . . . but those who satisfy the burden of denunciation are bound to swear an oath at the beginning to tell the truth, and then, when the dealings are complete, must swear to maintain secrecy even if they are priests.[23]

75. Ratzinger's 2001 instructions failed to correct the fundamental mistake made in *Crimen*, of confusing child sex abuse with sins

relating to the confessional and the sacraments. The latter were just ecclesiastical offences of misconduct in holy office, whereas child abuse is a serious offence under every national criminal law. It had no place as a 'delict' alongside such priestly misbehaviour as 'taking . . . the consecrated species for a sacrilegious purpose' or 'forbidden concelebration of the eucharistic sacrifice with ministers of ecclesial communities which do not have apostolic succession . . .' Horrific offences, no doubt, against Catholic ritual and tradition, but of no possible concern to anyone outside the church (or, perhaps, to many within). Child sex abuse, however, is rightly the concern of the entire community and the church's claim to exclusive and secret jurisdiction over those of its priests who are accused of committing it amounts not only to a confusion of thought but to an usurpation of the power of the state to punish crimes committed on its territory and against its children.

76. Canon Law procedure remains intolerably slow because all credible allegations must be reported to the CDF, which can order trial in Rome or tell the local bishop to proceed to a Canon Law trial himself. The 'investigator' is another priest, with no forensic experience or resources. The investigation is conducted clandestinely, with all parties and witnesses sworn to keep the 'pontifical secret' (p. 200). The witnesses and the evidence collected by the 'promoter of justice' need never be made available to police or prosecutors. Whether or not there is a 'guilty' verdict, the papers are sent to the CDF in Rome, where they are immune from court-ordered discovery, and bishops are enjoined to keep any copies of the evidence under lock and key, obtainable only by the drastic measure, to which Belgian police have recently had to resort, of obtaining a warrant for search and seizure to be carried out at the cathedral. If the CDF decides to hold a trial in Rome, there will be a further delay – and any 'sentence' imposed by the bishop will be reviewed there in any event. 'Punishments' remain both nominal and unlikely: any defrocking must be ordered or confirmed by the Pope himself, even when the guilty priest has asked for laicization. 'In cases where the accused priest

has admitted to his crimes and has accepted to live a life of prayer and penitence' the CDF will merely restrict his ministry, thus allowing a confessed child sex addict to continue in the church.

77. Ratzinger's supporters have suggested that his 2001 initiative shows he was concerned to do something about the rising tide of child abuse allegations, by making clear that they were henceforth to be supervised by his CDF in Rome and were not to be left to the discretion of local bishops. This suggestion is difficult to fathom, because his instruction to send all cases to Rome 'under the pontifical secret' meant that the local bishop could not possibly use his own discretion to report them to police – otherwise, by revealing the formal allegation and breaching papal secrecy, he would be liable to excommunication. It also served to delay any action against the accused priest: the CDF, a year or so later, would either decide the case itself or remit it back to the local bishop telling him to begin again. It is difficult to resist the conclusion that in 2001 Cardinal Ratzinger was aware of the sex abuse scandal that was about to hit the church, and instead of instructing bishops to abandon the secret and useless *Crimen* procedures, notify the police and let public justice take its course, he decided instead to increase the Holy See's control over all sex abuse allegations, confirming that this 'state' would henceforth have exclusive jurisdiction to punish crimes committed by its priests in other states, but under its own law. The Holy See had come to view the worldwide church as a nation, with its own Canon Law binding on its citizens – the priests of the church – in whatever country they might be found. In 2002, when shell-shocked US bishops raised with Ratzinger the possibility of cooperation with civil authorities in cases of child sex abuse, they were reminded, that 'the church reaffirms her right to enact legislation binding on all her members concerning the ecclesiastical dimensions of the delict of sexual abuse of minors.'[24] That the church's finest theologians thought that the acts of masturbating or sodomizing small boys had an 'ecclesiastical dimension' was astonishing enough. That Cardinal Ratzinger apparently believed the state of which he was the most powerful minister

had the right to run a secret legal system for sex abuse in friendly countries, in defiance of international law, was even more amazing. That he was still determined, in 2002, to protect priests who had committed it was the fatal error of rendering unto God the things that are Caesar's.

78. In 2010, five years into Benedict's papacy, and after all the shame and scandal, the church's procedures for dealing with clerical sex abuse of children remain completely unacceptable. The Vatican is determined to keep its Canon Law jurisdiction for this 'offence against morals' – ineffective, incompetent and unpunitive, as it has always been, still operated in secret and overwhelmingly protective of the accused priest. It refuses to adopt 'zero tolerance' for the universal church or to release victims from their promises of pontifical secrecy or to hand over evidence to law enforcement agencies about the paedophile priests who have been tried under Canon Law or dealt with informally in the past. The only apparent concession, made not in Canon Law or apostolic letter but put up on a Vatican public relations website in response to public outrage over the Pope's Easter silence, was an unofficial *'Guide to Understanding Basic CDF Procedure concerning sexual abuse allegations'*. It proposed that:

Civil law concerning reporting of crimes to the appropriate authorities should always be followed.[25]

79. The sudden appearance of this new suggestion in an informal website guide described as 'helpful to lay persons and non-canonists' was sold to the media on 12 April as evidence that the pope, despite his Easter silence, had acted at last. This was real reform, an order that bishops must report abusive priests. But the media which reported this news had been hoodwinked: the Vatican website has no papal authority to effect any change in Canon Law and the 'guidance' only purported to be an explanation of the existing 1983 Canon Law and the 2001 Ratzinger letter, neither of which contain any reference to a reporting requirement. The truth – that this aspect of the 'website guidance' was a public relations exercise – was revealed three months

later when the Pope published the 'New Norms' of Canon Law – *de gravioribus delictus* (Appendix D). It made no mention of any duty on bishops or anyone else to report cases of child sex abuse to civil authorities. Only when it was published did the Vatican spokesman, Father Lombardi, confess that a reporting requirement had been discussed but rejected – it was deliberately decided not to impose it as a new rule of Canon Law. So the website guidance was not law at all, although it has misled the media and the public and was probably calculated to do so. In any event, it was couched in careful language – it would only apply in places where there is such a civil law, and many countries, especially in Latin American and Asia, do not have specific laws requiring mandatory reporting, so in these places the police would not be alerted even were the guide followed. Many common law countries do not have specific reporting laws either, and bishops could wriggle out of the recommendation to report on the basis that by staying silent they were not 'assisting offenders' or involved in 'misprision of felony'. Why can the Vatican never bring itself to order bishops to report *all* credible allegations *immediately* to the *proper authorities*? Because the Holy See is not prepared to give up a Canon Law jurisdiction that gives it a power to protects its priests that is lost if they are put in the dock of a public courtroom. When they are, it is usually as the result of intelligence that does not come to police from any official church source.

80. There is a crucial flaw in the website 'guidance' in any event. In practice, the Canon Law process is so weighted in favour of priests that most who are found to have sinned have actually admitted it, often in the course of a formal confession. In consequence, the bishop could not repeat an allegation of child sex abuse to the police if it were made during the celebration of the sacrament of penance.[26] This cover-up is required by Canon Law, namely Canon 983(1):

The sacramental seal is inviolable. Accordingly, it is absolutely wrong for a confessor in any way to betray the penitent, for any reason whatsoever, whether by word or deed or any other fashion.

81. So even if Canon Law had been reformed as the website pretended, paedophile priests could continue to confess in complete confidence that the police would never be informed of their guilt. Whenever the subject of a bishop reporting a priest to police is broached in the Vatican, it is analogized to the anguish of a parent betraying a child – 'it is so hard,' said a CDF official, 'for a father to betray his son.' So long as the sacramental seal remains inviolable, in many cases, it will be impossible.

82. In July 2010 Pope Benedict made a new effort to address the sex abuse crisis with a promulgation – *de gravioribus delictis* (Appendix D) – that amended his 2001 apostolic letter and overruled the earlier website 'guidance'. It came after five of his European bishops had resigned, tens of thousands of the faithful had left the church in disgust, and the US Supreme Court had refused his request to review and overrule a judicial decision which leaves the Vatican open to questioning and disclosure duties in negligence actions in US courts. It was the moment for him to announce the abandonment of any reliance on Canon Law to investigate and punish sex offenders in the church, and to instruct his bishops, without equivocation, to report their reasonable suspicions to civil authorities. It was the moment to adopt for the universal church the US 'one strike and you're out' policy of automatically defrocking a clergyman convicted of child abuse. Alas for the church, and for his own reputation, he did not take this course. On the contrary, he endorsed Canon Law as the appropriate way to proceed against suspected priests, and actually enlarged the scope of its purported jurisdiction by directing that other sex crimes against national laws should be dealt with through its secret and priest-friendly procedures. These crimes – of possessing and distributing pornographic images of children, and of sexually abusing a mentally handicapped adult incapable of giving consent – are offences against the national law of most civilized countries. But henceforth they too, if committed by a priest, will not be reported to police, but consigned to the netherworld of Canon Law, where, as Article 30 of *de gravioribus delictus* again emphasized, they would be subject to the Pontifical

secret, any breach of which (even by negligence rather than design) would receive the most severe penalty (Appendix D).

83. The Vatican's spin-doctor, Father Lombardi, sought to deflect criticism by explaining that secret trials are necessary 'in order to safeguard the dignity of all the people involved' – and, one suspects, the reputation of the church. The right of the public to see justice done did not occur to him. As for the Pope's failure to include amongst the new norms any duty to call in the police, he admitted that 'collaboration with civil authorities' had been discussed but 'remains untouched'. (The notion that it is somehow 'collaboration' – with its overtones of assisting the enemy – to permit detection and forensic experts to investigate serious crime reveals the Vatican's almost paranoid fear of 'sacrificing its own'.) He went on to assert the church's preposterous claim that Canon Law can deal with serious crime: 'the penal code of Canon Law is complete in itself and entirely distinct from the law of states'.[27] The very fact that it is 'entirely distinct' disqualifies it from serving as an alternative to public justice, and involves the Holy See in a breach of international law by subverting the justice system of the friendly nation with which it has diplomatic relations.

84. The new claim that Canon Law can deal with priests who make or distribute child pornography is just as outrageous as the claim that it can deal with child sex abuse. Canon Law gives no power to seize computers, and has no forensic experts to examine hard drives or police to uncover networks of pornography distribution or doctors to examine victims. Yet now the Vatican is to assume jurisdiction over a criminal offence associated with child abuse (there have been allegations of 'pornography rings' among paedophile priests and of children being groomed by being shown obscene computer images) which most national criminal laws deal with by public condemnation, the prospect of gaol sentences and entries on a sex offenders register. The priest-offenders will, under Canon Law, remain unknown and will suffer merely an order for penance or at most a defrocking, with re-entry into a society where there will be nothing to stop them

re-offending, and no warning to others that they may offend again. As for the new Canon Law crime of sex with persons who have a mental disability, this is unsatisfactory in its terms because it protects only 'persons who habitually lack the use of reason' which is not the case with most of the sufferers from mental disorders who may become prey for priests. It does not cover physical disablement – schools for the blind or the deaf, and hospitals for the incapacitated, have been common stalking grounds for clerical sex abusers. But the central objection to this new Canon Law crime is that it overlaps with national laws that protect the vulnerable, and means that allegations will not be competently investigated, surveillance powers and forensic medical examiners will not be available, and the odds will be tipped against the complainant and in favour of the accused priest. There will be no public trial, any admission of guilt vouchsafed in the confession box will be utterly inadmissible, and indeed anyone rash enough to tender that evidence will be excommunicated.

85. There are some presentational changes in these new 2010 Canon Law norms. The church has at least understood that child sex abuse allegations can be made many years after the event, and the time limitation has been extended to twenty years after the victim's eighteenth birthday – although it would have been more sensible to abolish time limits altogether. (Why allow a victim to complain at age 38 but not when he or she turns 39?) It has also responded to criticisms over delay and the rarity of defrockings by enabling the Pope to 'dismiss from the clerical state' priests who admit or do not contest their guilt. He may at the same time issue the offender with a 'dispensation from the law of celibacy' which is usually difficult to obtain (it must come from the hand of the Pontiff) so this 'fast track' process may in this respect be advantageous to the offender, freed immediately to marry rather than to burn. As an example of the Vatican's defensiveness, the Pope has devised a special 'delict' to deal with any Catholic who might dare to 'record, by whatever means, or maliciously diffuse through the communication media, what is said in sacramental

confession by the confessor or the penitent'. This new Catholic 'crime' seems an attempt to deter police or journalists from wiring victims – actual or potential – and sending them into confession to tape evidence against priests accused or suspected of using the confessional for sexual grooming.

86. In other respects, however, the new norms merely amplify the objections to the old, by treating crimes like child sex abuse and possession of child pornography in the same way as sins like schism, heresy and apostasy. Priests who abuse small children are under these norms equated with priests who throw away 'consecrated species' or absolve their girlfriends in the confessional or attempt prohibited liturgies. Indeed, the promulgation of Benedict's 'New Norms' became a public relations disaster for the church because they included a new 'more grave delict' as serious as sodomizing a child, namely of attempting the ordination of a woman. Both the priest and the woman in such a case are threatened with the worst of all ecclesiastical punishments, namely 'major excommunication' (whatever that may be). The absurdity of this juxtaposition, coming a few days after the Anglican Church had decided to consecrate female bishops, was seen as an example of Benedict's misogyny, or his sexist theology (the ban on female priests, so a church committee reported back in 1976, has no biblical basis). For him to rewrite Canon Law to make this offence as serious as molesting a child was a setback for those of his defenders who blame John Paul II and claim that Benedict is now 'converted' to the need for action. In July 2010 the 'New Norms' made it pellucidly clear that Benedict was not prepared for his Church to hand his 'religious' over to secular law. 'Benefit of clergy' would remain canonically available to them.

4. The Lateran Treaty

I cannot accept your canon that we are to judge Pope and King unlike
other men, with a favourable presumption that they did no wrong. If there
is any presumption, it is the other way, against holders of power, increasing
as the power increases. Historic responsibility has to make up for the want
of legal responsibility. Power tends to corrupt, and absolute power
corrupts absolutely . . . There is no worse heresy than that the office
sanctifies the holder of it.

Lord Acton, 1887[1]

87. The Pope's claim to be the head of a state, entitled to use Canon
    Law wherever in the world it runs a church, turns on the issue of
    whether the Vatican (a tiny enclave in Rome) or the Holy See (the
    government of the Roman Catholic Church), or both taken
    together, can constitute a sovereign state as a matter of international
    law. Each has international personality, in the sense that they may
    enter agreements, sign treaties, hold conferences and swap repre-
    sentatives with other entities – be they corporations, religious
    organizations, charities or states. But upon the Vatican's claim to
    have more than just 'international personality' and to be a fully-
    fledged state, much depends. It brings many advantages, two of
    them especially prized: sovereign immunity for itself and its head
    in respect of any legal action, and direct access to the United Nations
    and its agencies, conferences and conventions in order to promote
    what it terms its 'apostolic mission'. But in exercising these priv-
    ileges the Vatican itself is aware that it is a curiosity: as it conceded
    when becoming a party to the Convention against Torture,

    The Holy See, on behalf of the Vatican City State, undertakes to apply it
    insofar as it is compatible, in practice, with the *peculiar nature of that state*.

Peculiar indeed, if this means that the Holy See's belief in hell must for that reason qualify its renunciation of torture. There are many more peculiarities in the Pope's claim to be the head of a state.

88. The Holy See's claim to statehood has at least some historical resonance: the Papacy played a minor role in international relations beginning in the fourth century AD, and later the Emperor Charlemagne created a territorial base for it in an area that is now central Italy. These 'papal states', of 4,891 square miles around and including Rome, were twice annexed by Napoleon and finally extinguished by the Italian army in 1870 as the culminating act of the *Risorgimento*, the unification of Italy. There is not much doubt that this invasion and occupation by Italian troops (after a French garrison defending the Vatican Palace had been withdrawn by Napoleon III) snuffed out the Pope's claim to be head of any state: Pius IX was allowed to stay, fuming and protesting in the Palace, and the Holy See continued to have diplomats accredited to it (in 1914, to reassure Catholics that God was on its side in the war, Britain re-established a relationship that had been broken in 1559), but neither had any subjects or territory over which they could purport to exercise sovereignty. As one leading textbook puts it, 'the Pope's personality was such as was consistent with his religious position and no more.'[2] In relation to this period from 1870 to 1929, an Italian court ruled that notwithstanding its diplomatic links with twenty-nine countries,

the Holy See could not be regarded as a foreign state . . . it cannot be said that between 1870 and 1929 the Pope had a territory of his own, however small, over which he could exercise his sovereignty.[3]

89. Was he suddenly endowed with 'sovereignty' by the Lateran Treaty in 1929? By that treaty Mussolini gave the Vatican City a certain independence from the law of Italy, making it the territory on top of which the Holy See nowadays relies for its claim to statehood. In due course more countries sent delegates to Vatican City and received papal *nuncios* in return. But neither city nor See was ever accepted as a member of the League of Nations,

and their offer to join the United Nations was rejected with some derision by US Secretary of State Cordell Hull in 1944. However, Vatican City and the Holy See were later allowed to sign international treaties, and in 1966 the UN Secretary-General U Thant agreed, without consulting UN members, that the Holy See might be accepted as a 'non-Member' state – but a state nonetheless. In that capacity it has continued to ratify many UN treaties and today is 'recognized' by 178 states with which it has diplomatic relations (although the majority do not send ambassadors). Recognition by other states, even to the extent of exchanging diplomats, does not automatically constitute 'statehood' in international law, a status that is objectively defined by the Montevideo Convention of 1933. Neither the Vatican nor the Holy See, or both together, satisfy that legal definition – a penny that dropped only after the Vatican overplayed its hand at a number of important UN conferences in the mid-1990s, when it used its 'statehood' to wreck family planning initiatives and efforts to improve the status of women.

90. The Vatican certainly rejoices in its pretension to statehood: it boasts that, as a result, 'the Catholic Church is the only religious institution in the world to have access to diplomatic relations and to be very interested in international law'. Statehood means that the international community recognizes the Papacy as 'a moral power *sui generis*, a sovereign and independent moral authority . . . the Pope with his pastoral ministry that involves the earth's peoples and those who govern them can inspire political leaders, give orientation to a great many social initiatives and contest systems or ideas that corrode the dignity of the person and thus threaten world peace'.[4] Pope John Paul II preened that 'the reason why the Holy See is in the midst of the community of nations is to be the voice that the human conscience is waiting for'.[5] That voice damns homosexuals as 'evil', gay civil marriages as 'evil and insidious', whilst abortion under any circumstances (even after rape by a father or a priest or to save the mother's life) is a deadly sin that should be placed beyond the temptation of women, who are also damned if they use any form of birth control other

than abstinence. The voice also describes as 'evil' anyone who engages in IVF embryo experimentation of any kind or for any humane purpose. It calls for an end to the use or distribution of condoms to save lives in HIV/AIDS-ravaged countries. It is a voice that condemns those who divorce, or marry without intending to have children, or (if married) have sex for pleasure alone, or view pornography or donate sperm to Artificial Insemination programmes or undergo pre-natal scans or enter surrogacy arrangements or contemplate euthanasia when terminally and intolerably ill. This is the voice that has been raised most loudly and consistently by Joseph Ratzinger a.k.a Benedict XVI – and it is not a voice that many human consciences in the west have been waiting *for* so much as waiting to leave far behind, although it is raised in chorus with a number of Muslim states that have laws which treat women as inferior and put homosexuals in gaol.

91. It is not my purpose to contest these aspects of Catholic dogma, other than to point out that they are highly controversial and highly political – the Vatican threatens to excommunicate Catholic politicians who support government policies that favour abortion and birth control. In 2002 Cardinal Ratzinger issued a 'Doctrinal Note' that made clear that Catholic politicians had a 'grave and clear obligation' to oppose any law that might tolerate abortion, IVF or embryo experimentation: support was 'impossible for a Catholic',[6] and they ran the risk of excommunication on exclusion from mass if they voted in favour (see para 150). In 2003 he used the same kind of spiritual blackmail to remind Catholic politicians of their solemn obligation to oppose homosexual unions because they 'go against natural moral law', they 'do not proceed from a genuine affective and sexual complementarity' and because all homosexual acts 'are a serious depravity'.[7] The Holy See lends its diplomatic efforts – powerful and effective so long as it is treated as a state – to promoting these fundamentalist beliefs.

92. The Vatican has put its case for statehood in various ways over the years. Its latest explanation to the UN, in May 2010, relies on

Canon Law to define the Holy See as 'the government of the Universal Church'. This description is self-indulgent – the Roman Catholic faith is large although not 'universal', and the Holy See should be no different from the government of any other church. The Vatican claims that it *is* different, because it is the government of a sovereign state:

The Holy See exercises its sovereignty over the territory of Vatican City State (VCS), established in 1929 to ensure the Holy See's absolute and evident independence and sovereignty for the accomplishment of its worldwide moral mission, including all actions related to international relations. (cf. Lateran Treaty, preamble and arts. 2–3.)[8]

93. Since the Holy See bases its claim to statehood squarely on the 1929 Lateran Treaty, it is necessary to examine that document in its historical context, where it may be seen from Mussolini's standpoint to have no dominant purpose of the kind alleged by the church (namely to enable it to accomplish its 'worldwide moral mission'), but rather to have been a bargain to shore up electoral support for the fascists, purchased by giving the church land, money and privileges in Italy and nowhere else. Vatican diplomats contrived to add some language which might give them a claim to favourable treatment over other religions in international law, but this was not an international treaty. No state other than Italy was a party to what was not a treaty at all, but an agreement between the Italian government and a church. This is not to suggest that states cannot be created by the unilateral action of other states – many in the world today were 'created' by colonial powers giving up claims to geopolitically distinct territories by way of granting sovereign independence to a defined people or ethnic group. But none have come about by way of conveyance of property in the form of a palace and its gardens.

94. It is important to understand the truth about the Lateran Treaty, however uncongenial this is to the Vatican and its diplomat supporters. The facts are indisputable enough to be found in school textbooks.[9] The Catholic Church, during the reign of Pius IX (1846 to 1878) became the sworn enemy of the advance of liberal

democracy in Europe; its intolerant and intolerable *Syllabus of Errors* in 1864 condemned freedom of speech and of conscience, and demanded that the Catholic Church be established as the only religion in every state. This call for tyranny was followed by the First Vatican Council (1869–70) with its proclamation of papal infallibility. Many leading Catholics, like Cardinal Newman, were opposed, and Catholic historian Lord Acton famously wrote to Gladstone that now 'we have to meet an organized conspiracy to establish a power which would be the most formidable enemy of liberty as well as of science throughout the world'.[10] (Even more famously, and in the context of attacking papal crimes, Acton pointed out that 'Power tends to corrupt and absolute power corrupts absolutely)'.

95. Pius IX was more concerned to stamp out liberty in his native land: he was the main obstacle to Italian unity, bitterly opposing the great struggle of Garibaldi and Cavour, Mazzini and Verdi. Nonetheless, after the Italian army occupied the papal states and Rome in 1870, the new nation's leaders tried to conciliate rather than extirpate the Pope. They passed *The Law of Guarantees*, allowing him to keep his palaces and to have free use of posts and telegraphs and to keep his own diplomatic representation. But Pius IX would have none of this: he stayed put, muttering, 'This corner of earth is mine. Christ has given it to me.' He demanded all his dominions back and engaged his battalions of Italians – an army of bishops, priests, nuns and officials who were running the country's Catholic schools, colleges and hospitals – to treat the new democratic state as illegitimate. Italian Catholics were ordered by the Pope not to vote or stand in national elections, and it was not until the First World War that the Vatican changed its tactics and backed the Popular Party, which supported the church and opposed votes for women. After the war the church feared this Catholic political party lacked the resolve to protect its interests against the rise of Italian communists: the country needed a much tougher response. The Bishop of Milan took the lead in befriending and championing Mussolini, who 'alone has a proper understanding of what is necessary in this country', and

allowed his fascist party banners to be waved in his cathedral.[11] The Bishop of Milan became Pope Pius XI in time to advise the king to appoint Mussolini as prime minister. (*Il Duce* immediately returned the favour by saving the Vatican Bank from collapse.) The Pope's support became crucial in 1925, during the crisis over Mussolini's responsibility for the murder of Matteotti, a courageous MP who had been threatening to expose fascist party corruption. This time, Mussolini rewarded the Pope by increasing state payments to priests and ordering that crucifixes should be displayed in all schools and courtrooms.

96. But there was more to be settled: Mussolini (a lifelong atheist) needed the church's positive endorsement of his future as dictator of a one-party state, as well as silence over his crimes, while the Pope approved the anti-socialism of the fascist movement and applauded its conservative views on the role of women and its encouragement of procreation. (He was to approve especially of Mussolini's 'battle for births' campaign, which chimed with his encyclical *Of Chaste Marriage*, declaring that since the only purpose of marital sex was the making of babies, all forms of contraception were 'an offence against the law of God and of nature'.) The Vatican was, however, nervous lest the fascists try to take over its schools and its 'Catholic action' social initiatives which nurtured its youthful faithful. So to achieve their mutual ends and to avoid a tug-of-war over the soul and spirit of young Italians, Pius XI and Mussolini began the secret negotiations in 1926 that three years later produced the Lateran Treaty. It had little to do with permitting the church to accomplish its world-wide moral mission: Mussolini needed the Pope to secure the electoral hegemony of fascism in Italy and the Pope was happy to agree in order additionally to secure the church's hold over Italian Catholic youth.

97. The Lateran Treaty and Concordat were unveiled at a grand ceremony in Rome on 11 February 1929. The Vatican newspaper announced 'Italy has been given back to God and God to Italy'. In the elections two months later Mussolini was publicly praised by the Pope as 'a man sent by providence' and the priests told

their parishioners they should vote for him. In consequence, Mussolini won 98.33 per cent of the vote.[12]

98. The terms of the Lateran Treaty provided for Italy to cede to the Pope the Vatican Palace and its gardens – 108.7 acres (1.2 square miles of land), and provided financial compensation for the loss of the papal states in 1870. An accompanying Concordat 'established' the Catholic Church as the official religion of the state of Italy, with Catholic instruction made compulsory in state schools, priests exempted from military service, church law applied to civil marriages and a guaranteed protection for the church's social and youth groups (so long as 'Catholic action' remained independent of politics). This amounted to a 'win-win' deal for both sides, and it was entirely Italy-centric. It was based on the presumption that the 'independent' Vatican would support the fascist state, which it did – despite a brief rift in 1931 over the control of its 'Catholic action' movement and in due course a concern – all too muted – about the 1938 anti-Jewish laws. Mussolini was unconcerned about the church's 'world-wide moral mission' and planned wars that made nonsense of its proclaimed 'mission of peace': the Pope and his bishops had no compunction in blessing Mussolini's army as it embarked in 1935 on its brutal and racist campaign to conquer Abyssinia, and his legions that left subsequently to bolster Franco's army in the civil war in Spain. Their arms were mainly supplied by a munitions factory owned by the Pope through an acquisition by the Vatican Bank.[13]

99. The Lateran Treaty cannot serve as a credible or creditable basis for the Holy See to claim statehood. The grant of 108 acres – the size of a large golf course – was not pursuant to any international treaty, but rather by the unilateral declaration of one sovereign state, through its agreement with a non-state entity that represented no local people, and it was governed not by international law but by the law of Italy and its very first article established Roman Catholicism as the state religion. A 'treaty' in international law is defined by the Vienna Convention as 'an international agreement concluded between states in written form and gov-

erned by international law'.[14] If the Holy See was not a state in 1929 (and the better view is that it was not), then the Lateran 'Treaty' is not a treaty at all but rather a 'Concordat'—a document evidencing an agreement between a state and a non-state entity. (Beginning with Hitler in 1933, the Holy See went on to sign many such Concordats, which as agreements between a state and the church can have no international law consequence. President Chavez is currently threatening to rip up Venezuela's Concordat with the Vatican, and many Germans feel it is time that the church was refused the tax breaks and other privileges granted in its Concordat with the Nazis.) Confusingly, the Lateran 'Treaty' was in fact accompanied by an actual Concordat giving the church in Italy further preferential treatment, so in reality what was concluded in 1929 amounted to two Concordats, which together provided for an internal Italian arrangement between a government and a church. This was an entirely different situation to that where a country gives up part of its territory to a people who need or demand independence: there were no 'Vaticanians' wanting freedom from Italy.

100. Yet this is the rock on which the Holy See still stands for its sovereignty and statehood: its explanation to the UN in May 2010 cites the preamble and Articles 2 and 3 of the Lateran Treaty. The opening paragraph of the preamble confirms that this was an agreement to settle the 'Roman question' in a way convenient to Mussolini's government (represented for ceremonial purposes by King Victor Emmanuel) and the Catholic Church:

Whereas, the Holy See and Italy have recognized the convenience of eliminating every reason of difference existing between them, to come to a definite arrangement of their reciprocal relations, which conforms to the justice and to the dignity of the two High Parties, and assuring to the Holy See in a stable way a condition of fact and right which guarantees to it absolute independence in fulfilment of its high mission to the world, by which the Holy See consents to recognize the Roman Question raised in 1870 with the assigning of Rome to the Kingdom of Italy and to the Dynasty of the House of Savoy as settled in an irrevocable manner.

That Mussolini's Italy had 'justice and dignity' is risible in retrospect and it was a pretence for the Holy See to condescend to 'assign' Rome to an Italy that had possessed it for the past fifty-nine years.

101. Later in the preamble comes the recital:

> . . . whereas it was obligatory, for the purpose of assuring the absolute and visible independence of the Holy See, likewise to guarantee its indisputable sovereignty in international matters, it has been found necessary to create under special conditions the Vatican City, recognizing the full ownership, exclusive and absolute dominion and sovereign jurisdiction of the Holy See over that City.

102. This is the language crafted by Italian diplomats on both sides, after three years of secret negotiations. It makes an unargued and unjustified assertion that by granting the governing body of the Catholic Church the 108 acres of land on which the Vatican Palace and its gardens stand, it will thereby be endowed with the sovereignty of a state under international law. Vatican lawyers had well in mind the international law requirement that a state should have some territory and the Holy See (in effect, the Pope and the Curia) had possessed none since 1870. They wanted the world to think (hence 'visible' independence) that giving the church government some land to govern would make it a state in international law. This was not necessarily correct, as the Montevideo Convention was soon to make clear. The reason they insisted on the insertion of this language was so that the Roman Catholic religion would be given a claim for preferential treatment over all other religions, in international law – and by today's international human rights standards, that is an illegitimate objective (see para 109).

103. The Vatican also relies on Articles 2 and 3 of this 'treaty'. The latter does no more than recognize the Holy See's 'sovereign jurisdiction' over the Vatican – merely a recognition by Italy alone that the church government of Pope and Curia govern the Vatican (although in practice most government functions, such

as policing and defence, are left to Italy, whilst local government functions – electricity, water, sewerage etc – devolve upon the Municipality of Rome.) By Article 2 it is only Italy – and no other state – which recognizes '*the sovereignty of the Holy See in the international field as an attribute inherent in its very nature in conformity with its traditions and with the exigencies of its mission in the world*'. But state sovereignty cannot be 'an attribute inherent in the very nature' of any religious organization, however large or international. The 'nature' of the Holy See is defined by its constituent parts of Pope and Curia: leaders and organizers of a major religion whose priests guide its members in preparation for an afterlife. This is not a body that can claim, as a necessary characteristic, the kind of sovereignty wielded by a nation state. It can only claim 'sovereignty' in the metaphysical sense of a spiritual power over adherents in many different countries, but this is not the kind of 'sovereignty' that international law can recognize.

104. As for the Catholic Church 'tradition', there had until 1870 been papal states with territory and subjects and a dictator Pontiff who exerted some international influence, but this was history – not tradition (and, as Professor Garry Wills puts it, 'the Pope is a freak of history – specifically, of medieval history'[15]). It was true that 'the exigencies of its mission in the world' made it useful or congenial for the Vatican to be a state. Any organization or person who conceives they have a mission to change the world would find that being a state 'conformed to the exigencies of that mission' by making it easier to achieve, for example by having special access to the UN and by demanding that other states receive and listen to its diplomats. But this is not a reason – much less a lawful basis – for being or becoming a state in international law. All religions and human rights organizations and most charities and corporations and Bob Geldof think they have some mission in the world, the exigencies of which require special recognition by the international community. The Roman Catholic Church alone has been permitted to achieve it, by an argument based on the Lateran Treaty – a case of pulling itself up by Mussolini's bootstraps.

105. There is one article of the Lateran Treaty which the Vatican rarely mentions. Article 24 reads:

> The Holy See, in relation to the sovereignty due to it also in the international sphere declares that it wishes to remain and will remain extraneous to all temporal disputes between states and to international congresses held for such objects unless the contending parties made Concordant appeal to its peaceful mission; at the same time reserving the right to exercise its moral and spiritual power.
>
> In consequence of this declaration, Vatican City will always and in every case be considered neutral and inviolable territory.

106. By this key article Italy guarantees Vatican City inviolability in return for abjuring any part in 'temporal disputes'. It was said by a leading international lawyer at the time that 'the article is a waiver, and nothing appears to have been further from the desire of the Supreme Pontiff than to exercise territorial power, as understood by the practice of nations'.[16] But statehood requires an ability to exercise territorial power over those who are citizens of the state, not merely 'moral and spiritual power' of the kind exercised by religions. The Pope said at the time that it was he, not Mussolini, who insisted on confining the Vatican City to a quarter of a square mile of palace and gardens: 'I have no desire to have subjects.'[17] But subjects are what countries must have, to be 'states' in international law.

107. The Pope's renunciation of any exercise of temporal power binds his successors, and his recent successors have reneged on it. They do not 'remain extraneous to all temporal disputes between states and to international congresses held for such objects . . .' They regularly condemn wars – no matter how just (for example the first Gulf War, to drive Saddam out of Kuwait, which he had unlawfully invaded). The Pope's criticism of the 2003 invasion of Iraq, however welcome in some quarters, was nonetheless a breach of Article 24, as was his criticism of Britain over the Falklands War, which ignored the illegal Argentinian aggression that started it. The public intervention on behalf of General Pinochet when the UK arrested and held him under the Torture Convention

was made by both the Pope and Cardinal Ratzinger in 1999, and was another breach of the promise to 'remain extraneous' towards temporal disputes. There are many other examples of how 'state-hood' has gone to the Holy See's head – or to the head of its head of state – who has so far exceeded Article 24 as to seek international status for Jerusalem and to recognize Taiwan as China.[18] At UN conferences, the Holy See frequently intervenes in disputes between states, especially between European and Middle Eastern states, siding with the latter on issues of birth control and family planning and women's and minority rights (see paras 147–155).

108. Its 'moral and spiritual power' is frequently exercised in temporal disputes in opposition to human rights – a recent example being Benedict's attack on the Equalities Bill as it went through the UK Parliament in 2010 as an 'unjust limitation on the freedom of religious communities to act in accordance with their beliefs' which he urged his bishops to fight with 'missionary zeal'.[19] There was a clause in the Bill which would require churches – like all other employers – to avoid discrimination in filling non-religious positions, and his fear was that they might have to hire, for example, a gay gardener to trim the cemetery hedges or be required to consider homosexual couples as foster parents. 'It actually violates the natural law upon which the equality of all human beings is grounded,' he announced – invoking (as he commonly does when attacking 'alleged rights, arbitrary and non essential in nature') an indefinable 'natural law', the doctrine of medieval schoolmen who lived 750 years before nature was decoded by the discovery of DNA and the human genome, and which just happens to coincide exactly with the teachings of the Catholic Church. Article 24 of the Lateran Treaty has long been forgotten by a Vatican which threatens to excommunicate politicians if they do not do what the Pope thinks comes naturally (see para 150). All these breaches of Article 24 mean that the Vatican should no longer be considered – by Italy or any other state – as 'inviolable territory'.

109. Although diplomats get tetchy when reminded of the unsavoury fascist rationale of the Lateran Treaty, the unprepossessing

origins of the Holy See's sovereignty does have this relevance to the legal question of whether the Vatican is actually a state. Those origins bear directly on the question of whether the Vatican City State was created for an illegitimate purpose. The South African puppet homelands were denied recognition because they were created in furtherance of apartheid, and to this day Northern Cyprus is denied statehood because Turkey 'liberated' it by illegal force. The legal objection to the creation of the Vatican City as a state is that the Lateran Treaty was devised to endow a church with statehood to promote its 'mission to the world', thereby discriminating against all other religions. Would the world recognize Mecca as a state if Saudi Arabia negotiated a Lateran-style treaty with its religious leader in order to further an extreme Wahabi 'mission to the world'? Would we be happy to welcome the Holy City of Qom into the councils of the UN if President Ahmadinejad were to negotiate a Lateran-style treaty with its senior Ayatollah? Would that guarantee him sovereign immunity for inciting the murder of anyone in Britain at whom he aimed a *fatwa*? It is astonishing how diplomats have come to venerate the Lateran Treaty: it is even suggested, quite wrongly, that Italy's democratic parties would have made the same deal with the Pope – although the great liberal leader Giolitti could not bear the sight of him and would not have given the Catholic Church, the enemy of democracy, the power that Mussolini granted it in Italy and would certainly not have inflicted its despised anti-democratic mission on the World.

110. The Lateran Treaty casts an extraordinary spell over diplomats unaware of its true history, or even, in the case of the UK's Foreign and Commonwealth Office (FCO), of its actual terms. In answer to a 'freedom of information' request made on my behalf to the FCO asking for documents relating to the decision to have separate UK embassies for the Vatican and for Italy, an astonishing reply was received from an FCO official described as 'Assistant Desk Officer, Papal Visit Team'. She wrote that 'The Lateran Pacts guaranteed the full sovereign independence of the Vatican City in international law' and that 'under the terms of

this Treaty, it is not possible for ambassadors to Italy to be representatives simultaneously to the Holy See – hence the need to maintain two separate embassies in Rome'.[20] This is nonsense: the Lateran Treaty says nothing of the sort, and even if it did the UK would not be bound, since it was not a party. Indeed, other states (like Australia until recently) combined the post of ambassador to Ireland and the Vatican. But the letter goes on: 'under the Lateran Pacts it is impossible for any state to merge its Embassies to Italy and the Holy See . . . they are in separate buildings . . . in accordance with the Lateran Pacts, the two ambassadors' residences remain located in separate parts of Rome'.

III. There is nothing at all in the Lateran Treaty that requires this separation. But when this was pointed out to the FCO, the response was that 'Article 12 of the Lateran Treaty covers issues relating to the diplomatic relations of the Holy See. It is the practice of the Holy See not to permit joint accreditation between Ambassadors to the Holy See and Italy. If you have further enquiries on this matter, they should be addressed to the Holy See'.[21] This is confirmation of (a) their ignorance of law and (b) their pusillanimity in the face of Vatican bluster. By Article 12, Italy undertakes to afford immunity to foreign diplomats accredited to the Vatican, and permits their headquarters to be based in Italian territory, but this does not mean that the embassies cannot be combined. However, in 2004 when Britain finally relinquished the luxurious villa in the Appian Way which housed its embassy to the Holy See, to save money on rent, security guards, gardeners and assorted flunkies by relocating it in the concrete monstrosity that is the UK's embassy to Italy, Cardinal Sodano protested loudly that this would be a breach of the Lateran Treaty,[22] and the UK capitulated by moving its mission to a separate building next door. It has cost the British taxpayers millions of euros, over the years, to maintain the charade of two separate and distinct embassies in Rome: one to Italy and the other to the Holy See. The latter performs no useful services for UK citizens. When I rang its bell recently during office hours I was gruffly informed that visits were by appointment only, and when I claimed to have lost my passport in the Sistine Chapel, I was referred to the UK's embassy to Italy, which handles all problems that mere citizens may have in Vatican village. It is astonishing that the FCO has been such a push-over, conceding a claim by Vatican diplomats that is wrong in law and is about a Treaty to which Britain is not a party. And speaking of parties, the UK's Vatican embassy hosted fifty-two of them in 2008 for 1,338 guests, and forty-four in 2009 for 1,206 guests, namely 'senior Vatican officials and others connected to Holy See diplomacy'. It is unlikely that the conversations with them over champagne and canapés raised questions about Vatican accountability for the sexual abuse of children.

112. Just what the UK's five-person embassy to the Holy See actually does is a mystery kept from UK citizens. Its website claims that it conducts a 'dialogue' on subjects related to human rights, but a Freedom of Information Act request for any memoranda, correspondence or other policy document relating to any 'dialogue' about human rights met with a flat refusal from the FCO, on the grounds that any disclosure of the information 'would be likely to prejudice effective relations between the UK and the Holy See'.[23] Decoded, this means that disclosure would cause embarrassment to the UK government, because the Vatican would of course already know of the content of correspondence and other 'dialogue' addressed to it by the UK ambassador. The FCO claim that all of it is 'confidential' cannot be correct. No doubt the British public would be very pleased to know, for example, that their diplomats had pressed the Vatican over the papal interdict on condom supply to HIV/AIDS-ravaged countries that has meant thousands of otherwise preventable deaths. But the British people are not allowed to know what human rights issues – if any – its Catholic ambassador to the Holy See is discussing with his fellow Catholics, at cocktail parties or anywhere else.

5. The Statehood Test

The Pope! How many divisions has the Pope?

> Joseph Stalin, dismissing a French suggestion that the Vatican might be
> invited to post-war conferences

113. Just four years after the Lateran Treaty, agreement was reached
on the definition of a state in international law. It was enshrined
in Article 1 of the 1933 Montevideo Convention on Rights and
Duties of States:

> The state as a person of international law should possess the following
> qualifications:
> - (a) a permanent population;
> - (b) a defined territory;
> - (c) government; and
> - (d) capacity to enter into relations with the other states.

114. These four requirements are essential although not exhaustive –
questions of the country's independence and capacity will also
be relevant. The importance of the Convention is that it provides an objective test that can be applied by a court, on the
evidence, rather than relying on the politically influenced (often
expedient) decisions by governments to open or close diplomatic
relationships. The argument that 'there are 170 states which have
diplomatic relations with the Holy See, so it too must be a
state' reflects the outmoded 'constitutive theory', developed to
deny the advantage of statehood to countries with a government
that most other countries refused to recognize, often for partisan
reasons – for example the pressure still imposed by China against
recognition of the obvious statehood of Taiwan – or when the
vast majority of states refused (out of misguided support for

Indonesia) to recognize the democratic republic of East Timor (now Timor Leste). The better view is the 'declaratory theory' that diplomacy and *realpolitik* should not be allowed to intrude on an international law question that can be settled objectively by applying the Montevideo criteria to the facts of the particular case.[1]

115. You do not have to be a lawyer to apply the Montevideo Convention to Vatican City. The most dimwitted tourist in St Peter's Square can recognize that before him stands not a state, but a palace with a basilica surrounded by museums and gardens. Its walls may be briskly circumnavigated in fifty minutes, entry requires no proof of identity but merely a bag search and, in the case of museums, a payment of €25 for a ticket – not a visa. The public rooms are for the most part repositories of religious art and artefacts (Nero's bathtub strikes a secular note), and the main crowd-pleasers, the Sistine Chapel and the Pietà, are owed to the genius of Michelangelo, whose eye for the male limbs, torsos and buttocks is often said to stem from a disposition that Cardinal Ratzinger would denounce as 'morally disordered'. Otherwise the opulent display is that of a wealthy church inviting contemplation of its promise of an afterlife: confession boxes offer absolution in different languages (although none in Latin, the official language of the Holy See), beside the mummified remains of several dead Popes. Gift shops beckon at regular intervals, offering Popemabilia – mainly mementoes of John Paul II (Benedict XVI, 'the German shepherd', does not sell as well), while post offices offer 'special issues' on religious themes. A request at the information office to be directed to various foreign embassies met with total incomprehension, but after lengthy inquiries produced some addresses that were all in Italy. The offices in the Vatican have to do with church matters: the Curia and its offices are also located in Italy, around St John Lateran, where the cardinals meet and talk in Italian except when electing a new Pope, when they vote in the Sistine Chapel and announce the result in Latin. Pope Benedict frequents Italy too, at his summer palace, Castel Gandolfo, guaranteed inviolable by the Lateran Treaty but excluded from Vatican sovereign territory. His appearance there

for the midday Sunday *angelus* is both a tourist attraction and a religious celebration, but hardly a state occasion: he emerges from a high window to applause, renewals of which he invites from different sections of the crowd by saying a few sentences in their language, while national flags are waved along with the insignia of various Catholic orders. Small children are held aloft and strain towards him, arms outstretched, while like a seasoned actor he controls the crowd by his quavering fingers, alternately silencing them and blessing them. But there is no mistaking the fact that all its members – invariably with cameras – are tourists who have come to Rome and not to the Holy See, to be blessed by the Pope as head of the church and not as the head of a state.

a) A Permanent Population

116. The Holy See has, by definition, no population at all and the Vatican has no 'permanent population' in any meaningful sense – it is a city without nationals or even residents. At one point it was said to have 416 'citizens', including 46 Curial cardinals, 89 Swiss Guards, 201 bearers of diplomatic passports and the Pope himself.[2] Additionally it has Italian workers – gardeners, museum attendants, cleaners and the like who walk to work across the road from Italy – and several thousand Curia employees working in offices in Rome (i.e. Italy) who are mainly Italians and are subject to Italian laws. There are a few hundred people who actually live within Vatican City and can be granted 'citizenship' by the Pope under its law 'because of their rank of service or employment', but these are peripatetic church dignitaries, or church officials and staff, or diplomats. For them, 'citizenship' is merely a temporary authorization to remain until their status or employment ends: it does not mean permanent residence.[3] There is a special provision for diplomats which extends citizenship to 'the wife [the sexist presumption is that diplomats will be male], children, parents, brothers and sisters', but his sons must leave when they are 25 and his daughters when they marry (another sexist provision). As the leading textbook by a Vatican diplomat

concludes, 'the population is very different from other states' because of the absence of any form of national community – citizenship is 'relative to a specific function which is wholly intended to serve the spiritual interests of the Catholic Church'.[4] Other than diplomats, the residents are Catholic officials – cardinals and bishops, priests and nuns, all of them celibate and hence debarred by that status from propagating citizens. The Vatican is a place where no Vaticanian is ever born, other than by accident – 'citizenship' of the Holy See cannot be acquired by birth. Its population is not 'permanent' in the sense that it can be self-perpetuated or entitled to remain for generations. Nationality is non-existent, since this is not a nation state – or any other kind of state.

117. The Vatican, whether it stands alone or is used to prop up the claim to statehood of the Holy See, cannot satisfy the requirement of a 'permanent population'. This demands, at the very least, an identifiable and stable community. The people of the Vatican are not a 'people' in any meaningful sense, but rather a transient Catholic bureaucracy, with visiting dignitaries and diplomats and servants, in a palace from which any of these 'citizens' may be expelled by the Pope at any time.[5] The Holy See, in short, lacks a stable human society– the only 'permanent' member of Vatican village is the Pontiff himself – and it appears from a recent television series that he often Pope-copters of an evening to his Italian residence, Castel Gandolfo (30 miles from Rome), where he dines from the produce of his organic papal farm whose Italian chef boasts of the taste of his 'lambs of God'.[6] He has no 'people' to enter in the Olympics or to play in the World Cup or to serve in any international peace-keeping mission (even the papal guards are Swiss). The national anthem of Vatican City, appropriately enough, is 'The Bishop of Rome' – the capital of Italy.

b) A Defined Territory

118. 'Vatican City' cannot properly be regarded as a 'territory' at all. In truth, it is a large palace built on top of land that was once

Caligula's private circus where Christians were thrown to the lions. It has a few attached buildings, but gardens take up two thirds of its 108.7 acres. The Palace – the basilica opens on to St Peter's Square – has buildings to the side that house a radio station, a bank and the official newspaper (*L'Osservatore Romano*) and various museums, whilst its secret archives (which may contain the CDF files relating to sex abuse) are flush against the Sistine Chapel. This territory is 'defined' only in the sense that a survey plan is attached to the Lateran Treaty, which comports with the reality that it conveys the ownership of property, despite the fact that it purports to be granting 'sovereignty' over a 'territory'. As a matter of simple English, and indeed of simple Italian, the Vatican is not even a city, let alone a city state: it is a palace entirely within an Italian city (Rome) which city is itself within a state, i.e. Italy. The alternative – that it is a state within a city – would be bizarre.

119. There is nothing 'territorial' about the Vatican: the palace and grounds have one proprietor, the Pope for the time being, and third parties are expressly forbidden from owning any of its real estate or lodging there without papal permission. There are in the world unusual 'microstates' which do have international sovereignty – Nauru with a population of 12,000 on ten square miles of bird droppings, and sinking Tuvalu, whose 11,000 people may eventually have to be evacuated to New Zealand (under a 'Toodle-oo Tuvalu' programme). But these are territories with territorians sharing a nationality and for whom they provide civic services. Vatican Palace has no nationals, and its basic services such as electricity and gas and water and sewerage are provided by Italy and by Italians.

120. Crucially, any state must be able to police its 'territory', but demonstrators, pickpockets and would-be assassins in the Piazza San Pietro are arrested by the *carabinieri* (the Italian police) and are placed in Italian gaols and tried in Italian courts. It makes no sense to have a state which is 'sovereign' over a territory yet cannot – or does not – exercise jurisdiction in respect of crimes

committed on it. Even micro Euro-states like Monaco and Liech-
tenstein have police forces to arrest offenders (unless they are tax
evaders). The Pope is indeed keeper of the keys to unlock his palace, but not to enter his territory, which has no customs or
immigration barriers. The 'defined territory' requirement is generally taken to mean that 'there must be a reasonably stable
political community and this must be in control of a certain
area'[7] – a description that would exclude atolls, lakes, rocks, ice
flows, battleships, volcanoes, Olympic stadia, cloud-capped towers
and garden-surrounded palaces. The Vatican City has been declared a World Heritage Area and has obvious cultural and
historical importance, but these factors do not satisfy this second
statehood requirement.

c) Government

121. If it makes sense to speak of a palace being 'governed' then the
Vatican has government: a proprietor (the Pontiff) and a governing council (the Curia). These personages are collectively called
the Holy See and it is at this point that one cause of confusion
should be cleared up: which one of them is the state? It cannot be
the Holy See because it has no 'territory' and it cannot be Vatican
City, a palace with no permanent population and no diplomats and
which has, as its 'government', the same body that rules the world-
wide Catholic Church. Vatican City exists not to support and
protect nationals but to provide business premises for administer-
ing the Roman Catholic Church – a church that is not itself a state.
The papal claim that the Holy See became a state once more in 1929
because it then acquired the Vatican City as its 'territory' is really a
fudge, because the Holy See does not 'govern' a palace (which virtually runs itself as a tourist centre, with help from municipal
authorities in Rome) but exists to govern the world-wide church.
The Pope is not Mayor of Vatican City, he is head of the church
and as such enjoys 'supreme and full power of jurisdiction . . . in
matters of faith and morals (where he is infallible) and to everything pertaining to the government and discipline of the church'.[8]

The Vatican is really an appendage of the church – its international headquarters, run by a pontifical commission which organizes employment contracts for servants, arranges the upkeep of the museum and deals with personnel matters and the Vatican observatory. The income of the Vatican derives from tourism – it has no income tax or property tax (there is no privately owned real estate) but does a brisk trade in papal blessings (for €96, heavily discounted for nuns). Its treasury is that of the church, which is swollen by tithes from adherents around the world and specifically from the annual collection of 'St Peter's Pence'. But all governmental, as distinct from administrative, functions devolve on the Curia which decides them as the government of the church based in Rome, outside Vatican City, rather than as the government of Vatican Palace. As one scholar points out:

> Not only is the 'government' (i.e. the Holy See) charged with overseeing a religion, rather than a nation, there is also no 'people' within the Vatican City over which such government has jurisdiction . . . The Holy See, which is no more than the administrative body of the Roman Catholic Church does not constitute a 'government' in the traditional sense.[9]

122. Nor in any other sense contemplated by the Montevideo Convention, which requires a state to have at least some degree of independence in the conduct of international affairs. The actual government of Vatican City, namely the Pontifical Commission, does not conduct international affairs at all: this is done from Rome by the Curia as the governing body of the world wide church. Other key government functions – defence, for example, and policing, not to mention hospitals and transport in Rome – are organized by the government of Italy, whilst the only law in the area is Canon Law – but that is silent as to commerce and tort and contract and crime, issues which must be decided in Italian courts. For example, Vatican Radio broadcasts to the world, but not from the Vatican: its transmitter is in Italy, and has recently been found to emit powerful electro-magnetic rays that pollute the atmosphere and have caused cancer and leukaemia in children living nearby. Its director, Cardinal Tucci, was initially treated as immune from prosecution, although this decision was

sensibly reversed on appeal and he has now been given a suspended gaol sentence by an Italian court. The Holy See cannot even punish crimes against its own head, as the world witnessed in 1981 when Pope John-Paul II was shot in St Peter's Square by Mehmet Agca. The would-be assassin was arrested by Italian police, held in Italian prison and tried in Italian courts, where his plea that he had been unlawfully extradited from a foreign state was rejected.[10]

d) Capacity to Enter into Relations with Other States

123. Both the Holy See and the Vatican have the capacity to make agreements with other states and frequently do so, by way of Concordats, or by joining agreements which are relevant or necessary to their operation (the Vatican City signed up immediately to the Universal Postal Union and the International Telecommunications Union). But this is not enough to satisfy the fourth qualification of statehood: many other entities, including wealthy individuals, have the capacity to deal with states by dealing with their governments. What criterion d) should focus upon is the question of what *kind* of relationships are formed with states: are they merely ceremonial or concerned with the Catholic religion, or do they approximate to ordinary diplomatic relations?

124. The establishment of diplomatic relations between states necessarily implies the establishment of consular relations, which are otiose for the Vatican. For example, under the 1963 Vienna Convention on Consular Relations,[11] consular functions include the issue of visas, but no visas are required for entry to Vatican land (the closest equivalent on the Vatican website is the opportunity to book ahead for guided tours and museum tickets: 'enjoy the visit without queuing – discover the Vatican secrets!' etc). Consuls for a state are mainly concerned with safeguarding the interest of its nationals when they are injured abroad or visiting them when they are imprisoned abroad, but as the Vatican has no

nationals, such consular duties are redundant. And any national of another state who is hit by falling masonry in a Vatican museum or pickpocketed in St Peters will not be helped by his state's embassy to the Vatican – these diplomats do not offer consular services, or any other normal embassy services. As for Vatican diplomats, they claim under the 1961 Vienna Convention to enjoy immunities, including inviolability of their person and their embassy and their diplomatic baggage. This exempts them from national laws, and makes it impossible for police to search nunciatures for evidence of harbouring or trafficking in paedophile priests.

125. Most importantly, Article 41(1) of the 1961 Vienna Convention provides that:

(1) Without prejudice to their privileges and immunities, it is the duty of all persons enjoying such privileges and immunities to respect the laws and regulations of the receiving state. They also have a duty not to interfere in the internal affairs of that state.

126. The Holy See, by operating a secret Canon Law process to deal with clerical child molesters, has done exactly that – interfering with the internal criminal law by not handing over those it knows to be guilty of crime; claiming entitlement to remove its guilty employees from the jurisdiction of national law and interfering with local justice systems by operating a Canon Law alternative. This amounts to a clear breach of Article 41, a breach which in most countries has continued for many years. Further breaches can be found in the 'spiritual blackmail' threats from the Vatican to have Catholic politicians excommunicated or denied access to churches or to communion if they vote to decriminalize abortion or in favour of laws stopping discrimination against homosexuals (see earlier para 150). The role of its *nuncio* includes gathering information on such politicians and reporting back to Rome so that the Vatican can consider whether to threaten them with excommunication them or a ban from mass. The reality is that the Holy See has, by exerting its Canon Law jurisdiction over crime, and by making spiritual threats to democratically

elected politicians, fundamentally ignored the Convention obligations of a state under Article 41 of the *Vienna Convention*, and should no longer be treated as if it is one.

127. Whilst diplomats are formally accredited to the Holy See, their role is unlike that at any other embassy or High Commission. Consular services for visiting tourists are provided by the ambassadors to Italy, with their residences and embassies in Rome, and most countries with 'diplomatic relations' with the Holy See actually have their missions *outside* the Vatican (i.e. in Italy).[12] It would save money to house them within the premises of their embassies to Italy, but this prospect enrages Cardinal Sodano, who has been prepared to make an exception only in the case of Israel, for security reasons (see paras 111–12). It is a frequent practice for governments to reward Catholic allies or dispose of Catholic enemies by appointing politicians, rather than career diplomats, to the Holy See ambassadorship, a sinecure congenial to their faith. Thus in 2010 the UK government offered the post to Catholic ex-minister Ann Widdecombe, and the Australian government, not for the first time, used it to lure a Catholic opposition leader from opposition.[13]

128. An example of how the Vatican has been allowed to insinuate its diplomats into the highest levels of the international legal order through the oversight or inertia of other states is provided by the widespread practice of making the papal 'plenipotentiary' (i.e. the local *nuncio*) the senior in order of precedence among the diplomatic community in national capitals, a role which should logically go to the longest-serving ambassador. This practice grew up in certain obsessively Catholic countries as a mark of religious respect, and at their insistence the 1961 Vienna Convention provided that its rules on diplomatic relations should be '*without prejudice to any practice accepted by the receiving state regarding the precedence of the representative of the Holy See*' (see Article 16(3)). This was merely a saving clause, but has been cleverly 'spun' as if it were a universal endorsement of this utterly unmerited practice, and many non-Catholic states such as Germany and Switzerland

and some in central Europe have fallen for it and made the papal *nuncio* the Dean of the Diplomatic Corps (who in New Zealand, for example, takes precedence on formal occasions over the Chief Justice and the Deputy Prime Minister). The man from the Vatican in those countries comes to represent the whole of the Diplomatic Corps, and so obtains special access to high levels of government – a diplomatic coup which has gone largely unnoticed.

129. Diplomatic exchanges between state representatives and the Holy See are generally secret, but the few which have been revealed show that it is not treated as a normal state, but rather as the Italian headquarters of the Catholic religion – which indeed it is. Pius XI spoke eloquently of 'our own dear native land, the country where the hand of God, who guides the course of history, has set down the chair of his Vicar on earth, in this city of Rome, being the capital of the wonderful Roman Empire, made by Him the capital of the whole world . . . guarantees for the liberty of the Roman pontiff [are] of incalculable benefit to Italy', as indeed they are, in tourist dollars and supportive diplomacy. Vatican politics remain Italy-centric, Italians take a significant proportion of Curia offices, and a recent analysis of the 100 papal *nuncios* revealed that fifty-one of them were Italian.[14]

130. Much of the 'diplomatic' traffic is to arrange papal visits and audiences with the Pope that are highly sought by political leaders and their families, whether Catholic (crypto-Catholic in the case of Tony Blair, who had four such 'audiences') or not (Mr Putin, for example, has also had four audiences with the Pope, and George W. Bush visited twice during his first year in office). The 'business' will generally concern the Catholic religion. For example, Australia's ambassador said in 2010 that a good deal of his time was being taken up with arrangements for canonizing the country's first saint: other diplomatic postings do not require a belief in miracles. He did not mention whether he was making any representations about the plague of paedophile priests (Australia has had more of them so far than most other countries) or disputing the Pope's views on family planning and

condoms. These do not appear to be the subject of the ineffably polite exchanges between diplomats. There is no sign of any state protesting about the Pope's condemnation of their law-abiding gay population as 'evil' and 'disordered'. It is a telling fact that the US State Department, which is required to issue an annual report on the human rights record of every state, never comments on the Holy See, and the UK Foreign Office similarly, in its annual report on human rights around the world, never notices the Vatican – not because it is above reproach, but because it is recognized as a 'santa clause state' (see para 12). The European Union has shown no interest in having the Holy See as a European state and Jacques Delors, on behalf of the European Commission, has told the European Parliament that it is highly unlikely that the Vatican would ever be admitted to membership.[15] So, if the Holy See is not a state in Europe where it is situated, why should it be a state anywhere?

131. Most jurists treat criterion (d) – capacity to enter into relations with other states – as requiring independence, evidenced, for example, by a nationality law of its own and freedom from foreign control. This test has invited some tricky distinctions: during the Cold War most of the puppet states of Eastern Europe were recognized because of distinctive and historical nationalities and borders, even though their foreign policy was controlled by the Soviet Union through the Warsaw Pact. The puppet homelands ('bantustans') during apartheid went unrecognized, because although tribally distinct they were a product of apartheid, and their government was tightly controlled by South Africa (they had an 'Embassy Row' in their capitals, but it boasted only the South African embassy). It is otiose to regard the Vatican City as independent in this sense: it has no nationals and all services essential for its survival – from policing and electricity to supply of food and all other commodities – depend on Italy. It is in reality no more than a palace, entirely contained within and dependent upon Italy for its very survival. The Holy See, as government of a church, is free to choose its theology and morality, although the 800 million members of its congregations

cannot be independent because they owe their allegiance to their various nations. No one can possess dual citizenship of a state and of a religion, and although the Vatican issues 'diplomatic passports' to its representatives they should be no more honoured than passports from Bophotswanaland or indeed from Disneyland (which is larger than the Vatican, has a larger population and dresses them in even more colourful costumes).

132. It might be expected that an issue of such obvious legal importance as whether the Holy See (or alternatively or additionally, Vatican City) is a state, would by now be soluble simply by consulting international law textbooks. This is a mistake. The starting point – *The Creation of States in International Law* – began in 1976 as a doctoral thesis by James Crawford: his second edition remarks (understatedly) that 'the legal status of the Vatican City and the Holy See has been the subject of much study and some controversy'. He still inclines to his earlier view that the Vatican City is a state but admits that some experts have denied this and that 'the position of the Vatican City is peculiar and the criterion for statehood in its case only marginally (if at all) complied with'.[16] Professor Gillian Triggs, correctly in my view, concludes that 'The Vatican City does not meet the criteria for statehood'[17] – it has no accredited diplomats, for a start, and serves as a territorial prop for the Holy See which ratifies most of the treaties. Crawford considers that the relationship between City and See is 'a matter for some perplexity' and cites 'the best modern study' of the issue which concludes (correctly in my view) that 'the Holy See is not a state in international law, but has an international legal personality of its own which permits it to take international actions such as the conclusion of treaties and the maintenance of diplomatic relations'.[18] Another leading textbook, *International Law*, sets out reasons to question 'the reality of the Vatican statehood',[19] whilst the late Professor Ian Brownlie's standard student textbook opines that the Vatican City claim is doubtful and that the personality of the Holy See, as a politico-religious hybrid, is 'even more difficult to solve' and can only be characterized by the way in which individual states relate to it.[20]

Many textbook writers compare it to another pumped-up Catholic entity, the 'Sovereign Military Order of St John of Jerusalem, of Rhodes and of Malta', which has had inter-state relations since the beginning of the Crusades. It too issues diplomatic passports and postage stamps, has diplomatic relations with over 100 countries and has buildings in Rome almost the size of the Vatican, but nobody classes it as a state, and in this respect (aside from the Lateran Treaty) it is indistinguishable from the Holy See. It is given merely 'observer' status at the UN, like other NGOs. There are law journal articles of considerable scholarship which relate to the question of Vatican statehood: the weight of more recent opinion appears to favour the negative view.[21]

133. Confusion over the 'statehood' status of the Holy See and Vatican City has been most confounded in respect of the Vatican Bank, which bears the Monty-Pythonesque name 'The Institute for Religious Works'. Under the incompetent and probably corrupt Archbishop Marcinkus (whose motto was 'You can't run a church on Hail Marys'), it became deeply embroiled with the mafia (Michelle Sidona) and with crooked Italian financiers (Roberto Calvi and Licio Gelli) and their right-wing freemasonries operating criminally though Gelli's P2 lodges. When the Bank of Ambrosiano collapsed in 1982, the Milan prosecutors accused Marcinkus of giving 'systematic support to Calvi in many of his illicit operations' and sought his arrest, so the Archbishop hurriedly moved from his luxury apartment in Rome to lodge within the Vatican, which claimed that there, under the Lateran Treaty, he was immune from arrest. The ensuing jurisdictional dispute was settled through political channels – the prosecutors lost interest in Marcinkus after the Vatican paid $250 million to local creditors and the Pope declared 1983 a 'Holy Year' in order to help the Italian economy by bringing vast numbers of indulgence-seeking pilgrims, with foreign currency, into the country.[22]

134. The Vatican has its statehood partly to blame for the sinister power attributed to it by *The Da Vinci Code*. An earlier (but more

factual) bestseller, *In God's Name*, by experienced journalist David Yallop, explored the mysterious demise in 1978 of John Paul I, found dead in his bed with anguish written on his features after only thirty-three days as the Vicar of Christ.[23] In that time he had determined to sack Marcinkus and rid the Vatican bank of its connections with Gelli, and Calvi and their proto-Fascist P2 lodges which (despite the Canon Law ban on freemasons) had attracted some senior Curia figures as members. John Paul I was a stripling, as holy fathers go, aged only 65 and in robust health: Vaticanologists began to whisper about the possibility of suicide, and even murder by poison. These rumours might have been quashed had he died in Italy, where the law requires an immediate autopsy. But Canon Law (unsurprisingly, given its obsolescence) says nothing about autopsies or inquests when death occurs suddenly or suspiciously. So Cardinal Villot (allegedly a P2 member) destroyed telltale documents and pill bottles he found by the side of the papal death bed, arranged for a Vatican doctor to take one quick look at the corpse to diagnose a heart attack, after which the embalmers arrived (summoned, so it is alleged, before the body had even been discovered) to transform the Holy Father's agonised features into a beatific smile for his lying-in-state in St Peters, outside the jurisdiction of the Italian courts. According to Yallop, he was probably poisoned by the P2 lodge to stop him from sacking Marcinkus and cleaning the corrupt freemasons out of the Vatican bank. The bank's complicity in Gelli and Sidona's financial crimes only became public after the collapse of the Ambrosiana bank and Calvi's likely execution (he was found hanging upside down under Blackfriars Bridge). High-ranking Catholics today concede that John Paul I's death was 'mysterious' and that 'rumours abound about the circumstances of his untimely demise' but 'nothing credible has ever been established'[24] – they do not explain that this is because his body lies in the depths of the Holy See, outside the jurisdiction of Italian coronial law and cannot be examined for traces of the poison (digitalis) that Yallop suggests was used to kill him. In 1983, five years after his death, Canon Law received its update under the imprimatur of John Paul II, but it still contained no provision for an autopsy or an inquest: the most significant change was to end the centuries-old ban on Catholics becoming freemasons.

135. The issue of Vatican Bank immunity continues: its operations and finances are cloaked in total secrecy, and US Justice Department investigators have been turned away, powerless in a 'foreign state' and unable to use their extradition arrangements with Italy. The bank has claimed state immunity in the US in long-running legal actions over its holdings of Nazi gold and its involvement in the massive Frankel insurance fraud. In the former action, brought by victims of the Ustasha holocaust in war-time Croatia, the Holy See sent a formal protest to the US government, demanding that it intervene to stop the disrespect to its sovereignty involved in allowing a case to proceed which accused the bank of stealing the property of 700,000 victims of fascism. On this occasion the White House refused and the Court described the bank's dealings as 'murky' and 'opaque'.[25] Because the Holy See is not recognized as a European state, the bank is not bound by European anti-money-laundering rules and controls. It is free from International Monetary Fund supervision and examination (doubtless the reason why the Holy See, so eager to join most international organizations, has declined to join the IMF). Unlike real states, the Holy See has no border checks and no exchange controls and no customs posts – which make its bank a useful vehicle for financial crimes and tax evasion.[26]

136. But for all the force of legal, logical and moral objections to the statehood of the Vatican, the fact remains that most states recognize it as sovereign, and state practice, however politically skewed, is a powerful formative influence on international law. Nonetheless, this branch of law only progresses by attention to principle, and it is altogether possible that a principled court – the International Court of Justice or the European Court of Human Rights or a court in a country where the government did not interfere with an immunity certificate would find the Vatican's claim unsustainable. That would mean that the Holy See, and Vatican City too, would have international legal personality and be capable of

signing treaties and dealing with governments as they have in the past, but they would not have the awesome diplomatic privileges that come with statehood, notably immunity for papal actions which cause damage or are of dubious legality. There is a strong moral case for the movement of international law from a set of rules for diplomatic expediency to a system of global justice based on norms that are not only objectively defined but also objectively determined, free from political pressure. That movement has been most noticeable with international criminal justice, which now indicts heads of state and in many cases (like that of Charles Taylor), rejects sovereign immunity, and it is a movement that demands objective judgements on questions of statehood. That is the challenge for international lawyers in the case of the Pope.

137. However the argument is finessed, neither Vatican City nor the Holy See satisfy the objective Montevideo criteria for statehood, whether considered separately or together. Even the head of the Holy See's permanent division at the UN admits as much:

'it struggles to be counted as a "real" state. Since 1870, it has had almost no real territory to defend. It has no economic or industrial interests in the usual sense of the term. It has almost no population . . . It has the Swiss Guards but no strategic defence to speak of . . .'[27]

Looked at from any direction, the edifice seen is a church – the Roman Catholic Church – with palatial headquarters and a supreme leader, his hands raised to give a blessing not a salute. It is, with 800 million nominal members, the world's largest NGO. It is a tribute to the adroitness of Vatican diplomats (and to the desire of political leaders to be blessed by the spiritual head of many of their subjects) that the church has maintained for so long its camouflage as a state on the world stage, and has achieved an influence in world affairs that is denied to all other churches and NGOs. That influence has come through its privileged position in the UN, as the only 'non-member state', with every entitlement of a member except the right to vote at the General Assembly and be elected to the Security Council.

6. The Holy See and the United Nations

Jesus said, 'my kingdom is not of this world. If it were, my servants would fight to prevent my arrest by the Jews. But now my kingdom is from another place.'

John 18: 36 (New International version 1984)

138. The story of how one religion came to infiltrate the United Nations, to such an extent that its diplomatic tentacles can reach out to affect the agendas of the most important international conferences, still has elements of mystery. When Vatican diplomats first canvassed its case for admission, back in 1944, US Secretary of State Cordell Hull told them 'as a diminutive state the Vatican would not be capable of fulfilling all of the responsibilities of membership in an organization whose primary purpose is the maintenance of peace and security'. He pointed out that in any event membership would be inconsistent with Article 24 of the Lateran Treaty, which guaranteed neutrality in return for the Pope's abandonment of temporal power (see para 105–8), certainly if it was required to contribute armed forces to a UN operation. The Vatican would of course be welcome to participate as a non-member, like other organizations or religions or NGOs, in the UN's social and humanitarian activities. But after the war, the Holy See and Vatican City, somewhat interchangeably, became parties to various international treaties: in the 1950s, for example, the Vatican City signed the International Wheat Agreement (although it grew no wheat), but later it was the Holy See which appended its coat of arms to various conventions – nuclear test bans, anti-personnel mines and chemical weapons – and although the prospect of it ever deploying these armaments was negligible, nobody seemed to mind. Whether

through bureaucratic inertia, or the desire to add another signature to a convention, no official ever seems to have challenged the right of the church to add its name – either as Vatican City or the Holy See.

139. The church gradually insinuated itself into the UN system, without ever inviting a determination as to its statehood. After its rejection in 1944 it turned up at a Food and Agricultural Organization Conference in 1948 and was granted observer status because of its 'special religious nature' – whatever the FAO took that to mean – its headquarters were in Rome and it was vulnerable to papal influence. From 1951 a Vatican diplomat attended meetings of the General Assembly and the World Health Organization as an observer and on an *ad hoc* basis, and UNESCO accepted it as a 'permanent observer'. In 1956, the Holy See arrived at a conference of the International Atomic Energy Commission and was for some reason accepted as a full member – a decision made by an obscure official and not subject to any vote. But with this collection of credentials, the Holy See then had itself elected without debate to the Economic and Social Council (ECOSOC) in 1956 and made this its springboard in October 1957 for raising the question of its status with the Secretary-General's office, which puzzled over whether it was talking to the Vatican City, or to the Holy See. It was at this point agreed that relations (of a non-specified kind) should exist between the UN and the Holy See, not the Vatican City, because the latter 'would have unduly stressed the temporal aspects of the Pope's sovereignty' – and would perhaps have drawn attention to the fact that the Vatican City lacked the Montevideo Convention qualifications for statehood.[1] This agreement did not mean UN acceptance that the Holy See was a state, but merely that it was the appropriate entity for further communications with the UN.

140. In 1964 the Holy See made its play for more power, by unilaterally informing Secretary-General U Thant that it was sending a permanent observer mission to UN head quarters in New York.

U Thant seems to have accepted this as a *fait accompli*, without referring it to the General Assembly or Security Council for approval. (The Vatican now claims that the UN 'invited' it to join in 1964 – in fact, the initiative came from the Holy See). In 1967 the Vatican followed up by sending another 'permanent observer' without objection to the UN's offices in Geneva. It was then accepted as a full member by the World Health Organization and other UN agencies, and turned up at their conferences to exercise full speaking and voting rights. Soon it had elevated itself to a 'non-Member state permanent observer', a status that it shared at the time with a few real states, such as Switzerland and North and South Korea.

141. Although the Secretary-General can in retrospect be criticized for allowing the Holy See this back-door entry, it is important to remember that Vatican policies were not particularly controversial at this time. In 1964 the great majority of states still criminalized abortion and homosexuality, whilst IVF children and embryo experimentation were not on the moral radar. As for contraception, one dramatic breakthrough had already been made when Pius XII approved the 'rhythm method' for married couples, and a Birth Control Commission had been established to advise the Pope on whether to permit artificial contraception as well as 'Vatican roulette'. It was not until 1968 that *Humanae Vitae* rejected the Commission's advice (which was overwhelmingly in favour) and damned all contraception use in all circumstances, putting the Holy See at odds with some UN programmes and making its special connection with the UN potentially problematic. (As one distinguished medical member of the Pontifical Commission spluttered, 'I cannot believe that salvation is based on contraception by temperature and damnation is based on rubber').[2]

142. Another subsequent factor in Vatican acceptability at the UN was the acceptability to the US and its allies of the election in 1978 of a profoundly anti-Communist Pope. Once John Paul II had demonstrated his pro-Western credentials, the Reagan adminis-

tration recognized the Holy See (1984) and other Western nations followed. In 1978 the Holy See had diplomatic ties with only eighty-five countries, many of them Catholic-populated states, but by the end of John Paul's reign the number had increased to 174;[3] even the Soviet Union, under Gorbachev, sent a diplomat. The Holy See may not have been a state, but it consorted with states and declined to mix on the same level with NGOs or to receive communications from non-state entities however important (like judicial commissions into child abuse) and insisted that it be formally addressed in its native language – Latin.

143. Until the UN's Cairo conference in 1995, the enormous political and lobbying clout that non-member statehood gave the Catholic Church compared with other rival religions and NGOs was barely noticed. Yet this religious denomination was now, as a result of its non-member statehood, a participant, not merely a consultant – a fundamental distinction spelt out by an ECOSOC resolution in 1968:

> A clear distinction is drawn in the Charter of the United Nations between participation without vote in the deliberations of the Council and the arrangements for consultation. Under Articles 69 and 70, participation is provided for only in the case of states not members of the Council, and of specialized agencies. Article 71, applying to non-governmental organizations, provides for suitable arrangements for consultation. This distinction, deliberately made in the Charter, is fundamental and the arrangements for consultation should not be such as to accord to non-governmental organizations the same rights of participation as are accorded to states not members of the Council and to specialized agencies brought into relationship with the United Nations.[4]

144. The message was clear – non-member states could be partners and participants at the UN through their observer status, whilst NGOs and religious organizations were merely 'consultants'. The distinction was further clarified in 1990, when the Red Cross was granted a 'special' observer status to allow it to participate in UN initiatives relevant to its role under the Geneva Conventions. Hitherto, it had merely been accorded a 'consultative

status' under Article 71 of the Charter, and so had not been allowed to speak at, or even regularly to attend, UN conferences. It complained bitterly that it had to spend a large amount of its budget in lobbying states (including non-member states) to take up its concerns, and had great difficulty at every level in putting its problems on the UN agenda.[5] Non-member states with permanent missions have no such problems – they have a right to be present as members in all UN bodies and are only refused the right to vote at plenary meetings of the General Assembly. As one international law textbook explains, 'in the case of the Vatican, state acceptance thus gives a particular religious community privileged access to international fora'.[6]

145. In 2002, after Switzerland – by then the only other 'non-member permanent observer state' – had democratically decided to become the 193rd member of the UN, the Holy See let it be known that it too wished to become a full member. The UN *nuncio*, Archbishop Miglione, was given the delicate task (as a member of his team coyly put it) 'to explore with national delegations and other experts the pros and cons of membership weighed against the alternative of an official clarification of our status as an observer'. In other, less euphemistic, words, the Vatican lobbied aggressively for eighteen months to crown its claim to statehood with full membership of the UN. It failed – and doubts about its legal status must have played a part in that failure, notwithstanding its power over Catholic states. (The office of the President of the General Assembly hinted only that the Vatican had been rejected for membership because 'not every country recognizes the Holy See as a state.') To save embarrassment and the prospect that its 'statehood' might be questioned, the Vatican turned to its alter ego – Italy's UN ambassador – who brokered a deal with the President of the General Assembly to put down a resolution which would 'clarify' the position of the Holy See, and give it similar rights to those accorded to Palestine in 1998 (in fact, it was given more). So by an agreement with the President – a rotating office which happened to be held at the time by devout Catholic cricketer Julian Hunte, from the

tiny tourist island of St Lucia – Resolution 58/314 on *Participation of the Holy See in the Work of the United Nations* was put on the agenda. It went through without a vote or a discussion.

146. This resolution recited inaccurately that the Holy See had become a 'permanent observer state' in 1964 (in fact, it had been a 'non-member permanent observer state') and confirmed its rights to participate in General Assembly debates (occupying as many as six seats in the hall); to make interventions and points of order and replies, to have its documents officially circulated, to co-sponsor resolutions and to take precedence ahead of Palestine and any other accredited observers, although it would not vote or nominate candidates. The resolution had not been debated, and according to 'See Change' (a coalition of 700 NGOs, many of them Catholic, which opposes the Holy See's policies) some UN missions were entirely unaware of it. It was a lost opportunity to settle the Vatican's true status, although it did confirm the privileges it had been exploiting for some years. The Vatican 'spun' this consolation-prize resolution as a great success and has presented it as a confirmation of its statehood (although it was nothing of the sort) and a few weeks later Cardinal Sodano awarded Mr Hunte its highest papal award for lay persons, making him a Knight of the Guard Cross. Ironically, this award contravened a Vatican ban on giving papal honours to pro-abortion politicians (as St Lucia's Catholics quickly pointed out, Hunte had cast the deciding vote to decriminalize abortion on the island, declaring 'I am a pro-choice man'). Sodano turned a deaf ear: evidently Hunte's services to Catholic diplomacy were more important than any disservice to the Catholic religion.[7]

147. The Holy See's 'permanent observer statehood' had first been exploited to wreck an important UN conference on population and development in Cairo in 1995.[8] Even before the preparatory conference to settle the agenda, the Vatican began a propaganda campaign over family planning and contraception proposals, alleging that 'reproductive health' meant abortion (a 'heinous evil') and tolerance of homosexuality (another 'heinous evil'). It

forged an unholy alliance with states like Libya and Iran to oppose the projected 'right to sexual health'. At the all-important 'prepcoms' (the preparatory conferences which settle the final agenda) the Holy See used its 'state' rights to the hilt. Accorded full membership, it objected to over 100 paragraphs of the initial draft which referred to any form of planned parenthood, then it called for special debates on these issues at the conference, to which it dispatched one of the largest delegations (seventeen diplomats) who blocked consensus and enlisted allies from the Catholic countries of Latin America and Africa to water down the language and avoid any possibility of recognizing that abortion or contraception might in any circumstances be tolerated or that anything might be done to help the victims of botched or backyard abortions. As a result, a conference that should have discussed population policy and international aid was hijacked by a church masquerading as a state, preventing consensus being reached on any proposal that might possibly challenge the proposition that the only acceptable human genital contact was that between husband and wife for the purpose of procreation.

148. The Vatican's proactive behaviour at Cairo made some statesmen realize that permitting the Holy See to claim statehood had been a mistake. The European Community resolved that the Vatican had led the Cairo conference 'up the blind alley of abortion' and prevented debate on overpopulation and development.[9] But at the next big UN event – the 1995 Beijing conference on women – the Vatican was up to its old tricks, played more subtly but played nonetheless, from its powerful position as a presumed sovereign state. Thus it was able to prevent consensus over a draft text by voting against (or threatening to vote against) any formulation at the precoms and on the conference floor with which it disagreed. Once again, it lobbied its allies – the Catholic states of Latin America, and some Muslim states – to oppose the inclusion of any language that sent a shudder up its spiritual spine – 'gender' and 'gender equality', 'sexual orientation', 'unwanted pregnancy', 'unsafe abortion', 'sex education', 'reproductive health', 'contraception', 'reproductive rights', 'sexual health', 'couples

and individuals' and even 'lifestyle'. Any phraseology that could conceivably concern abortion (even after incest or rape) or homosexuality was anathema to its delegation, which opposed the availability of condoms to curtail what was then the imminent plague of AIDS in the third world.[10] It had quickly adopted the arrogance associated with major power status – at the conference it tried to ban the attendance of one NGO, 'Catholics for a Free Choice', which opposed the church's stand on abortion.

149. Many priests and nuns working for Catholic aid organizations in remote or impoverished areas of Africa and Latin America ignore Vatican teachings and distribute condoms and IUDs and family planning advice, but Vatican diplomatic pressure has had serious effects on funding and direction of UN programmes such as the UN Population Fund, which suffered massive cuts (except for 'abstinence' campaigns) when Catholic and US evangelicals made common cause under the George W. Bush presidency. In third world cities, bishops insist that Catholic charities toe the Vatican line – and even in cosmopolitan Sydney, a life-saving needle exchange programme run by nuns was stopped by the personal intervention of Benedict XVI.[11] Catholic politicians threatened with excommunication generally comply with church instruction – in El Salvador, they even passed a dishonest law requiring all condom packages to carry the 'warning' that they offered no protection against AIDS.[12] For years, UNAIDS has been complaining that the Vatican's demonization of condom use is contributing to the spread of AIDS, especially in Latin America where almost 2 million have fallen victims to an epidemic which would be resolved in the region were condom use encouraged. In Brazil their laws not only criminalize abortion but require doctors to report to police when women come to hospitals bleeding from self-administered terminations. At present over 100 await trial. It is a strange Christianity that requires the reporting to police of injured women but not of molesting priests.[13]

150. The Holy See has exploited its statehood at the UN to exclude its religious critics and to inflict its fundamentalist morality – that

all sexual acts are wrong unless done for the primary purpose of procreation – on the UN's social and health initiatives. It leads a group of Catholic states – i.e. states with a majority of people (and hence of politicians) who are of the Roman Catholic faith. A powerful influence in the lobbies of UN conferences is the veiled threat of excommunication of leading politicians if the governments they run support a political or moral position with which the Pope strongly disagrees. This is the 'spiritual blackmail' devised by Cardinal Ratzinger during his CDF days and spelled out in his Doctrinal Note on *The Participation of Catholics in Public Life*, placing a 'grave and clear obligation' (i.e. one that might be enforced by excommunication) on every Catholic politician to vote according to the church's moral dictates. His new 'enforcer', Archbishop Burke, whom he appointed to head of the church's highest court, told bishops in 2009 to refuse communion to Catholic politicians, like John Kerry, Joseph Biden and Nancy Pelosi, who 'sin gravely' by voting in disobedience to the church's teachings (see para 91).[14] Holy See delegates have shown no interest in child sex abuse: their concern to protect children has always been phrased as a concern to protect them from being aborted in embryo, from being molested by homosexuals, from being unborn to couples intent on IVF programmes or sexual pleasure.

151. In 1996 the Holy See launched a campaign against UNICEF, encouraging states to withdraw contributions because it had sponsored a handbook for women in refugee camps, which provided information on how they could access maternity and family planning services.[15] In all its statements at the UN on 'gender equality' the Vatican uses a stock phrase: it 'recognizes the difference and complementarity of men and women' (which decodes to mean that they are not equal – women are to give birth to the children of men). In 2000, Cardinal Ratzinger launched a stinging attack on the UN's 'New World Order' because one of its goals was to reduce the world's population. 'At the base of this new world order,' he wrote ominously and mysogynistically, 'is the ideology of "women's empowerment", which erroneously sees the principal obstacles to a woman's fulfilment

as the family and matrimony . . . Christians have the duty to protest.'[16] Feminists who complain that the Vatican treats women as little more than a life-support system to a womb back their case with quotations like these from Cardinal Ratzinger.

152. In 1998, the Holy See delegates descended on the Rome conference called to establish the International Criminal Court (ICC). They had already tangled with Nato over its support for agencies which supplied 'morning after' pills to women pack-raped by marauding soldiers, and they scoured the ICC draft for any suggestion that making such rapes a 'crime against humanity' might be interpreted to justify a victim terminating an unwanted consequential pregnancy. The Holy See failed to stop the inclusion of rape, at least when undertaken on a widespread and systematic scale, or 'forced pregnancy', i.e. making women pregnant with the intent of affecting the ethnic composition of a population (an example being the Serb soldiers who raped Muslim women in order to 'make Chetnik babies'), but it insisted – as the price for consensus on the definition of crimes against humanity – that outlawing such atrocities should carry the rider that 'this definition shall not in any way be interpreted as affecting national laws relating to pregnancy'. In other words, in countries where the church had succeeded in having abortions banned by law, women who were raped in war would be forced to carry the children of the enemy soldier who attacked and impregnated them – often after killing, in their presence, their husband and children.[17]

153. The Holy See was also largely responsible for including in the ICC Treaty the most ridiculous clause ever devised. 'Persecution' had been defined in Article 7(1)(h) to include persecution 'on grounds of gender'. The very word 'gender' rang alarm bells for the Holy See, which led other homophobic Catholic and Islamic states to insist on appending Article 7(3):

For the purpose of this Statute, it is understood that the term 'gender' refers to the two sexes, male and female, within the context of society. The term 'gender' does not include any meaning different from the above.

154. This means, presumably, that governments can do what they like to transsexuals. Persecution (i.e. 'intentional and severe deprivation of human rights') is a crime if directed at men as men, or women because they are female, but homosexuals may still suffer the thumbscrew and the rack when this is 'within the context of society', i.e. approved by a gay-bashing government or a vicious state religion or culture. The inclusion of Article 7(3) at the insistence of the Holy See is a distasteful but realistic reminder that many states in 1998 still favoured the withdrawal of human rights from homosexuals, and that their political campaign was led by a major world religion.

155. The Vatican tried to have drug trafficking made an international crime, but was noticeably silent about paedophile trafficking, (for which it could have been liable because it had moved abusive priests from country to country). Its major initiative was to include a special clause exempting priests and their penitents from ever having to reveal the secrets of the confessional, irrespective of whether the penitent confessed to genocide or some other atrocity. This unattractive proposal was sensibly rejected, and the Holy See then petulantly refused to sign the ICC Treaty – a refusal that it maintains today, despite its pretensions to support human rights. On that subject, Cardinal Ratzinger showed his true colours in 1999 when he protested passionately to the UK against the arrest of the torturer General Pinochet. At first he used the high diplomatic channels which the Holy See is accorded as an assumed state, but when that failed he angrily went public, 'to repeat to the world that at no time can the sovereignty of any state, big or small, be violated, stripping the local government of the power to judge a fellow national'.[18] This was ironic, because the church's insistence on Canon Law for its priests was doing exactly that – stripping local governments of the power to judge fellow nationals of a particular vocation. It was also disingenuous, because (as Ratzinger well knew) Chile had no power at the time to judge Pinochet, who had given himself an amnesty. Ratzinger was asserting that no matter how great the crime, there should be no international accountability for political lead-

ers or heads of state: they should be tried in their own country, or not at all. (This would be of comfort to any Pope, because it would mean he could only be tried by the law of Vatican City, which gives him complete immunity and where in any event he is the supreme judge.) In other respects the Vatican has been hostile to the enforcement of human rights law, permitting priests and nuns accused of burning and bulldozing Rwandan churches (with Tutsis inside them), to take sanctuary in parishes in Italy, and obstructing the court's prosecutor, Carla del Ponte, when she asked for one priest to be surrendered. This was Father Seromba, hidden there for several years under an assumed name, who was later convicted of genocide. She relates how the Vatican's 'Foreign Secretary' even denied to her that the Vatican is a state in order to avoid her request for help in locating Croatian war criminals believed to be hiding in Franciscan monasteries.[19] It has recently been accused of permitting a local archbishop and a Catholic relief organization to assist Joseph Kony, head of the Lord's Resistance Army in Uganda, after his indictment by the ICC for international crimes – notably the use of children as sex slaves.[20]

156. Ironically the Vatican has made itself a party to treaties which call its own behaviour into question. For example, the Convention Against Torture and Other Cruel, Inhuman or Degrading Treatment (1984) was acceded to by the Holy See on 25 June 2002. It was required under this Treaty to submit a report on 26 July 2003 but it failed to do so: the next report date (26 July 2007) was also missed, and no report has ever been forthcoming – perhaps because international courts have now held that rape and child sex abuse can amount to torture when they serve such purposes as 'intimidation, degradation, humiliation . . . control or destruction of a person'.[21] The Inter American Court of Human Rights has found that rape constitutes 'psychological torture'[22] and this has been confirmed by the European Court of Human Rights, a court to which the Holy See, despite its anxiety to take almost every opportunity to advance the perception that it is a state, has not volunteered to become a state party.[23] Both that court and the UK's highest court have held that the special

vulnerability of children is an important factor in considering whether ill-treatment crosses the higher threshold to amount to torture, or at least the lower threshold to be classed as 'inhuman and degrading'.[24] There is no doubt that these courts would find clerical sex abuse of children to fall within the latter category and in many cases to amount to the more serious crime of torture, certainly in the significant percentage of cases where the victims are under 12 and have been raped or forced to have sex.

157. As a 'state party' to the Torture Convention, the Vatican is required to take effective action to prevent acts of torture and 'to make these offences punishable by appropriate penalties which take into account their grave nature' – a duty hardly satisfied by the inappropriate Canon Law penalties of penance or laicization. It has to be said that the definition of 'torture' in the Convention is narrower than the definition applied by international criminal courts for judging war crimes and crimes against humanity, and abuse of children by priests for gratification of their lust does not come within the narrower definition, which refers to acts undertaken by public officials or persons acting in an official capacity. Torture under the Convention includes the causing of severe mental pain, but requires a specific purpose, and the examples in the text ('for such purposes') do not include sexual gratification, although it could be argued that the stated purposes are not exhaustive. But another difficulty is the requirement that it be inflicted by or with the acquiescence of a 'person acting in an official capacity': is a paedophile priest 'acting in an official capacity' when abusing a child? Ironically, the argument would be stronger if the Holy See *were* a state, and the priest could be characterized as one of its officials, if clad in its vestments (uniform) and committing the abuse whilst officiating at confession or in the sacristy or whilst on duty with a youth group.

158. In any event, the Vatican's failure to comply with the Torture Convention's reporting obligations shows that it does not take its UN 'non-member state' duties seriously, although it takes every opportunity to use its non-member state privileges to have its

own theological dogmas define the help that the UN can give to the poor and the sick and the persecuted in the developing world. What shows the Vatican up for the hypocrisy that it peddles in international fora is the fact that it is not in favour of human rights at all. This can be seen from its failure to sign all the human rights treaties, with the exception of the *Convention Against Torture* (with its reservation) and the *Convention on the Rights of the Child*, which it has so fundamentally breached. The list of the Conventions that it rejects are quite staggering: they include the central human rights conventions – the *International Covenant on Civil and Political Rights* – with its Optional Protocol that invites a judgment on state practices; the *International Covenant on Economic, Social and Cultural Rights* (without ratifying this convention it should never have been allowed membership in the ECOSOC bodies in which its voice is so loudly raised), the *Convention on Migrant Workers* (ironic given its trafficking in migrant priests), the *Convention on the Rights of Persons with Disabilities* (for all its protestations for concerns for the disabled), the *International Convention for the Protection of All Persons from Enforced Disappearance* (introduced to do something about the death squads run by right-wing military leaders who were never threatened with ex-communication by the Church), *Convention on the Non-Applicability of Statutory Limitations to War Crimes and Crimes Against Humanity* (doubly ironic given the insistence on imposing time limits for complaints against paedophile priests) – and perhaps inevitably – the *Convention on the Elimination of All Forms of Discrimination against Women* – a refusal that reflects a long history of teaching in the Catholic church which is, according to Cherie Booth QC, 'based on the notion that women were somehow inferior. Women still do not get due respect in the Church'.[25] Pope Benedict XVI has had more than five years to ponder whether to ratify these Conventions.

159. There are some commentators – most prolifically, the Catholic journalist John L. Allen Jnr – who argue that it is for the public benefit that the Pope should remain above all human law as the head of a UN-recognized state so he can act as mediator of disputes between Catholic states. But a Pope can do this as religious

leader and does not need the bogus mantle of statehood. Besides, the best example of papal intercession was in the dispute between Chile and Argentina over the Beagle Islands, and that was thirty-five years ago. At that time, military leaders in the Catholic countries of Latin America were contriving to exterminate leftists (many of them young Catholics attracted to 'liberation theology' beliefs) by death squads and the murderous designs of Operation Condor; in Chile torture was an open secret and in Argentina leftist women prisoners were killed after giving birth and their children were adopted by army families. The Vatican rarely intervened, but instead forged friendly links with the military leaders responsible for the atrocities and whom the Pope would often honour by receiving when they visited Rome. In 1984 Cardinal Ratzinger took it upon himself, as head of the CDF, to condemn liberation theology and expel liberation theologists.[26]

160. Papal diplomacy at an international level has depended on charisma rather than statehood: its impact has been blunt and inconsistent. Many who admired John Paul II's stand against communist repression in his native Poland were shocked when he failed to stand behind courageous Catholics in Latin America like Archbishop Romero, whose last cry to the brutal Salvadorian military – 'I beg you, I implore you, I order you in the name of God: stop the repression' – provoked his assassination the next day. The pope's attack on the Sandinista government in Nicaragua and the priests who supported it served to sanctify the Reagan administration policy of backing the *contra* war in that country, and was unaccompanied by any concern for the suffering of the people.[27] He said little about apartheid, the other significant struggle of the time, and with the help of Cardinal Ratzinger he pulled the rug from under the courageous Catholics who had tried to stand up to Hastings Banda in Malawi and to Lee Kuan Yew in Singapore. He failed to develop a coherent 'just war' doctrine, most noticeably during the Falklands conflict when he lectured English Catholics that war was 'totally unacceptable as a means of settling differences between nations' then flew to Argentina and notably refrained from threatening

its Catholic military leaders with excommunication (or anything else) unless they withdrew from islands they had captured by unlawful aggression.[28] The Pope opposed the 1991 Gulf War although it had full UN support and there was no other practical way of liberating Kuwait from Saddam's unlawful invasion, and he opposed the UN-backed attack on Afghanistan in 2001 although it was the only way of dislodging Bin Laden and his al-Qaieda.[29] Benedict has wondered somewhat enigmatically, in relation to the 2003 invasion of Iraq, 'whether it is still licit to admit the very existence of a just war'; but a state which boasts a 'moral mission' is not much good to a world where massive attacks on human rights sometimes have to be met by force – very occasionally (as in the case of Kosovo) without UN-animity.

161. Allen argues further that papal immunity and UN statehood is necessary so the Pontiff can act as 'a neutral voice of conscience on the global stage'. The problem is that Benedict's voice is not neutral on matters of conscience: Allen himself has exposed Joseph Ratzinger's amnesia over his Hitler youth; his attempts to whitewash Catholic Church collaboration with the Nazis; his alliance with right-wing military and political forces in attacking liberation theology and the World Council of Churches; his hostility to women in the church; the almost primitive depth of his opposition to IVF babies (because the sperm is obtained through masturbation); his wish to stop married couples from ever using condoms 'even if one spouse is HIV positive and the goal is to prevent the spread of the disease'. Moreover, Benedict's 'infallible' edicts on faith and morality encourage homophobia – he describes being gay as an 'intrinsic moral evil' and promotes discrimination against gays 'in adoption and foster care, in employment of teachers and coaches and in military recruitment', using the kind of hate-preach which can be linked, so Allen suggests, to gang-beatings of gays and prostitutes in Latin America.[30] The articulation of such views is not 'the neutral voice of conscience' which can assert some unique moral claim to UN non-member statehood, so as to make maximum impact on the world stage.

7. The Convention on the Rights of the Child

Legislation is needed to protect children from all forms of exploitation and abuse, as in the case of incest and paedophilia . . . these scourges are an affront and a scandal to humanity. These various forms of violence must not go unpunished.

> Holy See, Statement to UN Special Conference on Children, 2002, para 23(a).

162. The most important Convention that the Holy See has ratified is the Convention on the Rights of the Child (1989). It accompanied its ratification with a solemn declaration that 'by acceding to the Convention . . . the Holy See intervened to give renewed expression to its constant concern for the wellbeing of children and families'. But it undercut this boast by several 'reservations', (i.e. statements that it will interpret or apply aspects of the Treaty in ways that may exclude or alter their legal effect).[1] It interpreted the phrase 'family planning education', for example, to mean 'methods of family planning which it considers morally acceptable, that is natural methods of family planning' despite the fact that education only in the rhythm method may not permit much 'planning' at all. More significantly – but so obscurely that no state party seems to have noticed its effect – it entered its reservation *'that the application of the Convention be compatible in practice with the particular nature of the Vatican City state and of the sources of its objective law . . .'*. The main source of Vatican law is Canon Law, which sets out a secret, ineffective and non-punitive process for dealing with child sex abuse by priests – a process which, as we shall see, is impossible to reconcile with certain key provisions of the Convention, and should be withdrawn if the Pope is serious about its obligations.

163. By becoming a party in 1990, the Holy See undertook to submit a report on its performance and did so on one occasion (March 1994). It claimed to have 'a profound esteem for children's personal dignity . . . from the moment of conception' and demanded that other states give 'particular protection' to orphans. It inveighed against contraception and sex education as causes of teenage promiscuity, supported breast feeding as good for the child 'and a way of spacing childbirths' and said not a word about clerical sex abuse. The Convention's Expert Committee blandly recommended that Catholic Church institutions and organizations ensure that 'the best interests of the child and respect for the view of the child be taken fully into account'.[2] This recommendation was certainly ignored in the orphanages of Ireland and schools for the deaf in the US, where child sexual abuse in this period was 'endemic'. The Holy See was next due to report on 1 September 1997 and then again on 1 September 2002: it did not do so on either occasion and indeed has never submitted another report,[3] a complete abdication of its duties under the Convention. The Committee of Experts should itself have commenced an investigation of the Holy See's compliance: had it done so, it would have found extensive breaches of its obligations under the following articles:

(a) Placing the Best Interest of Children First

> *Article 3(1): In all actions concerning children, whether undertaken by public or private social welfare institutions, courts of law, administrative authorities or legislative bodies, the best interests of the child shall be a primary consideration . . .*

The evidence shows that the primary consideration in dealing with children's allegations has been the good name and reputation of the Catholic church and the protection of the priesthood from scandal. The best interests of the child requires the church to act immediately to stop the abuse and protect other children by precluding any prospect of re-offending. That meant calling in the police and social welfare services and providing counselling to the child and the family – steps the Vatican resolutely refused to envision when it published its new Canon Law norms in July 2010.

(b) Duty to Investigate and Prosecuting Child Sex Abuse

> **Article 19(1):** *States Parties shall take* **all appropriate legislative, administrative**, *social and educational measures to protect the child from all forms of physical or mental violence, injury or* **abuse**, *neglect or negligent treatment, maltreatment or exploitation,* **including sexual abuse** . . .

> *(2) Such* **protective measures should, as appropriate, include effective procedures** *for the establishment of social programmes to provide necessary support for the child and for those who have the care of the child, as well as for other forms of prevention and for identification, reporting, referral, investigation, treatment and follow-up of instances of child maltreatment described heretofore, and,* **as appropriate, for judicial involvement** . . .

This placed an international law duty on the Holy See to make arrangements for reporting child sex abuse to law enforcement authorities – a duty that has been blatantly breached from the outset by subjecting all allegations to the 'pontifical secret' procedures of *Crimen* and then of the 2001 apostolic letter and most recently of the July 2010 decree, which insists on Canon Law jurisdiction over abusive priests.

(c) Duty to Investigate and Prosecute Child Sex Abuse

> **Article 34:** *States Parties* **undertake to protect the child from all forms of sexual exploitation and sexual abuse**. *For these purposes, States Parties shall in particular take all appropriate national, bilateral and multilateral measures to prevent:*

> *(i) The inducement or coercion of a child to engage in any unlawful sexual activity* . . .

The Holy See, through its responsible agency the CDF, took no 'national, bilateral or multi-national measures' other than by issuing the 2001 Ratzinger letter, which served to delay investigations of accused priests and failed to require notification to law enforcement agencies. The Holy See has most scandalously breached its obligations under Article 34, and remains in breach through its 2010 insistence on Canon Law process and 'pontifical secrecy'.

164. It is also relevant to note the Holy See's unwillingness to afford 'measures to promote physical and psychological recovery and social reintegration' to victims, required by Article 39, although they are usually provided for offending priests. Article 39 also requires state parties to take measures that 'foster the health, self-respect and dignity of the child' after the abuse. The Holy See continues to be in breach of this obligation other than in cases where it has been forced by court orders or settlements to pay compensation.

165. It is a serious reflection on the competence and resolve of the 'eighteen experts of high moral standing' who have been elected to the Committee on the Rights of the Child that they have done and said nothing about the Vatican's thirteen-year failure to deliver a report, during the period when widespread child abuse by its priests has been extensively publicized. The Holy See's grave and extensive breaches of the Convention on the Rights of the Child, and its contempt for its reporting obligations over the past thirteen years, should – if the other parties care – justify its expulsion. The other parties, and the UN itself, should care very much, because this is the one and only human rights convention that has near universal support, having been ratified by 193 states, with the exception only of the failing Somalia and the United States, which fails to ratify many international law treaties, although it has at least signed this one. It is the UN's 'showpiece' convention, and the virtual unanimity over its provisions means that they have force in customary international law. The Holy See's defiance demonstrates its unfitness for membership: its boast of 'constant concern for the wellbeing of children' is an egregious example of diplomatic hypocrisy.

166. Vatican diplomats may have prepared a devious defence for the Holy See by entering a 'reservation that it will only apply the Convention' when it is compatible with Canon Law. The sections

of the Convention dealing with child sex abuse are irrevocably incompatible with Canon Law, which favours the priest at the expense of the best interests of the child (a breach of Article 3(1)); which does not provide effective procedures for investigation, reporting, referral or judicial involvement (a breach of article 19(2)), and has secrecy provisions that preclude national, bilateral and multi-national measures (a breach of article 34). If the true purpose of the reservation was to maintain the church's claim to deal with abusing priests under its internal disciplinary system, and the exclusion of any cooperation with law enforcement authorities, it was a 'reservation' that amounted to a repudiation of key provisions in the Treaty's protection of children. Other state parties should have denounced it as such, and could have forced the Holy See to withdraw its reservation or repudiate the Convention.[4] No state party did so: the naïve or overly trusting legal advisors to the foreign offices of all governments of the world fell for the Vatican's trick. It was not until May 2010 that the Holy See 'fessed up' to the fact that its 1990 reservation about VCS law really did refer to Canon Law ('Canon Law is the primary source of the law of VCS'). Faced with exposure of the way that Canon Law had protected paedophile priests and permitted re-offending, it belatedly protested 'the fact that a given act may also be treated as a religious offence under penal Canon Law does not preclude prosecution according to the criminal law and procedures of any state'.[5] This claim, made in its report on the Optional Protocol (see below) is disingenuous and misleading. Canon Law – and *Crimen* and the 2001 Ratzinger apostolic letter and the 'New Norms' of July 2010 – do effectively preclude prosecution because from the moment a complaint is formally made, and for ever after, all participants in the process are sworn to total secrecy.

167. The other relevant treaty which binds the Holy See in its inflated capacity as a state is the Optional Protocol to the Convention of the Rights of the Child (2000) which it ratified in 2001. This deals *inter alia* with child prostitution, defined as 'the use of a child in sexual activities for remuneration or any other form of consideration'

(other forms would include spiritual consolation, absolution, vows of silence and other kinds of 'consideration' that priests can offer their child victims) and requires action under penal laws against pimps and procurers and persuaders, which would include priests and church officials who encourage or arrange paedophile activities. Article 6 of the Protocol obliges state parties to assist each other with providing all the evidence at their disposal – an obligation which the Vatican continues to evade. In 2008 it refused even to answer letters from the Murphy Commission in Ireland, and its *nuncio* then insulted the Commission and refused to appear before it. The Optional Protocol required the Vatican to submit a report in January 2004 (by which time the Boston scandal had hit the headlines) but the Vatican delayed its response until May 2010, when its position was almost defiantly defensive:

Obviously, children must be protected in cases where a proven abuse of a child's rights (e.g. neglect, physical or sexual abuse, violence) has been committed within the family. Beyond such cases, however, civil authorities must not intervene in the family and interfere with the duties and rights of parents, who are presumed to act for the well-being of their child, especially as regards matters pertaining to primary care, religion, education, association with others, and privacy.[6]

168. Reading between the lines of these weasel words, the Vatican is saying that only paedophilia committed within the family (e.g. incest) requires police investigation, but beyond such cases the police should not intervene. Catholic parents must be left alone by welfare agencies, so they will choose to make complaints about the treatment of their children in secret to the church which can persuade them as good Catholics to forgive the priest, or that their child's well-being would be better served by keeping away from police and courtrooms. Children and parents will be bound by the secrecy oaths they sign under canonical processes and the police and welfare services should not intrude into family matters in order to investigate. The Vatican's appeal to 'parents' rights' is too often an excuse for giving the church the opportunity to pressure victims and their families to forgive and forget. (The Cumberledge report said 'we are only too

aware of the pressure sometimes placed on those who have suf-fered abuse to forgive those who have abused them')[7].

169. This important first statement by the Holy See about the child sex abuse scandal – the only official report it has yet made to the UN – struck a defiant note. The scandal was addressed in a section headed 'The Roman Pontiff', who had, it proudly reported 'on many occasions publicly acknowledged the offences committed by some of the church's own members against the rights of child' (*sic*). But it insisted that the church was 'governed by an auto-nomous legal system' and had an 'inherent right acquired at its foundation by Jesus Christ and independent from any civil authority' to deal with offending priests merely by urging them 'to lead authentic Christian lives'. It spelt out the 'inherent right' that it claimed Jesus bestowed on it to deal with the rapists of children by the *pastoral path* (exhortation, preaching, correction), the *sacramental path* (confession), the *disciplinary* path (for example restricting their opportunity to give the sacrament, vetting priesthood candidates) and the *penal canonical path* which is disin-genuously described as 'penal sanctions, penal remedies and penances', although as explained in Chapter 4 above, Canon Law has no true 'penal' sanction of imprisonment, or even of a fine or an order for community service.

170. This passage – paragraph 26 of the Holy See report – contains the kernel of the case against Benedict XVI, who must have approved it. It defiantly proclaims the church's 'inherent right' to deal with criminal priests independently of criminal law, under an archaic disciplinary procedure that enables them to escape punishment for their serious offences against children. They will be forgiven their crimes of rape and indecent assault if they say their prayers or accept restrictions on their ministry, or seem amenable to exhortation – all in secret, and decided by fellow priests or by their bishop/father. This 'inherent right', as crafted by Vatican diplomats, is attributed to Jesus Christ – a claim that many Christians might find upsetting: Jesus is not on record as urging his disciples to protect abusers of children. On the contrary,

they deserve to be drowned in the depths of the sea, not hidden in the depths of the Holy See. It is plain from this paragraph, and from the new Canon Law norms laid down in July 2010 (Appendix D) that the Vatican will not, under this Pope, yield in its claim that the church is entitled to shelter suspected criminals in its midst from police investigation, public trial and any punishment that they deserve.

171. The remainder of the section on clerical sex abuse quotes from speeches by Pope John Paul II and Benedict XVI, in which they seek to shift the blame from the church to 'society as a whole. It is a deep-seated crisis of sexual morality, even of human relationships . . . the church will help society to understand and deal with the crisis in its midst,' apparently by 'clearly presenting . . . the church's moral teaching' and striving to promote 'healing and reconciliation'. This is presumptuous nonsense: there is no crisis in society as a whole, which universally condemns the molestation of children and demands deterrent punishment for its perpetrators. The crisis is in a church that unrealistically demands celibacy and chastity from its priesthood, then arms them with spiritual power and gives them practical opportunities to ventilate their sexual urges with fearful and distressed, but overawed, children. It does not monitor their behaviour, and when they are caught it does its best to hide them from public justice and treats them as repented sinners, to be given second and third chances in fresh parishes or different countries.

172. It is ironic to recall the words of the Holy See at the Special Session of the UN Conference on Children in 2002, just before the scandal emerged, urging the world to protect children from the 'scourge' of sex abuse by punishing their abusers.[8] (See quote at head of chapter.) That the Church has, by its own words, condemned itself, its leadership and its law for the inaction over the next eight years, is all too clear. What infuriates those who wish the church and its humanitarian missions well is that its Pope and Cardinals have been so resistant to reform. Benedict's major encyclical, *Caritas in Veritatae*, issued in June 2009, was full of

meandering generalities about the sad state of a secular world struggling with original sin: it made not a single mention of clerical sex abuse of children.

173. Amen to that – but the scourge of child abuse within the church itself had for many years gone unpunished as a result of the procedural deficiencies of Canon Law, the selfish desire to protect the church from scandal by harbouring and trafficking paedophile priests, and the negligent supervision of bishops by the Holy See through its CDF office, headed for the previous two decades by Cardinal Ratzinger. The misconduct of the Holy See shows the need for legislation in all countries to require mandatory reporting of child abuse allegations, the removal of time limits on prosecution and the empowerment of civil authorities to investigate organizations which control the upbringing of young people. In the case of the Roman Catholic Church, that means laws allowing civil authorities access to those institutions which have private dealings with child abusers and the children they abuse. It means that these institutions and their chief executives must have no immunity from police investigation or from criminal processes or from civil actions for negligent supervision. It means, in short, that the Pope, the Holy See, and the secret CDF archives must be made subject to national laws and the law of nations, and that the pretence of statehood and sovereignty, which has so far rendered them immune from these laws, can no longer be sustained.

8. A Case to Answer?

There is no denying the fact that the world-wide system of covering up cases of sexual crimes committed by clerics was engineered by the CDF under Cardinal Ratzinger.

Father Hans Kung, Open Letter to Catholic Bishops on Fifth Anniversary of Benedict's election as Pope

174. Does this serious charge, by Benedict's former friend and an eminent theologian, stand up? On any view, under Cardinal Ratzinger's direct authority, a policy was implemented between 1981 and 2005 pursuant to which complaints against perpetrators were hushed up by secrecy oaths and confidential settlements: priests known to be guilty were sent to other parishes or other countries despite knowledge of their propensity to re-offend; guilty priests were normally forgiven after penances of prayer and restriction of movement – very seldom were they defrocked and there is no case yet identified where the Vatican urged its bishop to submit the matter to the competent authorities for investigation and prosecution. The policy of the CDF was *never* to oblige or even request bishops to submit these matters to competent authorities and few did so voluntarily: the prosecutions that have taken place usually resulted from independent police action after some victim or other informant had complained directly to them. Under Canon Law the Pope is the immediate superior and absolute commander of Catholic bishops and priests: Canon 331 endows him with 'supreme, full, immediate and universal power in the church'. Bishops were are bound to comply with Holy See directives such as *Crimen* and the Ratzinger 2001 apostolic letter and the 'New Norms' of 2010 which all enjoined them to absolute secrecy. The CDF would have

known and approved of offers of 'hush money' compensation to victims in return for confidentiality, and the forcing of victims to sign confidentiality agreements under threat of excommunication. That policy, in the words of the Murphy Commission, was motivated by 'the avoidance of scandal, the protection of the reputation of the church and the protection and preservation of its assets' to which considerations 'the welfare of children and justice for the victim were subordinated'. This policy was continued in the 2001 Ratzinger letter, and in the 'New Norms' of 2010 by which the Holy See endorsed 'pontifical secrecy' and directed that *all* child sex abuse cases must be reported to the CDF, either for it to put the priest on secret trial or to give directions to the bishop on how to handle the case. The recent revelation that John Paul II directed the publication to all bishops of the commendation he awarded to a French bishop who refused to inform authorities about a paedophile priest is compelling evidence of the Holy See's policy of hiding priestly crimes from the competent authorities (see para 153).

175. That policy, sustained over the quarter century during which Joseph Ratzinger was head of the CDF and for the first five years of his Papacy, does raise serious questions, not only about the negligence in the organization of a world-wide religion but whether that negligence was so gross that it might entail civil or even criminal liability for individuals who should have foreseen the consequences and were best placed to avoid them. Many bishops certainly have a case to answer but so too does Cardinal Ratzinger: his 2001 letter directed that all sex abuse complaints should be sent to the CDF, either for trial or for remission to the bishops, under a 'pontifical secret' that effectively precluded their transmission to law enforcement agencies. As Prefect of the CDF, Ratzinger had 'command responsibility' for the behaviour of bishops and the priesthood. He must have known, from information reaching the CDF in the 1980s and certainly in the 1990s, that there was widespread and systematic abuse, but he never once embarked on a proper enquiry or updated the ancient *Crimen* procedures or ensured that criminal priests were really

punished and were disabled from offending again. In all his pro-
lific books, writings and lectures throughout the period, he never
once seems to have mentioned the time-bomb of clerical sex
abuse, which he of all Vatican heavyweights should have known
about and which it was his duty, as head of the CDF, to defuse.

176. True, he acted in 2001, but his apostolic letter reinforced the system rather than changed it, and brought him certain knowledge
of thousands of cases of child sex abuse. Still he did not act, and
although his supporters now blame Pope John Paul II for block-
ing any reform, his failure to speak out (and speaking out may
have damaged his chances of election as John Paul's successor)
was a moral failure which permitted the abuse to continue. After
his election as Pope he dealt with a few notorious cases – like that
of the Mexican Father Maciel – but only by 'inviting' retirement
and penance, *not* by defrocking them and making evidence of
their guilt available to civil authorities. A few years later, as a
result of public outrage, he met a few selected abuse victims in
the US, Australia and Malta, and began to speak out against
abuse, but it was not until mid-April 2010 (after the first suggestion that he might be liable to prosecution) that a direction went
up on the Vatican website which seemed to concede that bishops
should report their paedophile cases to civil authorities (and then
only in countries which had laws requiring such reports). In July,
he promulgated 'New Norms' which, quite incredibly, override
the website 'guidance' by making no reference to any duty upon
bishops to report confessed or strongly suspected predator priests
to the police, and even expanded the number of crimes by clerics
that the church could snatch away from the criminal law. Can he
be excused for command failures over thirty years, during which
the abuse of tens of thousands of children took place?

177. He has found an accomplished defender in Alan Dershowitz,
who thinks his tardy responses can be attributed to the church's
tradition of moving slowly, backed by its important commitment
to confidentiality and to Canon Law and to the essential value of
forgiveness and to its belief 'that matters affecting the faithful

should generally be dealt with in the Church without recourse to secular authorities'.[2] But these are all excuses – mitigating circumstances, perhaps, but not justifications for covering up serious crime. The notion that crimes committed by members of a church should be dealt with secretly and leniently within the church can now be seen as an effort to protect the reputation of the church at the expense of victims and of justice. As for the tradition of moving slowly, and at deliberate pace, the Vatican was warned of the 'time bomb' by the Paracletes way back in the 1950s (see para 17); even for an institution as old and as venerated as the Roman Catholic Church, half a century provides more than enough time to take action. They should have started in the seminaries, emphasizing to trainees that Canon Law was the system under which they would be judged for sins but not for sins of the flesh that count as serious crimes. Gary Wills, the eminent Catholic historian, accuses Benedict not of moving slowly, but of moving backwards:

Pope Benedict wants to go back to the Latin mass, with the priest turned from the people. He has cut back ecumenical initiatives, denying again the validity of Anglican orders, forbidding concelebration of Mass with Protestants, declaring (in *Dominus Iesus*) that all other churches are 'gravely deficient'. He wants to put nuns back in their habits. He is driving to canonise the anti-Semitic Popes Pius XI and Pius XII. These are further signs of the structures of deceit – of self-deception as the first step to defying 'wordly wisdom'.[3]

178. The possibility of redemption is a key to our humanity, and I too salute the Roman Catholic belief in forgiveness which has made it a doughty opponent of the death penalty and a supporter of merciful sentencing. I do not suggest for a moment that abusive priests should all go to prison for long periods, or necessarily go to prison at all - society's attitude to paedophiles, whipped up by the tabloid media, can be both brutal and ignorant towards people who are capable of reform and have done some good in their lives. (I know, because I have defended quite a few.) But forgiveness is not the prerogative of a bishop. It is a matter that must be weighed by a judge, taking into account the attitude of the

victims' families, together with previous good character and good works, the genuineness of his remorse and the prognosis for his re-offending. The church must remember that there are some crimes so heinous that forgiveness is inappropriate – which is why international law allows no time limits for prosecution of crimes against humanity, like genocide, mass murder, systematic torture and widespread rape of children.[4] The church is entitled to proffer forgiveness for perpetrators in the afterlife, but it has no right to bestow forgiveness for self-interested reasons on its own servants.

179. As for the shibboleth of confidentiality, this cannot possibly cover informal disclosures made to colleagues, deacons or bishops by priests seeking to unburden themselves of guilty secrets without facing up to the consequences. This would make other church servants their silent collaborators. Bishop Pican was rightly sentenced for remaining silent while he knew that further offences against children were being committed by his confidant. As for the inviolability of the confessional – often exempted from laws which mandate reporting – further analysis is needed. The church traces the inviolability of its seal back to Bad King Wenceslaus (IV) who in 1393 jealously demanded to hear the secrets divulged by his wife, and tortured her confessor in the hope of obtaining them, finally drowning him in a river when he refused to tell. This grisly tale does not say much for the wife, who could have saved her priest by waiving confidentiality, but it makes the point that penitents can confess in confidence that their confessor will take their sinful secrets to his grave. Not just adulterers, but bank robbers and contract killers may open their hearts and receive fatherly advice and remonstrance, just as they may have unburdened themselves in confidence as clients to lawyers or as sources to journalists. But there is a crucial difference – a number of crucial differences – when a priest, a servant of the church, confesses to a fellow priest, a servant of the same church, that he has exploited his service in their church to rape children put into his hands by parishioners of their church. What right has the confessor to make a decision to absolve such a man? He is

hopelessly conflicted, not only because his confessee is his brother, but because the confessor is a fellow servant of the church that will suffer reputational damage if the secret gets out. Moreover, the criminal sin has been committed under the auspices of the church, by using its power and mystery to entice or subdue the victim. In principle, the church should not be offering confession or absolution to its own priests in these circumstances, because by doing so it becomes an accessory after the fact to its employee's crime. It does not explain what should be said to a guilty but penitent priest, who is presumably absolved after promising to do penance and say prayers. How can any 'absolution' in these circumstances be a proper use of the prerogative of mercy accorded to the confessor by virtue of the sacrifice of Christ on the cross?

180. So what are we to make of this 'forgiveness' that the church extends to its own, without reference to the victims or the public? A priest, let us imagine, admits under the seal of the confessional to sodomizing a 9-year-old boy in the sacristy, for which he says he is repentant and he really means the Act of Contrition, which he recites by heart. What penance is imposed?

Nowadays, a penance may be to do something nice for your enemy every day for a week or a month. It may be to work in a nursing home or a hospital one day a week for a month. It may be to donate time to a soup kitchen . . . quite often the penance is a set of prayers, such as saying Our Father or the Hail Mary five or ten times. Whatever the penance is, it's merely token.[5]

It certainly is, as compensation for abusing children, before the confessor intones the stain-removing formula: 'may God give you pardon and peace and I absolve you from all your sins, in the name of the father, and of the son, and of the holy spirit, Amen.' Even if the priest does reform, his victims will still have to live with their own psychological damage. If he does not reform, then the confessor has his future crimes on his hands, and possibly on his conscience. Canon Law says there is utter confidence in this iniquity but civil law adopts the maxim of equity that:

'there is no confidence in iniquity'. That is why psychiatrists in the UK are exempt from duties of confidentiality to clients they think will re-offend and commit serious crime, while in the US they can be sued for failing to tell the police about the murderous plans of their patients.[6] The priest who takes the confession of a paedophile colleague, therefore, has no legal obligation to keep silent. If he realizes that the man is harming children, and will continue to do so, then Canon Law becomes the law of *omerta*, the rule of criminal gangs, not of Christians.

181. As a matter of ethics, the church has no business to offer absolution to its own criminals. It should adopt a rule that provides an exception to the seal of the confessional in the case of its own employees who confess to sins that are also serious crimes. Or, at very least, to those of its employees who confess to serious crimes, committed in the course of, or connected with, their clerical duties. In such cases, the confessor is surely under a morally imperative obligation to ensure that his paedophile confessee does not injure more children, by telling the bishop – preferably with the agreement of the priest himself. If that is not forthcoming then the church (it would have to be the Pope) should in these circumstances authorize a breach of the seal. There can be no ethical alternative, to avoid complicity in the paedophile's continuing crimes, since otherwise the church would continue to offer him the opportunity and the power to commit them in the knowledge (through its confessor) that they would be committed. Imagine a company whose letterhead and correspondence and facilities are used by an employee to perpetrate a successful and ongoing fraud against the company's clients. He confesses the crime to his boss, who keeps quiet about it and permits him continued access to the company facilities, sure that he will succumb to temptation to commit further frauds. The company – and the boss – would be liable for gross negligence, aiding and abetting fraud and so on. Open the curtains of the confession box and the similarity becomes apparent: through the knowledge imparted to its confessor, imputable to the church, it is an organization which condones the ongoing crime which it continues to

facilitate and cover up. The consequences will be explored further in the next chapter. To avoid them, the church must abandon its practice of absolving its own criminals.

182. Priests who oppose change are worried by their vulnerability to false accusations. But we do not exempt men from prosecution for rape merely because a tiny proportion of complainants bring false charges. The falsely accused priest has no more to fear than any other defendant in our criminal justice system – less, in fact, because the evidence of children (if the complaint is fresh) or of historic memory (if it refers to events many years before) are both categories that are problematic for prosecutors in the absence of corroboration. Of course, if there is corroboration and the case goes to trial, the defendant will be identified, which will be embarrassing for the priest and the church, but that is the case with every other defendant in a public justice system. There may indeed be great benefit to an innocent priest in having a false accusation investigated by police and forensic scientists at the very outset, when falsity can conclusively be established. In any event, it is not suggested that a bishop should call the police whenever he is told of a rumour or merely on suspicion: only when an allegation is made credibly or with confirmatory evidence should the obligation to report arise. So the danger of a false accusation is no excuse for failing to take action once suspicion becomes reasonable suspicion. There should be an exception to this rule in the countries where criminal justice is in disarray or where the government is attacking Catholic clergy and there is reason to believe that a prosecution would become a persecution. These obvious exceptions do not detract from the need for a general rule requiring mandatory reporting, but they do put the onus on the Vatican to set up its own rapid-reaction policing and forensic team to investigate these exceptional cases with a proper and open trial in Rome of clergy who are found to have a case to answer.

183. Benedict's most persistant defender is John L. Allen Jnr, who presents himself as a kind of 'Vatican lobby correspondent' with

an insight into the opaque politics of the Holy See. He admits that Ratzinger ignored or minimized child sex abuse whilst head of the CDF and was probably blameworthy for condoning a paedophile priest like Father Hullermann while Bishop of Munich. But Allen claims that Ratzinger had a 'conversion experience' circa 2003 or 2004, after studying the thousands of clerical sex abuse complaint files sent to him in response to his apostolic letter in 2001. It was through reading them that he came to understand the scale of the crisis, although at first he could do nothing about it because of the 'complex world of court politics at the Vatican' which protected even the most outrageous child abusers – such as Father Maciel Degollado, who was untouchable through his close friendship with John Paul II and other powerful conservative figures. But in 2006 – a year after his ascent to the Papacy – he used his power to force the dissolute Father Maciel at last to retire. In Allen's turbo-charged prose, this showed that Benedict had 'drunk the Kool-Aid' and 'become a Catholic Eliot Ness' because he 'became the first Pope to meet with victims of sexual abuse, the first Pope to offer a direct apology for the crisis in his own name, and the first Pope to break the Vatican's wall of silence'.[7] This reflects very badly on Benedict's predecessor, John Paul II, although a more measured view is that both men must share responsibility for ignoring the crisis and that Benedict's recent behaviour may not be the result of some Damascene conversion experience, but of the church's desperate need for damage limitation as both congregations and donations diminish.

184. It is not plausible to suggest that Cardinal Ratzinger spent almost a quarter of a century as head of the CDF in ignorance of clerical sex abuse until the very end. *Crimen* clearly states, and re-emphasizes, the need for bishops to inform the CDF immediately upon receiving any allegation of child abuse and again if they embark upon any Canon Law process.[8] Each bishop has a most solemn duty to make such communications: 'since they are of utmost importance for the common good of the church, the precept to make them is binding under pain of grave sin'

(i.e. under threat of excommunication).[9] So bishops must have told Ratzinger long before 2004, and he made no effort to change a system which was harbouring guilty priests. Allen's best evidence for Ratzinger's 'conversion', namely his handling of the case of Father Maciel, does not stand up. In 2006, Benedict issued Maciel with an 'invitation to lead a reserved life of prayer and penance'. But Maciel was a bigamist, pederast and drug taker, who fathered a number of children who say he raped them from the age of 7. He had several mistresses and wives (he told them he was a CIA agent with little time for domestic life) and he would regularly demand to be masturbated by young boys whenever he visited seminaries of the Legion of Christ – a conservative and deeply anti-feminist order that he had founded. The Vatican received sworn evidence from nine of his teenage victims in 1998 but then the CDF under Ratzinger took no action even as Mexican newspapers began to expose Maciel's vicious and hypocritical life.[10] Maciel was invited to the Vatican in 2004 to be blessed by his friend Pope John Paul II. Had Ratzinger undergone by this time the conversion that Allen claims, he would have tried to block this blessing and immediately upon his election in April 2005, he would have insisted on putting Maciel on canonical law trial or at least ordering him to be defrocked. If Benedict were really converted, he would have made the Vatican's evidence of Maciel's lifelong criminality available to the Mexican police. Instead, he waited for a year and then merely 'invited' this monster priest to lead a quiet life in the US away from the glare of the Mexican media.

185. Benedict's minimal and delayed response to the Maciel scandal is typical – he seems to act only when something *must* be done to limit the damage, and then he does as little as possible. Every action that Allen uses to suggest he is a Catholic Eliot Ness actually shows him up as the church's Inspector Clouseau. He may have been the first Pope to break the Vatican's wall of silence, but only when silence was no longer an option, given all the evidence that had mounted since 2002. It is true that he met abuse victims from Boston when he visited the US in 2008, but he did

not meet them *in* Boston: in what some described as an act of cowardice, he declined to visit that city of Catholic shame. He met other abuse victims in Sydney, ironically on World Catholic Youth Day, and in Malta, but these victims were carefully chosen by the church and included victims who had remained in its fold and had been compensated or were willing to forgive and forget. Allen says that Benedict's conversion has led to 'a determination to punish abusers', but this has not translated into orders that they should all be defrocked and reported to police. As for being 'the first Pope to offer a direct apology for the crisis in his own name', this was a reference to his statement that 'I am deeply sorry for the pain and suffering the victims have endured . . . as their pastor, I share in their suffering.' What sort of apology is this? There was no self-criticism, no insight into his personal responsibility or the failings of Canon Law procedures and the CDF. At Easter 2010, as the crisis reached its height, Benedict announced that his faith had led him 'towards the courage of not allowing oneself to be intimidated by the petty gossip of domin-ant opinion'.[11] For any commander who ignores as 'petty gossip' the clearest evidence of the serious sex crimes his subordinates perpetrated on little children, the law should provide a reckoning.

186. What else can be said in Benedict's defence? The Vatican spokes-man, says it is 'false and calumnious' to suggest that Ratzinger covered up abuses and abusers when head of the CDF: 'he han-dled cases with wisdom and courage'. Unfortunately, the cases that have come to light, such as Murphy and Keisle, show him procrastinating, and then acting in fear of scandal. 'As Pope he has dismissed many priests from the clerical state.'[12] But how many is 'many'? The Vatican never gives names or details and unless CDF records are independently examined, this kind of statement cannot be verified. Archbishop Vincent Nichols, Eng-land's top Catholic, stepped up to the plate to defend Ratzinger's 24-year tenure at the CDF but was hard put to think of any actual reforms he had accomplished in relation to child sex abuse other than including internet pornography offences and extend-ing the age of consent from 16 to 18 and the time for reporting

from five to ten years (now, to twenty). Nichols claims that Ratzinger instituted a 'fast-track' defrocking process, but because it is 'pontifically secret' there is no evidence of how it works: previously appeals took years and, as in the Keisel case uncovered by the Murphy Commission, unjustified appeals by priests against laicization orders succeeded. The Vatican vetoed the 'zero tolerance' approach agreed by American Catholic bishops in 2002, on the grounds that 'the terms of abuse were too widely defined, contradicted Canon Law and failed to protect an alleged sex offenders' right to due process'.[13] Later, the Vatican approved a watered-down 'zero option', but only for the US church. A rather better defence for Benedict is that he is simply very old – at 83, too old to outwit the reactionaries all around him in the Vatican and begin root and branch reform. John Paul II suffered from Parkinson's Disease in the last few years of his life: the tactics of Vatican sources who wish to exculpate him as well as Benedict are telling journalists that in his final years he was under the influence of his Polish assistant, the extremely reactionary and protective Stanisław Dziwisz, whom he made a Cardinal and who is alleged to have influenced his resistance to all reform. But responsible pontiffs should resign when the work gets too much and the *curia* should insist that they do, and not elect them, as they did Benedict, at the age of 78. This points again to the need for institutional reform.

187. There can be no doubt that Benedict is sincere in his abomination of priests who abuse children – at one stage, he dropped his characteristic circumspection and called them 'filth', although he then reverted to proffering them forgiveness (on the doctrinal basis that no earthly sin is incapable of heavenly pardon). He is genuine too, in his apologies to victims, however stage-managed these events have become. He can be credited with a wish to reform, unlike his predecessor, whose tolerance of abusers was an unexposed scandal, and notwithstanding the sexual ignorance of many of the elderly cardinals and Vatican officials promoted during the reactionary regime of John Paul II. It may be his age (he is 83) or the conservatism of his advisors, or simply the weight

of the jurisprudence of Canon Law, centuries of it going back to the Inquisition, which prevents him from taking a principled stand and renouncing the church's claim to deal with the sex crimes of its priests and bishops. The acid test came in July 2010, after public acceptance of the need to act and months to reflect on how to proceed. He failed that test: the hoped-for mountain of *de gravioribus delictus* brought forth a mouse: a ten-year extension on the Canon Law time limit for 'prosecution' of child sex offences, without any requirements of publicity or transparency or a single acknowledgement that they must always be reported to law enforcement authorities. Benedict has proved to be a Pope who cannot bring himself to take the hard action required to save his church from the consequences of having become a law unto itself.

188. It is all very well to ask God's forgiveness, as Benedict did when addressing 15,000 priests in St Peter's Square on 12 June 2010, but he was asking forgiveness for sin: he still had not grasped that what some of them had committed was a crime. At this time he began to ask forgiveness for himself, as well as for his errant bishops and priests, although he did not explain for what sin or delict he was personally in need of grace. Unless a civil action against the Holy See overcomes the immunity hurdle, either by establishing that the Vatican is not a state or else by making this state vicariously liable for its agents or for negligence in supervising them, there will be no court-ordered disclosure of CDF files and no full accounting for its failures. If the Pope wants forgiveness, it would appear incumbent upon him to establish a Commission of Inquiry to examine the CDF archives and give a full account of what was done – or left undone – during his prefecture. This was, after all, the period in which tens of thousands of children were bewitched, buggered and bewildered by Catholic priests whilst his attention was fixated on 'evil' homosexuals, sinful divorcees, deviate liberation theologians, planners of families and wearers of condoms. Until this fallible man admits his errors and abjures Canon Law as a substitute for criminal law, there can be no guarantee that he – or his successor – will learn from his mistakes.

9. Crimes Against Humanity

Crimes against humanity . . . can only come within the purview of this basic code of humanity because the state involved, owing to indifference, impotence or complicity, has been unable, or has refused, to halt the crimes and punish the criminals.

Judgment at Nuremberg[1]

189. If the Holy See really is a state, then the Pope as head of state is immune from prosecution or civil action under the law of any nation he may visit, and the Holy See may resist most (but not all – see Chapter 10) civil claims. But one law with an arm that may be long enough to feel the papal collar is international criminal law, specifically the law against the commission of *crimes against humanity*. Such crimes are part of customary international law and, in a somewhat narrower definition, fall within the jurisdiction of the International Criminal Court (ICC) if committed or continued after July 2002 when the court was established. Article 27 of its statute proclaims the irrelevance of official capacity by abolishing state immunity for Presidents and Prime Ministers – and for Pontiffs.

> This Statute shall apply equally to all persons without any distinction based on official capacity. In particular, official capacity as a Head of State or Government, a member of a government or parliament, an elected representative or a government official shall in no case exempt a person from criminal responsibility under this statute . . .

> (2) Immunities or special procedural rules which may attach to the official capacity of the person, whether under national or international law, shall not bar the court from exercising its jurisdiction over such a person.

190. Although the Holy See participated in the conference which drafted the ICC Treaty, and John Paul II even donated a very modest $3,000 to its trust fund for victims, it has refused to join the III states that have so far ratified it, perhaps out of concern that its ratification would give the court jurisdiction over the Pope. This fact has led some academics to think that Benedict XVI is safe, because other than a ratifying state only the Security Council can refer a case to the court, and then only if it endangers international peace and security, like Milosevic's ethnic cleansing of Kosovo or Bashir's war in Darfur, and child sex abuse does not fall into this category. Academics can sometimes overlook the blindingly obvious, and one blindingly obvious fact about Benedict is that Joseph Ratzinger is German,[2] and Germany ratified the Rome Statute (the ICC Treaty) on II December 2000. Under Article 12, the ICC may exercise its jurisdiction over the national of a state party, so Benedict is, potentially at least, within its range. The Pope and his officials would also be liable if their connivance in an international crime had crossed borders through diplomatic bags, email instructions or directives in Latin from the Pope or CDF to bishops or *nuncios* in countries which have ratified the convention – Germany, Ireland, Australia for example – in which case the court would also, under Article 12 of the Rome Statute, have jurisdiction to indict them. They would, of course, be safe from an international arrest warrant if they stayed in the Vatican, but they could not leave its precincts for hospital treatment in Rome and the Vatican does not have an airfield from which they could fly for treatment to another non-signatory state (unless the Pope-copter could reach Libya).

191. In considering the question of whether and in what circumstances systematic sex abuse of children amounts to a crime against international law, I shall first examine the ICC – an international criminal court which is up and running, but which has some statutory limitations one of which (the 'elements of crime' point) might well exculpate the Vatican. However, this is not a problem for customary international law, which may be invoked (subject to the immunity question) in national courts

which have universal jurisdiction over crimes against humanity. So far as the ICC is concerned, the first question is whether a case against Vatican officials would be admissible. Since the ICC is a court of last resort, it will only take cases which states are unwilling to investigate and genuinely prosecute. If the Pope stays in the Vatican, this test is easily passed: the King of Vatican City will never prosecute himself. The case must also be of 'sufficient gravity', and clerical sex abuse, although horrific, is not equivalent to mass murder. Given its scale, however, and its impact on victims, and in particular given the Vatican's refusal to abandon Canon Law and to hand priests over to the civil authorities, this admissibility test could be satisfied. Of much greater difficulty for an ICC prosecution is the rule that the offence must have been committed after July 2002 (when the ICC came into existence with sixty ratifications of its treaty). There is certainly evidence that the Vatican was turning a blind eye to sex abuse after this period, and as late as July 2010 was still refusing to direct that criminals should be reported to law enforcement authorities, but much of the evidence of its dereliction of duty is from the 1980s and 1990s.

192. It may seem odd that the Pope – by definition, a man of peace – could conceivably be liable to prosecution for a crime generally associated with war. When I first suggested that such a prosecution was not inconceivable, some critics, including the Pope's US lawyer, fell into the trap of claiming that crimes against humanity can only be committed during a war. They are wrong. The 'crime against humanity' was first defined in Article 6(c) of the Nuremberg Charter, to include inhumane acts against a civilian population 'before or during the war'. The notion that such a crime could not be committed in peacetime was specifically rejected by the ICTY (the UN Tribunal which deals with crimes against humanity and with war crimes in the Balkans) Appeals Court in the *Tadic* case:

> It is by now a settled rule of customary international law that crimes against humanity do not require a connection to international armed conflict . . . [international law] may not require a connection between crimes against humanity and any conflict at all.[3]

193. This issue was specifically decided at the Rome Conference in 1998 which settled the ICC Treaty, where a proposal to link crimes against humanity with international armed conflict was decisively and derisively rejected by all major powers except China. The record shows that the US delegate stated that 'if situations arising in times of peace were not covered the court would be denied the jurisdiction over many of the crimes it should address'[4] and the Russian, Canadian, Israeli, French and Australian delegations all agreed. Elizabeth Wilmhurst (who would later resign from the Foreign Office over the illegality of the invasion of Iraq) pointed out on behalf of the UK that, as a matter of customary international law, crimes against humanity could be committed in peacetime. In consequence, there is nothing in the ICC Statute that provides that such crimes can only be committed during war, or limits ICC jurisdiction to crimes committed in periods of armed conflict, and the pre-trial Chamber of the ICC decided in 2010 that the prosecutor could continue his investigations into crimes against humanity committed during electoral violence in Kenya, although there was no 'armed conflict' as such.[5]

194. The next – and very important – question is whether the factual basis of the allegation – the *actus reus* – falls within the definition of a 'crime against humanity'. It can be said with some confidence that the sexual abuse of young children is implicitly covered in Article 7 of the ICC Statute. It defines the 'crime against humanity' to include 'rape' and 'sexual slavery' or 'any other form of sexual violence of comparable gravity',[6] as well as 'other inhumane acts of a similar character intentionally causing great suffering, or serious injury to body or to mental or physical health'.[7] Clerical sex abuse has demonstrably grave effects on mental health and indeed is a cause of psychological torment: it is committed in betrayal of fiduciary duty by priests and church officials, often against the very young and very vulnerable (for example in orphanages and homes for deaf or otherwise handicapped children). International courts have held that recruitment of children to be soldiers and specifically the recruitment of girls to be 'comfort women' or sex slaves,

amounts to a crime against humanity, as does forcing members of a group to marry against their will.[8] So clerical sex abuse which is part of a 'widespread or systematic practice' can constitute a crime against humanity and such crimes, in the words of the ICC explanatory memorandum, amount to *'particularly odious offences in that they constitute a serious attack on human dignity or grave humiliation or a degradation of one or more human beings. They are not isolated or sporadic events but are part of a wide practice of atrocities tolerated or condoned by a government or de facto authority.'*

182. Clerical sex abuse where it has been most carefully studied has not comprised 'isolated' or 'sporadic' acts. On the contrary, the Murphy Commission described it as 'endemic' in Catholic boys' institutions in Ireland, and class actions have so far netted almost $1.6 billion for over 10,000 victims in the US, where the John Jay study conservatively estimated over 4,000 guilty priests. Similar patterns have been observed in Germany, Malta, Australia and Canada. This has been a widespread and systematic criminal activity, and it can be credibly alleged that the perpetrators have been harboured and helped to evade justice by rules endosed by successive Popes and CDF prefects. But can it be said that the abuse amounts to an attack directed against a civilian population? This means *'a course of conduct involving the multiple commission of acts* [i.e. rape, child abuse etc.] *against any civilian population, pursuant to or in furtherance of a state or organizational policy to commit such attack'* (Article 7(2)(a)). Here the Pope would have several grounds for defence –

(1) that the victims were not attacked as part of a 'civilian population';
(2) that he had no intention that any child should be abused; or
(3) that there was no Holy See 'policy' to commit the abuse.

196. The first defence would not hold much water – the victims were all vulnerable civilians, and this requirement of 'an attack against a civilian population' has been broadly interpreted to include, for example, attacks on patients in civilian hospitals, or forcing women in particular areas of Sierra Leone to marry soldiers. The ICTY has ruled that the requirement of an 'attack' is not limited

to the use of armed force; 'it encompasses any mistreatment of the civilian population'.[9]

197. A more important second ground of defence for the Pope would be that he did not have the necessary mental element – the *mens rea* – to be guilty of the widespread crimes of his paedophile priesthood, because he had no intention, in his twenty-four years as the head of the CDF, that a single child should be harmed. This can be accepted without hesitation, but does it go far enough to exculpate Joseph Ratzinger from criminal responsibility if charged with aiding and abetting the international crime of systematic child abuse? The answer would depend on the evidence, because the international law doctrine of 'command responsibility' fixes a superior – political or military leaders, Popes, presidents and prime ministers – with liability for the international crimes of their inferiors, even if they did not specifically know that such crimes were being committed and even if they were positively opposed to their commission, if they nonetheless negligently failed in supervision or, once apprised of the crimes, failed to punish them or to report them to police or other 'competent authorities' for investigation, prosecution and punishment.

198. The command responsibility principle received its classic formulation from the US Supreme Court in a case involving General Yamashita, the Japanese General whose troops ran amok in the Philippines in his absence towards the end of the war. To his plea that he was a hundred miles away from the scene of their crimes and that as a man of honour he had no wish for, and was indeed outraged by, the rapes and other atrocities committed by his soldiers, the court replied:

> a person in a position of superior authority should be held individually responsible for giving the unlawful order to commit a crime, and he should also be held responsible for failure to deter the unlawful behaviour of subordinates if he knew they had committed or were about to commit crimes yet failed to take the necessary and reasonable steps to prevent their commission or to punish those who had committed them.[10]

199. This rule may seem harsh, but it is a necessary concomitant of power: those who seek and obtain power over the lives of others will be held liable when their underlings commit offences if they have been seriously negligent in their supervision or insouciant about investigation and punishment. The command responsibility principle can be recognized in the indictment of East German leaders Erich Honecker and Egon Krenz, whose policies encouraged border guards to kill civilians who tried to escape over the Berlin Wall: these leaders ensured that the guards were never punished for shooting to kill (Honecker was himself killed by cancer before he could be tried but Krenz was sentenced to six years as an accessory to manslaughter). The command responsibility principle as it applies to non-military commanders like the Pope (the test for military commanders is more stringent) has been given the following formulation in Article 28(b) of the ICC Statute:

RESPONSIBILITIES OF COMMANDERS AND OTHER SUPERIORS

Article 28 (b) . . . *a superior shall be criminally responsible* for crimes within the jurisdiction of the court committed by *subordinates under his or her effective authority* and control as a result of his or her *failure to exercise control properly over such subordinates*, where:

i) the superior either *knew, or consciously disregarded information* that clearly indicated that the subordinates were committing or were about to commit such crimes;

ii) the crimes concerned *activities that were within the effective responsibility* and control of the superior; and

iii) the superior *failed to take all necessary and reasonable measures* within his or her power to prevent or repress their commission or *to submit the matter to the competent authorities for investigation and prosecution.*

200. It is under Article 28(b)(iii) that any prosecution for serious negligence in respect to clerical sex abuse would be considered. There can be no doubt that for all the time that Joseph Ratzinger was Prefect of the CDF, he had command responsibility for the decisions of the Holy See office charged under Canon Law with overseeing (and after 2001, with directing) how allegations of

clerical sex abuse were handled. The abuse itself was widespread and systematic, certainly in the US, Ireland, Australia and parts of Europe, places where it has been properly investigated. (It is reliably predicted to have been even worse in developing countries, where no proper investigation has yet taken place.) (See para 37) It is likely that Cardinal Ratzinger would have known of its scale, because bishops were ordered under *Crimen* to report all cases to the CDF. He was responsible for the system under which allegations were processed in utter secrecy, without national law enforcement authorities being informed. He should have known of the trafficking of paedophile priests, since the CDF authorized this in a number of cases. But what he actually knew or else consciously disregarded can only be established by inspecting the Vatican 'secret archives' located on tourist maps next door to the Sistine Chapel, although more probably found at the Curia offices in Rome. (It would be necessary to override Holy See immunity to obtain them, because the Vatican has not allowed access to papal papers after 1939.)

201. The full force of the command responsibility principle has been explored in a number of international criminal trials, albeit in the context of hierarchical military leadership. It is not necessary for the prosecution to prove that the superior's inaction *caused* future crimes. As Professor Cassesse puts it in the leading textbook on international criminal law,

> A superior breaches his *duty to report* to the appropriate authorities crimes committed by his subordinates unbeknownst to him. Here the superior knows that a crime has been perpetrated and fails immediately to draw the attention of the body responsible for the investigation or prosecution of the crime. In this case, the superior is liable to be punished for the specific crime of failure to report. This offence is plainly different from that of his subordinates: he is responsible if, upon becoming cognisant of the crime of his subordinates, he deliberately or with culpable negligence fails to report them to the appropriate authorities for punishment. Here the superior's conduct may not be held to have caused, or contributed to the cause of, the criminal offence.[11]

202. In short, superiors in positions of authority – *a fortiori* heads of state – are legally bound to make their subordinates criminally responsible, and the duty is not satisfied by making them responsible only to an ecclesiastical disciplinary system which does not provide for 'punishment' as that word is usually understood. A bishop is not a 'competent authority' for the purposes of Section 28(b)(iii) because Canon Law provides him with no statutory power to investigate or to punish other than by directing prayers or penance. The 'knowledge' requirement is met by awareness that priests (the 'subordinates') are committing child sex abuse or are likely to do so – ignoring the information coming to the CDF is no excuse, because that would be to 'consciously disregard' it. It is clear from the case law that command responsibility arises when the superior has 'information of a general nature' about the crimes and the likelihood of their commission – to be fixed with liability he does not need to know the details of specific crimes or criminals (for example, commanders have been held responsible for the actions of troops whom they knew included mentally unstable characters or were prone to drunkenness).[12] The Pope and the head of the CDF have effective responsibility for the conduct of priests, and the question under Article 28(b)(iii) is whether they failed to take 'all necessary and reasonable measures within their power' to prevent or repress child sex abuse or to direct their bishops to 'submit the matter to the competent authorities for investigation and prosecution'. Quite clearly, at this point, Joseph Ratzinger would have a case to answer, both as Prefect to the CDF (1981–2005) and thereafter as a Pope who still – as recently as the 'New Norms' in July 2010 – refuses to impose a rule that these crimes must always be reported to the police.

203. It must be said – and has been said by courts which have convicted military leaders on the command responsibility principle – that because the commander does not share the perpetrator's vicious intent, and may actually abhor his crime, the sentence should be moderate and merciful. The state of mind the prosecutor must prove is really that of gross or serious negligence amounting in

effect to turning a blind eye to information upon the receipt of which there arises a moral duty to act. The question in the hypothetical case of the Pope is whether he should have known about the crimes of his subordinates or whether, if he did become aware of them, he should have realized that it was reasonable and necessary, in order to stop or deter offending, to lift 'pontifical secrecy' and to order bishops to call in the police rather than merely 'warn' or 'reassign' offenders to other parishes or send them for therapy that was known rarely to work. The state of mind necessary for committing the offence of 'failing to report the matter to the competent authorities for investigation and prosecution' could range from wilful blindness to truculence based on some belief that Canon Law was better and more forgiving than criminal law or that since the Holy See was a state, its servants were not amenable to punishment other than by its own range of spiritual penances.

204. If anyone bent on prosecuting the Pope for a crime against humanity under the Rome Statute had a case so far, a major problem is now encountered. The statutory definition – which generally reflects the definition of these crimes in customary international law – was tampered with by state parties shortly after the court came into existence. They endorsed a lengthy document called *Elements of Crime*, which purported to explain the Article 7(2)(a) requirement that the assault on civilians must be *'pursuant to or in furtherance of a state or organizational policy to commit such attack'*. Although *Elements of Crime* makes clear that this need not be a military attack, it says that the state or organization must 'actively promote or encourage such an attack against the civilian population.'[13] It could never be said that the Pope or the CDF under his rule were *active* in encouraging sex abuse, however much the Canon Law failed to deter it and however much they should have been aware that 're-assigning' paedophiles was a green light for re-offending. But how can this be consistent with command responsibility, as defined under Article 28? The truth is that it cannot be consistent, so those who drafted *Elements of Crime* produced a watered-down version of Article 28(b) for such cases. They said that a policy

. . . may, in exceptional circumstances, be implemented by a deliberate failure to take action, which is consciously aimed at encouraging such attack.
The existence of such a policy cannot be inferred solely from the absence
of government or organizational action.[14]

205. The diplomats who drafted this part of *Elements of Crime,* adopted
by the sixty original parties to the ICC Statute in September
2002, might almost have had the Pope in mind: their watered-
down version seems tailor-made to exempt him from command
responsibility because it is difficult to characterize his failure to
act as 'consciously aimed at encouraging' the abuse. The *Elements of Crime* project was in fact an initiative of the United
States, at a time (before the Bush administration) when it was
cautiously 'on side' with the Court. The watering-down of the
command responsibility principle had more to do with protecting the likes of some future Richard Nixon or Henry Kissinger,
than it did with protecting the Pope, and was promoted particularly by Turkey and other states concerned to avoid the drawing
of inferences against their military leaders who failed to restrain
forces attacking insurgents. But the fifty-page *Elements of Crime*
document adopted by the ICC prepcom in June 2000 and
endorsed by the Assembly of State parties in September 2002 is
now a 'source' of law which the Court must apply. However, the
application of *Elements* comes *after* the ICC's own statute, which
overrides all other sources, so the *Elements* can merely 'assist the
Court in the interpretation and application' of the statutory
obligation of a crime against humanity (ICC Statute, Article 9).
Under Article 9(3), the *Elements* 'shall be consistent with the Statute' and they are plainly inconsistent with the statutory definition
of 'command responsibility' under Article 28,[15] as well as with the
broad principle in *Yamashita*'s and international customary law.

206. This serious and unresolved issue needs to be settled, especially
since this watered-down version has no place in customary law.
Article 15 of the ICC Statute provides a means of doing so, were
victims of clerical sex abuse or an NGO prepared to take up
their case, and provide information to the ICC prosecutor which

he considered reasonable enough to warrant an investigation of the Vatican. He would first submit it to a pre-trial chamber of three judges, requesting them to authorize him to commence a formal inquiry. In these preliminary proceedings, at which victims are entitled to make representations, the issue of whether the case fell within the jurisdiction of the Court could be decided – i.e. whether widespread sex abuse by Catholic priests as overseen by the Vatican amounted to an 'attack on a civilian population' for the purposes of Articles 7 and 28 of the ICC Statute, notwithstanding the restrictive definition in the *Elements of Crime*. Indeed, the crucial issue would be whether such definition satisfies the Article 9(3) requirement that it be compatible with Articles 7 and 28 of the Statute. There are further provisions in Articles 18 and 19 which enable the pre-trial chamber to give preliminary legal rulings before there is any question of indictment.

207. At a preliminary stage, the Vatican could challenge the jurisdiction of the Court and victims could also make submissions, as could other state parties, especially Germany, the state of the Pope's nationality, which (since the ICC is a court of last resort) could render the case inadmissible by demonstrating that its own law enforcement authorities had commenced a genuine investigation into whether its national had been complicit in covering up abuses committed throughout the world by Catholic priests. The initial decision as to whether the case warranted action by the ICC would be made by the Court's prosecutor, Luis Moreno Ocampo, who has considerable experience in this area as a result of defending paedophile priests in his native Argentina and he could be relied upon to make reasonable decisions about taking the matter forward. It would provide a suitable test case for clarifying the meaning of the 'state policy' requirement in the definition of a crime against humanity, and its relationship to the command responsibility principle. However, it must be recognized that the ICC is still at an early stage (its first prosecution has started and stopped and it has not yet completed a trial) and it is buffeted by adverse political pressures (most notably from African states irate at its arrest warrant issued for President Bashir)

so it is likely to be resistant to proceeding against the Pontiff – even if such an action were to demonstrate that it was not only concerned with African leaders.

208. There is one alternative which would avoid the *Elements of Crime* problems in the ICC, namely a prosecution in a country where courts accept 'universal jurisdiction' to try crimes against humanity. Confusingly, any such prosecution would be brought under customary international law and not under the Rome Statute, and customary law has the advantage of not having any requirement that the attack should to be pursuant to a 'policy' of a state or organization,[16] or the further *Elements* restriction that the state must 'actively promote or encourage' the attack. Under customary law it is sufficient for the prosecutor to prove that 'the practice [i.e. systematic and widespread clerical child abuse] was accepted or tolerated, or acquiesced in by the state or organization',[17] which is closer to the case that might be made against the Vatican and the CDF. The charge would be of aiding and abetting a crime against humanity, by enjoining perpetual secrecy on victims and operating a Canon Law process that eschewed punishment, and was calculated to give assistance, encouragement and moral support to incorrigible paedophile priests.

209. If the Pope is the head of a state, the power to prosecute him outside a UN court has been severely restricted by the International Court of Justice in its *DRC (Congo) v Belgium* decision,[18] that a foreign minister (and *a fortiori* a state head) must enjoy immunity wherever he goes, in order to carry out his functions. (This rationale would only protect the Pope on a 'state visit' and not on a visit where he carried out only religious functions as head of the church, such as a 'World Youth Day' event.) However, if the Holy See is not a state, then its leader would be amenable to trial at a court with universal jurisdiction were he to come within its territory, either on a papal visit or as the result of the execution of an international arrest warrant, which a national prosecutor could arrange to be issued by Interpol, or the more effective European arrest warrant. One consequence of ini-

tiating such an action is that it would require a court to settle the legal issue of the Holy See's statehood, and if the action took place in a European country then this decision might ultimately come before the European Court of Human Rights.[19] Any such case would be brought under customary international law and not the Rome Treaty for the ICC, so it could deal with events prior to July 2002.

210. An appropriate place to consider such an action might be Belgium, where a police inquiry supervised by an investigating magistrate is already underway into high level church complicity in child sexual abuse. In June 2010 police actually detained for a day the country's nine Catholic bishops and its papal *nuncio*, while they seized some church computers and took 475 case files from a church-appointed commission that had become moribund.[20] If Belgian law enforcement authorities are to proceed with this criminal investigation, it would be logical for them to look beyond the bishops, and to examine the responsibility of the Vatican. The Pope should be prepared to disclose documents from the Vatican's secret archives that would be highly relevant to the prosecutor's investigation and which may indeed alleviate suspicion, for example if the files show that behind the scenes he did what he could to confront the problem. In the more likely event that he would refuse to disclose relevant material, the issue by a Belgian court of a European evidence warrant directed to disclosure of the CDF files (most likely held outside the Vatican, at the CDF offices in Rome) would raise a host of important legal issues about Italy's compliance duties to the Council of Europe, and about Vatican statehood if the CDF files were to be hastily relocated to the Vatican's secret archives alongside the Sistine Chapel.

211. These prospects of action in Europe against the Holy See, and even the Pope, may seem far-fetched. But the European Court of Human Rights has refused to allow international law to be hogtied by the deals done in the 1920s by Mussolini. A law from this era requiring the display of a crucifix in every state school in

Italy has been declared, 80 years on, to be an unlawful interference with the right of parents to have their children educated in a way which respects beliefs other than those of the Catholic Church. An attempted justification by reference to the role of the Catholic religion in Italian history and traditions was firmly rejected – parents and children alike had the right to believe in different religions or in none at all.[21] The European Court has also condemned provisions of the 1929 Concordat, which applied in Italy to allow Vatican courts to annul marriages at a husband's request without notifying his evidence to the wife or offering her a lawyer. The Court declared that Canon Law breached the European Convention guarantee of fair trial.[22] There is long-standing authority in common law countries that the Canon Law of the Roman Catholic Church is foreign to the law of the land and has no place in it: there must be expert evidence called by a party before a court can take notice of it.[23] In at least one nation – the US – the constitution (which prevents the establishment of any religion) has stopped the expenditure of taxpayers money on papal visits,[24] in marked contrast to the UK, where Anglican, Jewish, Muslim and atheist taxpayers must partly pay for it. In France, a bishop has been punished for harbouring a paedophile priest without informing the police. These are but straws in the wind, but it blows in directions that are beginning to rattle the stained-glass windows of St Peter's.

212. There has been much idle speculation as to whether the Pope could be arrested on his visit to Britain. Confusion has been caused by the arrest warrant related to the war on Gaza issued by a London judge against former Israeli Defence Minister Tzini Livni in December 2009, which caused her to cancel her visit. But that warrant was issued for a 'grave breach' of the Geneva conventions, a crime which can only be committed in the course of armed conflict.[25] Universal jurisdiction in relation to crimes against humanity is limited under Section 51 of the International Criminal Court Act 2001 to offences committed in the UK, or outside it by UK nationals, so the grant of an arrest warrant is unlikely and the papal visit would, if the courts accept (as the

government does) that the Pope is a head of state, be covered by diplomatic immunity under the Diplomatic Privileges Act 1964 (applied to heads of state by Section 20 of the State Immunities Act). Universal jurisdiction laws in other European countries such as Belgium and Ireland are much broader, and are not limited to crimes against humanity during a war.

213. The UK does have a law against attempting to pervert the course of justice, which can be committed by concealing the fact of a criminal offence or by assisting an offender to escape justice, whether or not a police investigation has started,[26] and most Commonwealth countries punish 'misprision of felony', i.e. withholding knowledge of a serious offence from law enforcement authorities. (Roger Mahony, the cardinal in Los Angeles, is currently under grand jury investigation for doing just that.) An agreement by a Vatican official with a local bishop to assign a priest known to be guilty to another parish or country or even to deal with him by secret process might therefore be charged as conspiracy. In the UK this would be a matter for the decision of the Director of Public Prosecutions, and would depend upon evidence that a priest known to have offended in the UK had his crime kept secret by arrangement between his local bishop and the head of the CDF or some other Vatican official. This could not have happened in the UK after 2001 if the Nolan recommendation to report all cases to the police was in fact followed, but cover-ups of this kind were common in Europe, where investigating judges are beginning to follow a trail that could lead them to the Vatican.

214 Readers who are not lawyers, and indeed those who are lawyers like Jack Straw (who, as Elizabeth Wilmshurst pointed out at the Iraq inquiry, is 'not an international lawyer'), will doubtless think this chapter excessively technical and complicated. This is an abiding problem with international law, especially its criminal law, which should in principle be simple enough for potential criminals to understand. However, it must be remembered that this branch of law was frozen by the Cold War for fifty years

after its first emergence at the Nuremberg and Tokyo trials and is still at an early stage of development. The cases on 'command responsibility' all deal with political and military leaders in the context of a continuing war – there has been no significant prosecution yet for crimes committed in peacetime. But that must be the next stage in the struggle for global justice: there is need to pioneer the prosecution of leaders whose states systematically commit serious crimes against their own people, innocent of anything other than dissent. The paradigm persecutor is also a theocracy, although a barbaric one: in 1988 Iran murdered thousands of its political prisoners after the war with Saddam had ended, and most of its present rulers, including its Supreme Leader, were implicated. They now approve the stoning of women taken in adultery, the torture of political prisoners and the assassination of opponents abroad. It must be hoped that, in due course, international law will develop its very real potential to threaten heads of state with accountability if they oppress their own people or their own faithful, or turn their eyes, blinded with a mote, to crimes that their own agents are committing. Crowning irony though it may be, the Vatican's decision to opt for statehood makes it responsible to an international law which is developing mechanisms to require states to act responsibly.

10. Can the Pope be Sued?

'The bishop of the Roman church, in whom continues the office given by the Lord uniquely to Peter, the first of the Apostles, and to be transmitted to his successors, is the Head of the College of Bishops, the Vicar of Christ and the pastor of the universal church on earth. By virtue of his office he possesses supreme, full, immediate and universal ordinary power in the church, which he is always able to exercise freely.'

Canon 331

215. The act of sexually abusing a child is not only a crime – it is a tort (a civil wrong) of assault and battery to the person occasioning a physical or psychological injury for which the victim can sue to obtain financial compensation. The direct perpetrator, if a priest who has by definition taken a vow of poverty, will rarely be in a position to meet a damages award, but in most cases his employer – the bishop or diocese for which he works – will be a 'joint tortfeasor' and hence vicariously liable because the wrongful act was committed in the course of employment. Bishops may, alternatively, be held directly responsible for their negligent failure to supervise the priest or to take sufficient care of the children in his charge, for example by ignoring their complaints or providing no effective investigation. In most cases, therefore, plaintiffs will have no need to look to Rome to find a defendant with deep pockets: usually dioceses have insurers who will take over civil actions by subrogation, and decide whether to fight or settle them. The courts in common law countries have developed rules for employers' liability for sexual assaults committed by employees, generally finding vicarious liability where the wrongful act by an employee is connected with his employment, as in most clerical abuse cases.[1] There are, however, exceptional cases:

in the US, dioceses are corporate entities which makes them easy to sue but unviable as defendants if they declare themselves bankrupt. And in some common law countries the Catholic Church remains an unincorporated association which does not exist as a juristic entity and cannot be sued in its own name – so unless the plaintiff can identify the officials who exercised an active or managerial role and can therefore be held personally liable, his action will fail.[2] There are, in other words, meritorious claims which cannot for technical or legal reasons be met by local church defendants, so some plaintiffs have good reason to consider taking action against the Holy See or the Pope.

216. There is nothing objectionable, in principle or in justice, about seeking redress from an organization (or its leader) that is ultimately responsible for the damage: legal actions serve not only to compensate the injured, but to provide the best incentive for the organization to exert its powers of control to prevent similar harm from being done in future to others. The doctrine of *respondeat superior*, by which an employer is held responsible for actions of agents and employees, irrespective of any direct authorization, has the policy rationale of encouraging greater care in their selection and control. The Pope appoints and dismisses bishops, and is ultimately responsible for disciplining priests: Canon 331 of the Code of Canon Law gives him supreme power in the church. The Holy See has had no difficulty in calling clergy to account for errors of doctrine or morality, no matter where in the world they are based, through its moral and legal authority over subordinates in Catholic religious orders that are bound by obedience to the Pope 'as their superior' (Canon 590). It follows that allowing plaintiffs to sue the Holy See for clerical sex abuse 'could have a significant policy effect by encouraging better safeguards and more stringent oversight at the highest level of the church's administration . . . and emphasizse cooperation with law enforcement, while requiring church leaders to account for their effectiveness in overseeing their personnel and protecting the members of the faithful entrusted to their care'.[3] Given these obvious public interests, is there any

good reason why, in appropriate cases, plaintiffs should be dis-barred from suing the head or governing body of the Catholic Church?

217. The first hurdle for them to surmount is state immunity, which protects against civil suit as well as criminal action. In the case of *Doe v Roman Catholic Diocese of Galveston-Houston and Joseph Cardinal Ratzinger*, the second-named defendant had become Pope Benedict XVI by the time the action was heard. As Cardinal Ratzinger, he was alleged to have approved the *Crimen* system of concealment: his 2001 letter, so the plaintiffs pleaded, 'is conspiratorial on its face in that it reminds the archdiocese that clerical sexual assault of minors is subject to exclusive clerical control and pontifical secrecy'.[4] However, the US State Department filed a 'suggestion of immunity' under the hand of Bush lawyer John Bellinger III which recited that 'the apostolic nunciature has formally requested that the government of the US take all steps necessary to have this action against Pope Benedict XVI dismissed'.[5] American courts deferentially treat such State Department 'suggestions' as diktats, and the case was dismissed on the Bellinger certification that the Pope was 'the sitting Head of State of the Holy See . . . a foreign state'. There was no argument about whether it was a state, because the government's 'suggestion' was treated as conclusive. Courts in some other countries are not prepared to defer to the Executive to this extent and might hear argument on whether the Holy See satisfies the Montevideo criteria. In Britain, although Section 21 of the State Immunity Act provides that a 'certificate of statehood' from the Foreign Secretary shall be 'conclusive evidence' of whether a country is a state,[6] in the case of the Holy See the courts would probably be prepared to examine the correctness or at least the rationality of the minister's decision to grant the certificate, in light of international law. As Lord Woolf pointed out in the Pitcairn Island case,

today it can no longer be taken for granted that the courts will accept that there is any action on the part of the Crown that is not open to any form of review by the courts if a proper foundation for the review is established.[7]

But if the Holy See is a state, the Pontiff cannot be brought before any civil court, even for wrongs that he committed when he was Cardinal Ratzinger.[8] Were he to resign, of course, he could be made a defendant – the case of ex-King Farouk (who was held liable for his mistress's Paris debts for Dior dresses after he was deposed) shows there is nothing so 'ex' as an ex head of state. An ex-Pope, however, is an oxymoron.[9]

218. The Holy See is a different matter. Even if it succeeds in establishing that it is a state, it will not have complete immunity from civil process. State immunity, after all, is a hangover from centuries past, where great sovereign nations regarded themselves as equals: their 'comity' would be upset if they permitted their courts to entertain actions against other nations. But when states and their nationalized corporations began to engage in international ventures which could do serious damage by breaching contracts or causing injuries, this had to change, and most countries now have national laws that restrict the immunities of states that engage in commerce or undertake activities that, through negligence, cause personal injury to individuals in the country in question. The European Convention on State Immunity reflects these exceptions, and in the UK the State Immunity Act (SIA) of 1978 and in the US the Foreign Sovereign Immunities Act (FSIA) incorporates them in broad terms. There is an exception for states that engage in commerce, but it is difficult (although not impossible) to argue that the Holy See engages in commercial transactions with its dioceses: it could be said to supply them with organizational and doctrinal services in return for financial contributions (for example 'St Peter's pence'). Where it is more clearly vulnerable to immunity loss when it is made a defendant to actions for negligence; for example 'for proceedings in respect of . . . personal injury . . . caused by an act or omission in the United Kingdom' (SIA s 5). Or when 'money damages are sought . . . for personal injury . . . occurring in the US and caused by the tortious act or omission of that foreign state or any official or employee of that foreign state while acting within the scope of his or her employment'.[10] Other advanced

nations restrict immunity in similar terms, so there would be no immediate bar to a civil action against the Holy See in relation to child sex abuse committed by a priest employed by the Catholic Church in the country where the action was brought, so long as a causal connection could be plausibly alleged with negligent orders or directives or decisions issued from the Vatican.

219. As in all tort claims, much would depend on the particular facts. The Vatican obviously does not direct priests to offend, or approve in any way of sex abuse. The cases brought against it in the US by victims of re-offending priests have been based on the theory that the abuse would not have happened had the Vatican directed its bishops to inform law enforcement authorities of the evidence of the original abuse, or had not ordered or approved reassignment to other parishes or to other countries – all being directives given with foresight of the risk that the priest will re-offend. These decisions are taken in the Vatican, outside the country where the claim is brought, and to succeed against the Holy See the plaintiff has to show that the directive was communicated to and complied with by the local bishop.[11] An alternative approach has been to argue that bishops are employees of the Holy See, acting within the scope of their employment and under instructions from the Holy See when they negligently failed to warn parishioners about paedophile priests and failed to report allegations of child abuse to police.

220. The English Court of Appeal has recently cut through some of these problems by asking whether there was a sufficiently close connection between the defendant's employment as a priest and the sex abuse he inflicted on a boy to make it 'fair and just' to impose vicarious liability and make the church pay. This was a strong case because the victim was not a Catholic, but was picked up whilst admiring the priest's sports car. Nonetheless, the Court held that his church was liable: a priest has 'a special role, which involves trust and responsibility in a more general way even than a teacher, a doctor or a nurse. He is, in a sense, never off duty.'[12]

His clerical garb 'set the scene' by emitting a moral authority that can bewitch a small boy.

221. The only case that has as yet reached the US Supreme Court – where in 2010 the Vatican suffered a serious setback – is *Doe v Holy See*.[13] The plaintiff had been molested at the age of 15 by a priest at a monastery in Portland. Ten years previously the same priest had admitted to sexually abusing a child at a church in Ireland, so he had been furtively trafficked to work as a counsellor at a boys' high school in Chicago, where (as he later admitted), 'temptation to molest was maximized'. After three victims complained, he was sent to Portland where the plaintiff became his next victim. The case against the Holy See was based on its controlling power over the Catholic Church, its process of appointment and removal of bishops and through them its responsibility for disciplining priests. In this case, despite knowing of the priest's dangerous propensities to abuse children, it negligently placed him, time and again, in a position to do so, and negligently failed to warn those coming into contact with him, including the plaintiff and his family, and negligently failed to supervise him. The Court rejected the Holy See's technical defence that its conduct did not occur in the United States, on the basis that it was sufficient that the injury and some of the conduct alleged to be negligent took place there, even if other aspects of the negligent conduct took place at the Vatican. The state of Oregon, where the action was brought, had an extended law of employer liability which covered crimes committed by an employee as a result of being given the opportunity to commit them by his employment, and the Holy See was potentially liable on the basis that 'an employer who has knowledge of an employee's predilection to sexually abuse young boys unreasonably creates a foreseeable risk by allowing the employee uninhibited access to young boys'.

222 The Vatican, pursuant to its strategy of avoiding trial at all costs, took an appeal against this ruling all the way to the Supreme Court, where it had the support of the Obama administration in

an *amicus* brief filed by Solicitor-General Harold K
some inconsequential submissions about Oregon
FSIA which did not persuade the Court. He did
the Holy See 'is recognized as a foreign sovereign
an indication that, like the Bush administration
White House will support the Pope's claim to imm
case, however, proceeded under the FSIA exceptio
ity, and the Supreme Court rejected the Vatican
review the decision of the Court below. In practic
means that the Vatican tactic has misfired and it m
to trial, or at least make some evidential disclosure
treatment of paedophile priests and perhaps ever
Pope (although it is certain to proffer only a m
answer questions on oath in a recorded deposition.

223. In another ongoing US case, *O'Bryan v Holy See*,
argue that *Crimen*, (Appendix B) which promulga
that all proceedings under Canon Law must be swa
tifical secrecy, operated to block police enquiries
have prevented their molestation. The Holy See, in
has argued that *Crimen* procedures could be avo
bishop deciding to handle the matter informally. If
course, there was nothing from the Vatican in its
that *bound* him not to report the allegation to police
event *Crimen* itself did not *expressly* prevent a bishop
plying with civil reporting requirements. These
appear specious: the emphatic concern throughou
with 'pontifical secrecy' and all concerned are bound
excommunication not to divulge anything, at any sta
parties. While bishops might choose to deal with
mally, i.e. by measures that did not amount to pena
erring priest, the Canon Law insistence on secrecy a
the very outset, starting with the 'denunciation' or
that begins the process and which has to be signed b
plainant under a secrecy oath. A decision to disp
complaint 'informally' – for example by warning and r
the priest or sending him for 'treatment' – would

made after it had been formally received, in which case the bishop would be bound not to report it to outsiders. The Holy See's brief (its pleaded case) gave no examples of a bishop *ever* deciding to report to the police or other civic authority.

A number of actions against the Holy See under the tort immunity exception of the FSIA have been brought in the US, although only *O'Bryan* has advanced to a stage where the Vatican has been called upon to answer allegations that its agents breached their duty of care to children or negligently failed to inform parents or report known or suspected offenders to the appropriate authorities. Cases against the Vatican proceed slowly, because its lawyers – fairly enough – take advantage of every technicality in a highly technical and novel proceeding. (For example, since it is an FSIA rule that all foreign defendants must be served with legal papers in their own written language, the Vatican insists that all such documents must be translated into Latin.) *O'Bryan* is based on the proposition that bishops are employees or agents or officials of the Holy See, and that it is enough for liability under the FSIA to show that the Holy See exerts 'substantial control' over them. This is certainly the position under Canon Law, which asserts that the Pope possesses 'supreme, full, immediate and universal' power in the Church, as head of the College of bishops which has 'supreme and full power over the universal church'.[15] The theory goes that Christ constituted his twelve (male) Apostles as a College, headed by Peter, the 'rock' of the church or (an alternative metaphor) the man entrusted with the 'keys' to the church or (another alternative) the disciple who was made shepherd of the faithful flock. The Roman Pontiff as successor to Peter as Vicar of Christ can do no wrong – at least when he proclaims a doctrine pertinent to faith and morals – and the College of Bishops exercises authority over the universal church, but only with papal approval through an ecumenical council.[16] So much for theology: the problem for plaintiffs is to characterize it as a relationship that can give rise to legal liability: they must prove either that the Holy See employs, controls or directs its bishops and its priests, or at least that it controls or directs its

bishops in their dealings with the priests whom they (the bishops) employ.

225. The importance of *O'Bryan* is that for the first time in a common law court the Vatican has been unable to wriggle out of liability on technical grounds, and has been obliged to file a pleading that contests the merits of the plaintiff's case that the Holy See is vicariously liable for its bishops – the only basis upon which the action was permitted to proceed.[17] The Vatican pleading is a masterpiece of equivocation: it sets out what the Pope's relationship with Catholic bishops is not, but declines to say what it is. It contends only that the Holy See does not have day-to-day control over bishops; it does not provide them with any employment benefits or workers' compensation; it does not pay their social security or withhold tax or lay down specific hours for them to work or hire their servants or gardeners for the Cathedral, and so forth. These are all factors that assist in determining whether a person is an 'employee' for the purposes of US law and the application of its vicarious liability rule, but they do not answer the question which would be posed in most jurisdictions to decide whether the Holy See is liable in law, and which would as a matter of common sense tell whether the Vatican has moral responsibility, namely whether it controls the way that bishops deal with clerical sex abuse allegations, and whether the Canon Law directives that have come to them from Rome caused or contributed to their negligent handling of the plaintiff's case.

226. In *O'Bryan*, the plaintiffs cite Canon Law and Catholic teaching to show that the Holy See has absolute and unqualified power over archbishops, bishops and their dioceses. The Vatican does not dispute this head on, but pleads that the Pope/bishop relationship is a non-justiciable issue that a court is unfit to decide: it is 'inseparable from complex issues of theology, religious doctrine and ecclesiastical governance' and is 'one of the most complex and sensitive issues in the life and history of the church'.[18] The Vatican claims that a civil court 'would be forced to wade deeply' into Catholic doctrine and that 'explaining the

relationships between the Pope and the bishops is extraordinarily complicated even for the best theologians'.

227. This argument – that the issue is non-justiciable because a secular court is not equipped to decide it – is disingenuous. The mafia too is complicated and hierarchical, with its own rites and rules of *omerta*. There *is* a relationship between the Pope and the bishops which any judge is capable of analysing and characterizing once the facts are established by evidence. It may be a canonically and historically sensitive matter, but it cannot be difficult for the court to decide what that relationship is, once communications between the Vatican and the diocese in question are disclosed.[19] If it be the case (as can reasonably be inferred from Canon Law, *Crimen* and the Ratzinger 2001 letter), that the Pope and his CDF Prefect between 1981 and 2005 had ordained a system in which priests who committed crimes would be shielded from prosecution and punishment, or if in the case of *O'Bryan* or his fellow plaintiffs', they had negligently directed that an abuser be reinstated or trafficked or permitted to minister in circumstances where his propensity to re-offend was foreseeable, then they would be liable to pay damages. In such cases, making the Holy See a defendant (either as a joint tortfeasor or a body vicariously liable for its employees) would achieve a measure of accountability.

228. It does strike an odd note that a state should claim that historical and theological complexity makes it impossible to describe the relationship between its head and its arms (in this case, between its Pope and its bishops). It serves to underline how the Holy See cannot fit the Montevideo Convention criteria for statehood: what other state cannot define its own government, because its political process is wrapped in the fog of theology? Whatever international entity the Holy See may be, it is *sui generis*. But nothing in its distinctive character can justify its failure to own up to its responsibilities for the abuse of children. Its inability to volunteer the truth when asked by official inquiries smacks of more than defensiveness – it is a reluctance to confront the abuses

of the recent past and a determined refusal – exemplified by the 'New Norms' issued in July 2010 – to give up its claim to a Canon Law jurisdiction which has, in many cases led victims through a secret, almost Kafka-esque, maze at the end of which they have received neither retribution nor compensation.

229. The refusal of the US Supreme Court to stop the action against the Holy See in *Doe* and the advance made by the plaintiffs in *O'Bryan* (where the facts are much weaker) suggest that some US victims may obtain redress against the Vatican, under the FSIA exception, in US courts notwithstanding a government determined to recognize it as a state. Similar arguments may succeed in other countries, most of which now have FSIA-style legislation. But one important means of redress for foreign plaintiffs which has been used to sue for human rights abuse is unique to America, namely, the Alien Tort Claims Act (ATCA), passed in the heady days of revolutionary independence, 1789. It permits foreigners ('aliens') to sue defendants responsible for civil wrongs ('torts') 'committed in violation of the law of nations'.[20] Since it was famously used in 1980 to bring a torturer to book in the case of *Filartiga v Pena-Irala*, it has been deployed against multinational corporations responsible for assaulting or negligently causing emotional distress in developing countries – against Unocal, for example, for using slave labour and hiring army units in Burma to terrify local opponents of its oil pipeline. Some rogue state leaders have been served with writs (left with the doorman of their New York hotels whilst they were visiting the UN), and although they usually do not stay around for the verdict (a jury awarded $750 million to victims of Radovan Karadzic, who stayed in hiding) the trials can be cathartic for victims, and the Vatican would have political difficulties if it did not pay up (and the US assets of the Vatican bank might be used to satisfy the award).

230. This is not to understate the difficulties that would face victims from Ireland or Germany or Malta (or anywhere outside America) in mounting an ATCA claim against the Vatican. Apart from

proving that widespread and systematic clerical sex abuse of children is a crime against humanity imputable to the Vatican, they would have to show that it violates a specifically defined norm 'accepted by the civilized world' – the narrow test for liability under ATCA laid down by the US Supreme Court in the 2004 case of *Sosa v Alvarez-Machain*.[21] This is certainly arguable – violations that have been held actionable include cruel, inhuman or degrading treatment and prolonged arbitrary detention and unpaid forced labour, and compared with these abuses the systematic sexual abuse of children can be classed as a crime condemned 'throughout the civilized world'. This is clear enough from the near unanimous ratification of the Convention on the Rights of the Child and may thereby be distinguished from the South African Apartheid Litigation, an unsuccessful ATCA case based on the Apartheid Convention, which very few states had ratified at the time. The plaintiffs would have further to show that the Vatican aided and abetted violations by bishops and priests by providing 'knowing assistance' or moral support, or by failing, as civilian leaders, to prevent or punish the violations committed by their subordinates. (The Unocal case was sent to trial by the Ninth Circuit appeals court on the basis that it was open to a jury to find that the corporation had aided and abetted the crimes of its Burmese agents by acts or failures to act which made 'substantial contribution' to the commission of the crime.) Where these hurdles have been jumped, the plaintiff's case may still die in the ditch of sovereign immunity – the relation between an ATCA claim and an FSIA immunity exemption has not been authoritatively tested. What US tort law – and international criminal law – may have in store for the Vatican cannot be predicted, but the very fact that there are ways round its sovereign immunity should give the Pope (and his insurers) pause to reflect. Why not, at least for the future, remove the prospect of any such claims, by giving up on Canon Law and directing bishops to report priests and monks reasonably suspected of molesting children, to the police?

11. Reflections

The Christian believer is a simple person: bishops should protect the faith of their little people against the power of intellectuals.

Bishop Ratzinger, sermon defending the expulsion of Hans Kung,
31 December 1979

231. The Roman Catholic religion counts hundreds of millions of adherents throughout the world, entitled to worship and manifest their faith according to its lawful traditions and doctrines. The Pope, as head of the church, serves as part of its iconography, endowed in certain respects with a quasi-divine infallibility and a spiritual charisma that is projected in a manner which suggests that those who believe in his God must also believe in him. Many Catholics dispute his teachings on the evils of homosexuality or family planning or divorce or contraception or indeed on liberation theology, but nonetheless derive succour from the church which he administers and rules. The observances of the Pope and his cardinals bring comfort and joy to members of their flock and are manifestations of a religion guaranteed protection under human rights treaties, notwithstanding that some of its moral dogmas are inimical to human rights. So the Vatican's work will go on, unabated and unrestricted, irrespective of whether it is denied the status of sovereignty. Statehood is no part of its catechism and no requirement that its believers are obliged to accept: its crux, the Lateran Treaty, and its offspring, the 1933 Nazi Concordat, were deals with historical devils that can be excused but cannot be regarded with pride or as part of a church tradition. Denial of statehood would mean loss to the papacy of the power of impunity and loss of the state soap box at the UN, a privileged platform to propound its controversial doctrines. It

is time that the Vatican began to reflect on the advantages that would follow for the Roman Catholic faith if it were uncoupled from its pretence of earthly power.

232. The evidence summarized in this book reveals three stunning, shameful and incontrovertible facts about the governance of the Catholic Church since Joseph Ratzinger became an archbishop (1979), the head of the CDF (1981) and Pope (2005):

a. Tens of thousands, perhaps[1] even a hundred thousand children and teenagers, mainly boys, have been sexually abused by the clergy, and most have been caused serious and long-term psychological damage.

b. Thousands of clergy, known to be guilty of very grave crimes of a kind which most perpetrators have a propensity to commit again, have not been defrocked. They have been harboured by the church, moved to other parishes or countries and protected from identification and from temporal punishment – usually a prison sentence – under Canon Law protocols that offer them forgiveness in this world as well as the next.

c. The Holy See, a pseudo-state, has established a foreign law jurisdiction in other friendly states pursuant to which, in utter secrecy, it has dealt with sex abusers in a manner incompatible with, and in some respects contrary to, the law of the nation in which it operates, and has withheld the evidence of their guilt from law enforcement authorities.

233. These three facts are incontestable – and inexcusable. There have, of course, been efforts by the church to excuse them, but they are either irrelevant or irrational. Originally, in November 2002, Cardinal Ratzinger was asserting that the crisis was no more than a 'manipulated and planned campaign by the media: less than one per cent of priests are guilty of acts of this type'. This is demonstrably false: 4.3 per cent was the understated John Jay College figure and others put it as high as 6–9 per cent and warn that it might be higher if clergy misbehaviour in the developing world is ever subject to the kind of investigation that has been undertaken in Ireland and in America. The Pope and his

Secretary of State, Bertone, then attributed the phenomenon to homosexual infiltration of the priesthood and to 'gay culture' – implying that gays are potential paedophiles – but the link has long been exploded by the John Jay study and the Vatican's own 2003 Commission.

234. Many good Catholics, led by the eminent theologian Hans Kung, consider that the blame lies not only with the fallibility of the Pope and the secrecy and incompetence of the Vatican and the irresolution of its bishops, but with the rule that requires priests to remain celibate – a rule of no biblical origin (Christ's disciples appear to have been married), but a dogma introduced in the eleventh century and almost abolished by the sixteenth-century reformers. A strong case can be made, on compassionate and on theological grounds as well, for permitting Catholic priests to marry, which would encourage more recruits to join the clergy and would alleviate the problem of some 'problem priests'.[2] But marriage does not 'cure' paedophilia. Many offending priests are not paedophiles: their disordered personality is often ascribed to loneliness in their private lives or to the drugs and alcohol they take to oblivianize it. There is no overwhelming obstacle to their departing from the priesthood if they seek conjugal sex, and for this reason some do depart, while others lead a double life. The priests who molest children are frequently those who are the most punctilious in religious observance and in good works. The suspicion must be that for many, the combination of spiritual power, genuine affection and sexual craving led to acts which were committed because – and only because – there was no deterrent in the form of any likely prospect of arrest and punishment.

235. These men believed, with good reason, that they would get away with it, because priests usually did. They believed – with bad reason although it must have seemed the case – that they had exemption from local law because where sex abuse was concerned they had the grace of the bishop and the protection of a Canon Law which would rarely convict them, never punish them and only occasionally defrock them. They were led to believe

that they had a form of dual nationality: they were subject to local law if they killed or robbed or parked illegally, and subject to church law if they sinned, whether by giving the sacrament to Baptists or Presbyterians, or by raping small children. They believed that the Holy See was a sovereign state with exclusive sovereignty over them in respect of child sex abuse, and the spiritual power to seal the lips of their victims. And every erring priest who underwent prayer and penance was promised forgiveness in this world and redemption in the next. Jesus may have said that those who make children suffer are to be drowned in the depths of the sea, but Pope Benedict XVI told his paedophile priests in Ireland that penitence offered them a life after death-jacket.

236. The Vatican's pretension to statehood cannot be separated from its child abuse crisis, because that crisis has exposed the fact that the church has operated a parallel, para-statal jurisdiction, forgiving sins that host states punish as crimes. Vatican critics have long harped upon how priests manned the 'ratline' that permitted some of the worst Nazis to make their escape to South America, but the real 'ratline' that it has been offering is an escape route to child sex abusers – not so much a 'get out of gaol free' card as a freedom never to be at risk of gaol. Through a mixture of arrogance, negligence, and recklessness borne of belief in its state immunity and its overweening desire to be a political actor on the world stage, the Pope and his army of cardinals, *nuncios*, archbishops and officials have run a church in which children have been suffering widespread and systematic abuse.

237. That the Vatican has escaped serious international censure, let alone prosecution, for its behaviour is something of a wonder. Any other organization, and any state, that turned a blind eye to the molestation of so many children, and that not only refused to punish the perpetrators but set them up to re-offend, would be condemned at the UN and at international conferences, would be made the subject of vitriolic reports by Amnesty International and by Human Rights Watch, and there would be calls to refer

the cause to the ICC Prosecutor. But it is hard to think of the Vatican as a pariah state: the beaming benevolence of John Paul II and the doddering decency of Benedict XVI confound any suggestion that they could possibly be responsible for human rights abuses. It is this two-facedness of the Vatican that enables it to operate without being called to account: the abuses are all on its state-side, with its pseudo-trials under Canon Law and its traffic in paedophile priests, but it can turn the other cheek to reveal joyful adherents and exquisite liturgies and a priesthood and sisterhood that work with courage and dedication for the poor and the sick. For all the damage that papal sex obsessions have done to the fight against HIV/AIDS in Africa, for example, those who actually risk their own health to succour patients in malaria-ridden outback clinics are, as often as not, the Pope's devotees. They are moved to self-sacrifice in the cause of compassion, and they endow the Catholic Church with the aura of goodwill that protects the Holy See from condemnation and from action that might otherwise be taken to limit its privileges. Perceiving the Pope as the incarnation of goodness is for many Catholics a form of wish-fulfilment: his iconic status is part of their religious experience, and woe betide the politician in any democratic country with a significant Catholic population who calls for Benedict to be called to account for covering up child sex abuse. In the 2010 UK election debates, the only two issues on which all three party leaders were agreed were firstly their complete opposition to the Pope's teaching on homosexuality and abortion and birth control, and secondly, on their sincere wish to welcome him on his visit to the UK.

238. The Pope will not find himself in handcuffs during his papal excursion to beatify Cardinal Newman (who made it plain in his lifetime that he wanted no posthumous sainthood). The very idea of putting the Pope on trial is no more realizable in 2010 than arresting Henry Kissinger or George W. Bush or Robert Mugabe or other world leaders whose diplomatic immunities take symbolic shape in the thickets of security guards surrounding them when they venture abroad. But some unrealizable ideas are useful

nonetheless, and the idea that this or any future Pope *could* end up in the dock over their command responsibility for grave breaches of international conventions that protect children is an idea that serves as an affirmation of the rule of a law that no one is above. It also delivers the gravest of warnings: if you insist on being a state, then you cannot complain if you are treated as one. Reform will come quickest, ironically, by hoisting the Vatican with its own petard and treating it as a rogue state rather than as a religion. As a state it has committed unfriendly acts against many other states by hiding felons from the consequences of their crimes and by asserting the supremacy of Canon Law to the exclusion of local criminal law in relation to sex abuse by priests. For this breach of the Vienna Convention, its *nuncio* should be carpeted and self-respecting states should recall their Vatican ambassador from Rome (or, calling Cardinal Sodano's bluff, save money by combining their office with that of the ambassador to Italy). For its grave breaches of the Convention on the Rights of the Child, it should be censured if not expelled, and human rights organizations should begin a close examination of how its doctrines and their propagation through diplomatic channels are damaging international efforts for human progress. Those countries which claim to care about human rights and maintain diplomatic relations with the Holy See might try sending ambassadors with instructions to protest at the sex abuse and sexism for which this 'state' has become notorious. Although it would be much to the benefit of the Catholic Church if its papal politicians would renounce the Holy See's claim to statehood and concentrate with more humility on their religious mission, power and ceremonial splendour has corrupted their thinking and they have convinced themselves that this status helps them to convert the world, or at least to be the most respected religion in it. The only way to cure this delusion may be to treat them like a pariah state and demand that they comply with the Conventions they have breached.

239. It should not be necessary to invoke human rights law against a great church, especially one whose founder laid down the Judeo-Christian ethics that have contributed considerably to the

principles of that law. The criticisms in this book are not directed against members of the Catholic faith, which has admirably withstood the test of time (over 2,000 years of it) or against the rituals which will doubtless continue to offer comfort and miracles to believers until time's end. The last people I would wish my arguments to encourage are those whose 'no popery' graffiti is spray-painted on Belfast walls, or those who view the Holy Father as some sort of anti-Christ, with the full-throttled hatred which can still be read in the Act of Settlement (1701) – the constitutional law which excludes Catholics from accession to the British throne and which, disgracefully, successive governments have declined to amend. Religious hatreds have caused too much murder and mayhem in the world, and the objective of the human rights movement is to ameliorate them, through the taxonomy of tolerance in the Universal Declaration of Human Rights and its successor treaties. They guarantee rights for rites, for religious worship and teaching, drawing the line only at hate-preach and discrimination and any church conduct that damages devotees or others with whom they interact. For the Vatican, the best solution to the problem of clerical sex abuse must be to take human rights seriously. That means putting the 'paramountcy principle' of the Convention on the Rights of the Child into Canon Law, along with mandatory reporting and zero tolerance. Then the Vatican should underscore this commitment by ratifying all the other human rights treaties it has for so long ignored, and proceed to reconsider some of its moral dogmas in light of what those treaties say about individual freedom.

240. So what must Benedict XVI himself do to earn the forgiveness that he seeks as a religious leader and to bring himself, as head of a presumed state, within the law of nations? First and foremost, and throughout the world, he must abandon his claim to judge priests under Canon Law for the sex abuse of children. The church simply has no right to remove priests from the criminal justice system of the country where they work, and for which Canon Law (with its sclerotic process and its tribunals biased in favour of the defendant) can never be an acceptable alternative.

The rule must be that any credible allegation of sex abuse made to any church official must be reported to the police, even in countries where there is no legal duty to make such a report, with Canon Law proceedings stayed until the criminal proceedings are completed. It is only then that Canon Law could become relevant, merely as a post-trial disciplinary process and not as a substitute for a public prosecution. For every priest convicted and imprisoned for child sex abuse, the ecclesiastical penalty should be mandatory laicization. If the church is to keep credibility, it cannot allow convicted child molesters to remain in holy orders. It may forgive them, after sufficient prayer and penance and perhaps prison, but it must never forget the offence by which they betrayed their calling. Even an acquittal should not preclude ecclesiastical penalty: bishops should be instructed to arrange for expert observers to attend every criminal trial because there may well be evidence against the acquitted priest that warrants disciplinary action, although it falls short of justifying a conviction beyond reasonable doubt. In such cases, a Canon Law penalty of penance or reprimand would not place acquitted priests in double jeopardy, as these penalties do not place them in jeopardy at all.

241. There is more, on a pastoral level, that requires Vatican approval and encouragement. Respect for victims and their families, obviously – a great defect in Canon Law is that it imposes no obligation on the church to heal those it has damaged. There must be a duty laid on priests, however hard for them to bare, to 'blow the whistle' on those of their brothers whom they learn are taking liberties with children. This does not mean running to the media, although this must remain as a last resort if superiors refuse to act, or are part of the problem or the cover up. And – however hard this may be to accept after colleagues have been prosecuted – there must be a duty to congratulate and succour the whistle-blower. The case of Father Maurie Crocker, sent to 'Coventry' and left to sink into depression and suicide after he had exposed a vicious clerical paedophile ring (para 42) should never be permitted to recur. But there is another side of the coin that the righteous angry should not forget, and it is the horror for the

priest who is wrongly accused, and the anguish for the priest who is guilty – perhaps of taking advantage of a child only once, or with minimal invasiveness. The paramountcy principle requires them to be named, and the shame will cover them, their mothers and their fathers and their sisters and their brothers and their cousins and their aunts (many priests come from large Catholic families). In taking steps that may lead to prosecution the church must suspend judgment until conviction and do its best to help them through the ordeal, paying for capable legal defenders and ensuring that they have counselling and support. It should automatically defrock those who are convicted (i.e. zero tolerance) but that should not stop it offering them benefits and spiritual support. It is at this point that its tradition of forgiveness is most needed, because forgiveness will not be forthcoming from other sections of society. To hate the sin but love the sinners is an appropriate religious approach to its guilty priests, and once the church accepts the need to cooperate with the secular arm of the law in dealing with offenders it should have no inhibition in striving for their redemption.

242. It is being said, by reactionaries in the Curia, that the worst has past: the church has learnt its lessons from the scandal and bishops everywhere are now on guard against paedophile priests, so there is no need for further reform. It may well be that public obloquy in 2010 has made bishops more attentive to the problem. But still the Vatican declines to make the 'zero tolerance' lead of the US Bishops a universal rule and there has been no action yet on the Cumberledge Report recommendation that England should have papal dispensation from provisions of Canon Law that contravene the paramountcy principle. The 'cover-up cardinals' who blame the whole phenomenon of clerical sex abuse on gays in the church and Jews in the media and moneygrubbing lawyers in the courts are still in their high positions, and what passes as reform for Pope Benedict is a pettifogging change to Canon Law to allow victims to complain up to the age of 38, rather than 28, but not after they turn 39. The fact that the complaint will go forward (if at all) under conditions of pontifical secrecy, with no

proper investigation, no aftercare and a trial process favouring the defendant, does not move the elderly males who run the Vatican, promoted in the era when John Paul II refused to advance those who gave less than enthusiastic support to his teachings on birth control and homosexuality, and when his *nuncios* turned into spies, reporting to Prefect Ratzinger on deviations from doctrinal correctness by up-and-coming priests and Catholic politicians. The notion that 'the worst is over' overlooks the nature of the beast – the incurable condition of most paedophiles and ebophiles, who will simply take more precautions to avoid discovery, or the damaged characters of weak and sex-starved men who succumb to opportunistic temptation – and opportunities will continue in a church that teaches children from their earliest rational age to obey the priest, the agent of God. The only reform that could tackle the evil of clerical child abuse at its source would be to raise the age, from seven to at least twelve, at which Catholic children are first given communion and confession, which inculcates their unquestioning reverence for the priesthood. But the Catholic church will never, I suspect, release its hold on the very young or understand that this is the real reason for its sex abuse problem: as I write, the Vatican newspaper is urging that the age of first communion actually be reduced to five or six.

243. It may be that more is yet to come: after paedophile priests, promiscuous and predator priests will enter the spotlight. There have already been revelations of the extent to which the church protects priests who conduct sexual relations with women and who have had children in consequence. In 2010 it emerged that in the US, Britain, Europe and Australia the church had responded to claims from partners deserted by priests by offering financial support for their children only on condition that they kept secret the identity of the father. These clandestine and often exploitive relationships, forged by priests through their spiritual power over parishioners, have entangled 2,000 women in the US, who are involved with an organization that is bringing law suits – in this case, paternity suits.[3] The vow of celibacy is widely disregarded: a recent survey in Poland showed that 54 per cent of priests would

like to have a wife, while 12 per cent owned up to already having one. When Cardinal Schönborn of Austria (where 22 per cent of priests are said to be in heterosexual relationships) called for a rethink, the Pope caused him to withdraw the suggestion because it contravened 'the principle of holy celibacy'.[4] Notwithstanding the lack of biblical support for the rule this Pope and John Paul II would not give way. They tried to suppress reports from Catholic charities CAFOD and Caritas which leaked in 2001 about the frightening behaviour of promiscuous priests in Africa during the HIV/AIDS crisis who began to force themselves on nuns on the assumption that they would be free of the virus. When caught, these priests would be moved to another parish whilst the nun in question would be expelled from her convent and made destitute. When this scandal was exposed by the *National Catholic Reporter*, the Vatican shrugged it off as a local African problem – a few months before it described clerical child abuse as 'an American problem'.[5]

244. These changes are the minimum required of the Pope if he is to make amends for the scandal to which his dereliction of duty at the CDF has contributed. He should go further, of course, and ensure that CDF files are inspected regularly by an independent (and non-Catholic) commissioner or panel of experts, whose public reports would provide a degree of transparency and accountability, together with reassurance that the Vatican is at last putting the interests of children before its own reputation and sense of self-importance. Sadly, when last heard from, Benedict XVI and Bertone were as truculent as ever on this score. After Belgian police had politely detained the country's nine cardinals whilst they looked for evidence of child sex abuse (para 210), Benedict condemned their action as 'deplorable' and insisted that sex abuse must be handled by Canon Law procedures as well as civil law, 'respecting their reciprocal specificity and autonomy'. Plainly he still does not understand that there is no reciprocity at all between Canon Law and criminal law – the former means of disciplining priests for sin must give way to the law under which they should be prosecuted and punished for crime. It has no 'autonomy' that can possibly be allowed to get in the way of police

investigation of a criminal case. But Bertone rejected this principle hyperbolically: 'There are no precedents for this, even under communist regimes', he raged, although the cardinals had suffered no more than a brief confiscation of their episcopal cell phones.

245. What will be required of the Vatican, as a signal of a new commitment to put children first, is the complete abandonment of Benedict's claim that the Holy See has the right to deal with suspected felons under an obscure, inefficient and secret ecclesiastical process. But Canon Law provides a form of power, and perhaps Benedict's fatal flaw is his attraction to power – to the pomp and circumstance of statehood, to the queues of world leaders who come to bend at his knee and kiss his fisherman's ring, and to the satisfaction of having delegates promote his ideology with six seats at UN conference tables. Journalists often tell how this kindly old man offers to share his food with them, but an analysis of his behaviour suggests a man in thrall to power and unable to give any of it up – even for the sake of innocent children. When it ratified the Convention on the Rights of the Child, the Holy See quoted the words of John Paul II, to the effect that children 'are that precious treasure given to each generation as a challenge to its wisdom and humanity'. John Paul II himself, as we now know, failed that challenge by cosseting notorious child molesters and turning a blind eye to the mounting toll of child victims. So did his closest lieutenant, Joseph Cardinal Ratzinger. On the question of whether Benedict XVI is capable of the wisdom and humanity to protect the children of his church, the jury is out.

Appendix A: A bishop on the stand

These extracts are taken from the official transcript of the deposition of Bishop Curry in one of the cases brought against the church in Los Angeles for negligent supervision of paedophile priests. This case was brought by a victim of Father Michael Baker, who began molesting children in 1974: he confessed to Bishop Curry and Cardinal Mahony in 1986 that he had interfered with two boys. Curry is being asked to explain how he dealt with this knowledge. After brief 'treatment' with the Paraclete Order in New Mexico, Baker was back in the ministry. When a young boy was observed coming out of his bedroom, Bishop Curry was meant to investigate. Baker was transferred to other California parishes – nine in total, where he regularly re-offended for the next fifteen years.

Q: Did you believe in 1986 that you could be cured of molesting children?

A: I don't know that I had any belief about that.

Q: Did you know in 1986 that molesting a child was a crime?

A: Yes.

Q: Did you call the police?

A: No.

Q: Why?

A: He came in under . . . a confidential understanding with the church confessing to something that he had done and I believed that that was a confidential matter.

Q: If he came in and told you that he had murdered children, would you have called the police?

A: I don't know what I would have done in that I never dealt with such a thing.

Q: In any event, you didn't call the police?

A: No.

Q: Did you talk to the Cardinal about calling the police?

A: I don't remember doing so. What I remember is that we said that he would need to be removed from ministry right away and that he would be sent to treatment.

Q: Okay. And when you say, 'sent to treatment,' what do you mean?

A: That he would be sent to a residential treatment facility.

Q: And what was he going to be treated for?

A: For the problems that he had confessed to.

Q: Meaning molesting kids?

A: Yes.

Q: So he was going to go to treatment to get him to stop molesting kids?

A: Yes.

Q: Who selected where he was going to go to get this treatment?

A: I probably did.

Q: Where did you send him?

A: We sent him to Servants of the Paraclete in Jemez Springs, New Mexico.

Q: And what is Servants of the Paraclete?

A: It's a religious community.

Q: It's a group of priests and brothers?

A: Yes.

Q: And what do they do?

A: What I knew of, that they ran that facility.

Q: . . . did you understand that the boys he molested were younger than 12 years old or older than 12 years old?

A: No, I didn't.

Q: You don't know?

A: No.

Q: Did anybody ask him how old the children were?

A: Not at that time.

Q: Did the Cardinal ask him what he had done with these boys?

A: I don't remember that.

Q: Did the Cardinal ask him the names of the boys?

A: Again, I don't remember.

Q: Did you ever discuss with the Cardinal the need to find these boys so they could get some help?

A: I don't remember doing that.

Q: You don't remember the Cardinal ever instructing you that these families needed to be found, these children he had molested, so the Archdiocese could help these boys?

A: I don't remember that.

. . .

Q: . . . Did you and the Cardinal ever discuss whether it would be appropriate to call Child Protective Services or the police on Father Baker?

A: No, I don't think so.

Q: . . . Was there ever a discussion about notifying the parishes or the places that Father Baker had served prior to coming to see you, to see if there were other people that he had hurt that the Archdiocese could give help to?

A: No.

. . .

Q: How did the Archdiocese determine it was appropriate to return Father Baker to ministry?

A: We believed that he wanted to change his life.

Q: And why did you believe that?

A: Because he came and reported himself and confessed and we didn't want to put him in a situation where he would be involved with children.

Q: So besides telling Father Baker that he was not to be around children, what other steps did the Archdiocese put in place to protect kids, if any?

A: We put him in an assignment where he was not involved with children. And we told the pastor of the parish that he was to live at that he was not to be involved in any ministry with children.

Q: Did you tell [the pastor] that Father Baker was a child molester?

A: I don't remember doing so.

Q: Well, did you think that it was important for [the pastor] to know?

A: I thought it was important that he know that he was not supposed to be around children.

Q: You didn't tell him he was a molester, but you told him he wasn't to be around children?

A: Yes.

Q: Why didn't you tell him he was a molester?

A: I don't know.

Q: Were you trying to hide it?

A: No.

Q: Did you and the Cardinal meet with Father Baker after he came back from the Paracletes?

A: I don't remember.

Q: Was Father Baker returned to ministry?

A: Yes.

Q: Did you understand that when a child's molested, that there can be catastrophic consequences to that little boy or little girl?

A: I didn't have a clear understanding – I didn't have a deep understanding then.

Q: Did it occur to you in any way that these children might be hurt?

A: Yes.

Q: Did the Cardinal ever ask you about the children, ever make any inquiry of their status?

A: I don't remember.

Q: You don't remember the Cardinal ever asking you about how are these children doing, have we made outreach to their families, have we tried to help them?

A: No, I don't remember.

Q: If the Cardinal had directed you to find the victims, would you have found them?

A: I don't know that.

Q: If the Cardinal said 'Monsignor, I want these boys found, I want their families found, I want to help them,' would you have done that?

A: I don't know whether I could have.

Q: You would have tried, right?

A: I don't know. I think so.

Q: If the Cardinal told you to do something, you would use whatever facilities and ability you had to do it; is that correct?

A: Yes.

Q: But he never told you to find the kids, did he?

A: Not that I remember.

Q: Now, did you have a discussion about notifying the parishes where Baker had served with the Cardinal?

A: No.

Q: Did it occur to you, while you were Vicar for Clergy, that there might be other kids that Father Baker had abused besides these two boys?

A: I don't remember thinking about that.

Q: You don't have any knowledge that anybody at the Archdiocese, Bishop, ever has tried to find those two kids, do you?

A: I don't.

Q: Is it true, Bishop, that the reason you didn't find the two kids is you were concerned they might call the police?

A: No.

Q: Why didn't you try to find the kids?

A: I just didn't know who they were and where they were and I thought one was in Mexico.

Q: Well, if you wanted to find them, what could you have done?

A: I don't know at that time.

Q: Could you have gone to the parish records and seen if they were registered?

A: No.

Q: No?

A: I didn't have a last name.

Q: Did you ask Baker for the last name?

A: No.

Q: You could have asked Baker for the last name, right?

A: Yes.

Q: You didn't even ask the last name of the victim, right? Is that your testimony?

A: Yes.

Q: So you didn't ask the last name of the victim, you didn't ask the name of the other victim; is that right?

A: Right.

Q: Why in the world not?

A: I don't know.

Q: Isn't it true you didn't want to know?

A: No.

Q: Well, then why didn't you ask?

A: Because I wasn't accustomed to dealing with those issues at that time. It was the first time I had dealt with it.

Q: Why didn't you hire somebody or bring somebody on that was accustomed?

A: Because I wasn't skilled in the matter.

Q: Did the Cardinal ask the last name?

A: I don't remember.

Q: If you had the name of the boys, could you have checked the parish register?

A: Which parish?

Q: Wherever it happened.

A: I didn't know where it happened. I didn't ask.

Q: Did the Cardinal ask where this happened?

A: I don't remember.

Q: Did the Cardinal ask what parish it happened in?

A: I don't remember that.

Q: His pastor was made aware he wasn't supposed to teach [kids]?

A: His pastor was aware he was not supposed to be involved in ministry to children.

Q: Was that in writing?

A: I don't remember.

Q: What was the pastor supposed to do if he saw him, you know, violating his – he was around kids?

A: He was supposed to let me know.

Q: Okay. Now, was he allowed to hear confessions?

A: For children?

Q: Well, yeah.

A: I don't think so.

Q: How would you prevent that? Was there an 'adults only' sign on the confessional?

A: No, but involving confessions for school children or for religious education children would be out.

Q: If he is hearing confession on a Saturday afternoon, he can't control who comes in the confessional?

A: I just don't know whether he was hearing confessions.

Q: You don't have a recollection of whether he was prevented from that?

A: No.

Q: Now, he was allowed to say mass at the parish he was living at?

A: Yes.

Q: And he was allowed to have altar servers with him?

A: I believe so.

Q: They are usually children, right?

A: Yes.

Q: And would the children dress in the same – to put on the cassocks and altar boy garb or altar girl garb – in the same area of the sacristy that Baker dressed in?

A: I don't know what the sacristy they had there was.

Q: Have you ever heard of a child being molested in the sacristy, Bishop?

A: I have.

Q: How many times have you heard that?

A: I don't know.

Q: Did you have a concern, did it ever occur to you that Baker might molest children in the sacristy?

A: I can't answer the question because I don't understand.

Q: When is the first time you learned that children were sometime molested in the sacristy?

A: I don't know.

Q: Did anybody ever warn the altar families, the altar servers at parishes where Baker was working while you were Vicar for Clergy that he was a molester?

A: No.

Q: Did it ever occur to you, while you were the Vicar for Clergy, that might be something a family should know before they let their children serve mass with Father Baker?

A: No.

Q: That never occurred to you?

A: No.

Q: Well, did he give children communion?

A: Yes.

Q: Did he have altar boys?

A: Yes.

Q: And altar girls?

A: I assume so.

Father Baker, having confessed to molesting two boys and having been placed on the 'restricted' ministry described above, was soon involved in a 'boundary violation'. Father Dyer reported to Bishop Curry that a young boy had been observed leaving the priest's bedroom.

Q: Did you ever, during your time as Vicar for Clergy, tell Father Baker he needed to stop this conduct, being alone with children or molesting children or you were going to call the police?

A: I told him that – obviously, that he had to stop the boundary violations.

Q: Okay. And what did he say?

A: He said he would.

Q: You made it really clear to him after the Dyer incident that this was wrong, it was a boundary violation and that it needed to stop, correct?

A: Yes.

Q: And you told him that it violated his aftercare contract, did you?

A: I believe I did.

Q: And did you tell him if he did it again, you were going to remove him from ministry?

A: No.

Q: Why not?

A: I don't know.

Q: Did the Cardinal tell him or anybody tell him that if he did it again, there was going to be a consequence?

A: I don't remember.

Q: Did anybody try and find the boy's parents to tell the parents what had happened?

A: Not that I know of.

Q: Was there ever a discussion about trying to find the boy's family, so they could ask their child if Father Baker had hurt him?

A: No, I don't remember that.

Q: And you don't know to this day who that child is?

A: No.

Q: Have you ever wondered in retrospect whether Baker actually molested that little boy?

A: I just don't know.

Q: I asked you if you have ever wondered about it.

A: I just – no, I don't wonder. I just don't know.

Q: In terms of the aftercare program, was there ever an arrangement to be sure that Father Baker was never alone in the rectory?

A: Not that I know of.

Q: After the boundary violation with the boy that Dyer reported, was there any type of change in his supervision that made sure that he was never alone in the rectory?

A: Not that I know of.

Q: Okay. So did he give an explanation as to why the boy was in the rectory?

A: I – I believe he did.

Q: And what was that?

A: I think he – I forget. But I think he asked – that the boy was looking for counselling or something like that.

Q: So he was counselling the boy?

A: I'm not sure. I really can't remember the details.

Q: Did you think that was a good explanation?

A: I don't know at the time.

[Many years later when LA police finally heard about Father Baker's re-offending, they subpoenaed records of this incident and through astute detective work they traced the boy – now aged 32 – who disclosed that he had indeed been sexually assaulted by Baker, and had been traumatized by the experience, which he had not dared to speak about for fear of its effect on his profoundly Catholic mother. The church eventually paid him $1.2 million compensation for its negligence in failing to investigate Father Dyer's report. The cross-examination of Bishop Curry turned to another of the church's methods of dealing with paedophile priests – sending them to University to study Canon Law.]

Q: Now, part of the duties of the Canon lawyers at the Archdiocese was to provide advice and provide canonical services in a variety of areas, including priest penal matters; is that correct?

A: Yes.

Q: Did you think it was a good idea for the Cardinal to appoint a child molester to the Canon Law office?

A: He was dealing with marriage cases entirely.

Q: Father X was a child molester, a convicted child molester and he was assigned to the office that handled priest penal cases; is that accurate?

A: I don't remember any case that he handled of that kind.

Q: After he got out of the Servants of the Paraclete and finished probation, you sent him to Catholic University to get a degree in Canon Law; is that correct?

A: I think so, yes.

Q: So you made a convicted child molester a Canon lawyer and placed him in the office that was to prosecute priest penal cases, including priest child molestation cases; is that accurate?

A: The Archdiocese, the office would recommend to the Cardinal, but I don't know that the office was there to prosecute.

Q: Before the Cardinal appointed Father X to the canonical law office and allowed him to go to law school to become a canonist, did you discuss with him any objections you had to a convicted child molester getting a degree in Canon Law?

A: No.

Q: Who supervised Father X when he was in law school – at Canon Law School at Catholic University?

A: I'm not aware of that.

[The cross-examiner then put to the Bishop an article from the Los Angeles Times *about Baker's re-offending after his confession and the Dyer incident.]*

Q: The article states, 'In addition, Baker continued to have frequent access to children over the next fourteen years while he was assigned to nine different parishes. Six of the churches where Baker worked had elementary schools adjacent to the rectory.' Is that true, Bishop?

A: I believe it is.

Q: Why in the world would you assign Father Baker to a parish that had a school, sir?

A: Because we had an agreement with him that he would not be involved in the school or in any ministry to children.

Q: You put a paedophile priest in a parish with a school; is that correct, sir?

A: We appointed Michael Baker, who said he had abused children in school – in these parishes that had schools.

Q: I take it you alerted the principal that there was a paedophile living next to their campus, right?

A: I didn't talk to the principal.

Q: Did the Cardinal direct you or anybody else to your knowledge at the Archdiocese to call the principal of those schools and advise him or her that there was a priest who had admitted to molesting children living at the parish where the school was located?

A: No.

Q: Do you think that would have been a good idea, Bishop?

A: Do I think that now?

Q: Yeah. Do you think that would have been a good idea?

A: I would – what I've learned since, yes.

Q: What did you learn since that changed your mind about notifying principals that a child molester was living basically at the school?

A: He was living at the rectory. He wasn't living at the school.

Q: Okay. Well, do you know how close the parish schools are to the rectory in these places?

A: Yes.

Q: Why did you not notify the principals of the schools at the parishes he served at that he had admitted molesting children?

A: Because we had an agreement that he was not to be involved with children and I believed that he wanted to change his life and follow that policy.

Q: How would that – how would notifying principals that he had previously abused kids change that?

A: I don't know.

Q: Bishop, did you know what he had done was a crime?

A: Yes.

Q: Did you know, Bishop, when you put Baker in parishes and schools, that he had committed a crime?

A: He confessed to a crime, yes.

Q: And you knew that he had committed a crime against children, correct?

A: He confessed that.

Q: And you knew that you were putting him in close proximity to children when you assigned him to parishes with schools, correct?

A: Yes.

Q: Okay. Did you tell the Cardinal or ever have a discussion with Cardinal Mahoney that that was an extremely bad idea?

A: No.

This particular case was eventually settled in 2010 by the payment of $2.2 million in compensation to the victims of Father Baker.

Appendix B: Extracts from
Crimen Sollicitationis

INSTRUCTION OF THE SUPREME SACRED CONGREGATION OF THE HOLY OFFICE

ADDRESSED TO ALL PATRIARCHS, ARCHBISHOPS, BISHOPS AND OTHER LOCAL ORDINARIES

INSTRUCTION
ON THE MANNER OF PROCEEDING IN CAUSES INVOLVING THE CRIME OF SOLICITATION

TO BE KEPT CAREFULLY IN THE SECRET ARCHIVE OF THE CURIA FOR INTERNAL USE. — NOT TO BE PUBLISHED OR AUGMENTED WITH COMMENTARIES — PRELIMINARY MATTERS

1. The crime of solicitation occurs whenever a priest – whether in the act itself of sacramental confession, or before or immediately after confession, on the occasion or under the pretext of confession, or even apart from confession [but] in a confessional or another place assigned or chosen for the hearing of confessions and with the semblance of hearing confessions there – has attempted to solicit or provoke a penitent, whosoever he or she may be, to immoral or indecent acts, whether by words, signs, nods, touch or a written message, to be read either at that time or afterwards, or he has impudently dared to have improper and indecent conversations or interactions with that person.

2. Bringing this unspeakable crime to trial in first instance pertains to the *local Ordinaries* (i.e. Bishops or Abbots) in whose territory the Defendant has residence, not only by proper right but also by special delegation of the Apostolic See; *and it is enjoined upon them, by an obligation gravely binding in conscience, to ensure that causes of this sort henceforth be introduced, treated and concluded as quickly as possible before their own tribunal.* Nevertheless, for particular

and grave reasons, in accordance with the norm of Canon 247, §2, these causes can also be deferred directly to the Sacred Congregation of the Holy Office, or called to itself by the same Sacred Congregation. . . .

4. The local Ordinary is judge in these causes for Religious as well, including exempt Religious. [*'Religious' here refers to deacons and monks and other church officials who have not been ordained*.] Their Superiors are in fact strictly prohibited from involving themselves in causes pertaining to the Holy Office (Canon 501, §2). Nonetheless, without prejudice to the right of the Ordinary, this does not prevent Superiors themselves, should they discover that one of their subjects has committed a crime in the administration of the Sacrament of Penance, from being able and obliged to exercise vigilance over him; to admonish and correct him, also by means of salutary penances; and, if need be, to remove him from any ministry whatsoever. *They will also be able to transfer him to another place*, unless the local Ordinary has forbidden it inasmuch as a complaint has already been received and an investigation begun.

5. The local Ordinary can either preside over these causes himself or commit them to be heard by another person, namely, a prudent ecclesiastic of mature age. . . .

7. The promoter of justice, the advocate of the Defendant and the notary – who are to be prudent priests, of mature age and good repute, doctors in Canon Law or otherwise expert, of proven zeal for justice (Canon 1589) and unrelated to the Defendant in any of the ways set forth in Canon 1613 – are appointed in writing by the Ordinary. . . . The Defendant is not prohibited from proposing an advocate acceptable to him (Canon 1655); the latter, however, must be a priest, and is to be approved by the Ordinary.
    . . .

11. Since, however, in dealing with these causes, more than usual care and concern must be shown that they be treated with the utmost confidentiality, and that, once decided and the decision executed, they are covered by permanent silence (Instruction of the Holy Office, 20 February 1867, No. 14), all those persons in any way associated with the tribunal, or knowledgeable of these matters by reason of their office, are bound to observe inviolably the strictest confidentiality, commonly known as the *secret of the Holy Office*, in all things and with all persons, under pain of incurring automatic excommunication, *ipso facto* and undeclared, reserved to the sole person of the Supreme Pontiff, excluding even the Sacred Peniten-

tiary. Ordinaries are bound *by this same law,* that is, in virtue of their own office; other personnel are bound in virtue of *the oath* which they are always to swear before assuming their duties; and, finally, those delegated, questioned or informed [outside the tribunal], are bound in virtue of *the precept* to be imposed on them in the letters of delegation, inquiry or information, with express mention of the *secret of the Holy Office* and of the aforementioned censure.

12. The oath mentioned above . . . is to be taken . . . in the presence of the Ordinary or his delegate, on the Holy Gospels of God (including priests) and not in any other way, together with an additional promise faithfully to carry out their duties; the aforementioned excommunication does not, however, extend to the latter. Care must be taken by those presiding over these causes that no one, including the tribunal personnel, come to knowledge of matters except to the extent that their role or task necessarily demands it.

13. The oath to maintain confidentiality must always be taken in these causes, also by the accusers or complainants and the witnesses. These persons, however, are subject to no censure, unless they were expressly warned of this in the proceedings of accusation, deposition or questioning. The Defendant is to be most gravely admonished that he too must maintain confidentiality with respect to all persons, apart from his advocate, under the penalty of suspension *a divinis*, to be incurred *ipso facto* in the event of a violation.

  . . .

TITLE ONE THE FIRST NOTIFICATION OF THE CRIME

15. The crime of solicitation is ordinarily committed in the absence of any witnesses; consequently, lest it remain almost always hidden and unpunished with inestimable detriment to souls, it has been necessary to compel the one person usually aware of the crime, namely the penitent solicited, to reveal it *by a denunciation* imposed by positive law. Therefore:

  . . .

23. In receiving denunciations, this order is normally to be followed: First, an oath to tell the truth is to be administered to the one making the

denunciation; the oath is to be taken while touching the Holy Gospels. The person is then to be questioned according to the formula (Formula E), taking care that he relates, briefly and fittingly, yet clearly and in detail, everything whatsoever pertaining to the solicitations he has experienced. In no way, however, is he to be asked if he consented to the solicitation; indeed, he should be expressly advised that he is not bound to make known any consent which may have been given. The responses, not only with regard to their substance but also the very wording of the testimony (Canon 1778), should immediately be put in writing. The entire transcript is then to be read back in a clear and distinct voice to the one making the denunciation, giving him the option to add, suppress, correct or change anything. His signature is then to be demanded or else, if he is unable or does not know how to write, an 'x'. While he is still present, the one receiving the testimony, as well as the notary, if present, are to add their signatures (cf. No. 9). Before the one making the denunciation is dismissed, he is to be administered the oath to maintain confidentiality, as above, if necessary under pain of excommunication reserved to the local Ordinary or to the Holy See (cf. No. 13).

28. . . . the Ordinary, if he has determined that the specific delict of solicitation was not present, is to order the acts to be put into the secret archive, or to exercise his right and duty in accordance with the nature and gravity of the matters reported. If, on the other hand, he has come to the conclusion that [the crime] was present, he is immediately to proceed to the investigation (cf. Can. 1942, §1).

TITLE TWO THE PROCESS

Chapter I – The Investigation

. . .

33. . . . once the Ordinary has received any denunciation of the crime of solicitation, he will – either personally or through a specially delegated priest – summon two witnesses (separately and with due discretion), to be selected insofar as possible from among the clergy, yet above any exception, who know well both the accused and the accuser. In the presence of the notary (cf. No. 9), who is to record the questions and answers in

writing, he is to place them under a solemn oath to tell the truth and to maintain confidentiality, under threat, if necessary, of excommunication . . . He is then to question them concerning the life, conduct and public reputation of both the accused and the accuser; whether they consider the accuser worthy of credence, or on the other hand capable of lying, slander or perjury; and whether they know of any reason for hatred, spite or enmity between the accuser and the accused.

. . .

Chapter II – Canonical Measures and the Admonition of the Accused

42. Once the investigative process has been closed, the Ordinary, after hearing the promoter of justice, is to proceed as follows, namely:
    a) if it is clear that the denunciation is completely unfounded, he is to order this fact to be declared in the acts, and the documents of accusation are to be destroyed;
    b) if the evidence of a crime is vague and indeterminate, or uncertain, he is to order the acts to be archived, to be brought up again should anything else happen in the future;
    c) if, however, the evidence of a crime is considered grave enough, but not yet sufficient to file a formal complaint – as is the case especially when there are only one or two denunciations with regular *diligences* but lacking or containing insufficiently solid subsidiary proofs, or even when there are several [denunciations] but with uncertain *diligences* or none at all – he is to order that the accused be admonished, according to the different types of cases, by a *first* or a *second* warning, *paternally*, *gravely* or *most gravely* according to the norm of Canon 2307, adding, if necessary, the *explicit threat of a trial* should some other new accusation be brought against him. The acts, as stated above, are to be kept in the archives, and vigilance is to be exercised for a period with regard to the conduct of the accused;
    d) finally, if certain or at least probable arguments exist for bringing the accusation to trial, he should order the Defendant to be cited and formally charged.
43. The warning mentioned in the preceding number (c) is always to be given in a confidential manner; nevertheless it can also be given by letter or by a personal intermediary, but in each case this must be proved by a document to be kept in the secret archives of the Curia, together with information about the manner in which the Defendant accepted it.

44. If, following the first warning, other accusations are made against the same Defendant regarding acts of solicitation which occurred prior to that warning, the Ordinary is to determine, in conscience and according to his own judgment, whether the first warning is to be considered sufficient or whether he should instead proceed to a new warning, or even to the next stage.

   . . .

Chapter III – The Arraignment of the Accused

   . . .

48. When the Defendant, having been cited, has appeared, before the charges are formally brought, the judge is to exhort him in a paternal and gentle way to make a confession; if he accepts these exhortations, the judge, having summoned the notary or even, if he considers it more appropriate (cf. No. 9), without the presence of the latter, is to receive the confession.

49. In such a case, if the confession is found, in light of the proceedings, to be substantially complete, once the Promoter of Justice has submitted a written opinion, the cause can be concluded by a definitive sentence, all other formalities being omitted (see below, Chapter IV). The Defendant however is to be given the option of accepting that sentence, or requesting the normal course of a trial.

50. If on the other hand the Defendant has denied the crime, or has made a confession which is not substantially complete, or even rejected a sentence summarily issued on the basis of his confession, the judge, in the presence of the notary, is to read him the decree mentioned above in No. 47, and to declare the arraignment opened.

   . . .

52. After this, the questioning of the Defendant takes place in accordance with Formula P, with the greatest care being taken on the part of the judge lest the identity of the accusers and especially of the denouncers be revealed, and on the part of the Defendant lest the sacramental seal be violated in any way. If the Defendant, speaking heatedly, lets slip something which might suggest either a direct or indirect violation of the seal, the judge is not to allow it to be recorded by the notary in the acts; and if, by chance, some such thing has been unwittingly related, he is to order it, as soon as it comes to his attention, to be deleted completely. *The judge*

must always remember that it is never permissible for him to compel the Defendant to take an oath to tell the truth (cf. Canon 1744).

. . .

TITLE THREE PENALTIES

61. 'One who has committed the crime of solicitation . . . is to be suspended from the celebration of Mass and from the hearing of sacramental confessions and even, in view of the gravity of the crime, declared incapable from hearing them. He is to be deprived of all benefices, dignities, active and passive voice, and is to be declared incapable for all these, and in more grievous cases he is even to be subjected to reduction to the lay state [*degradatio*]'. Thus states Canon 2368, §1 of the Code [of Canon Law].

62. For a correct practical application of this canon, when determining, in the light of Canon 2218, §1, fair and proportionate penalties against priests convicted of the crime of solicitation, the following things should be taken into particular account in evaluating the gravity of the crime, namely: the number of persons solicited and their condition – for example, if they are minors or specially consecrated to God by religious vows; the form of solicitation, especially if it might be connected with false doctrine or false mysticism; not only the formal but also the material turpitude of the acts committed, and above all the connection of the solicitation with other crimes; the duration of the immoral conduct; the repetition of the crime; recidivism following an admonition, and the obdurate malice of the solicitor.

63. Resort is to be had to the extreme penalty of reduction to the lay state – which for accused religious can be commuted to reduction to the status of a lay brother [*conversus*] – only when, all things considered, it appears evident that the Defendant, in the depth of his malice, has, in his abuse of the sacred ministry, with grave scandal to the faithful and harm to souls, attained such a degree of temerity and habitude, that there seems to be no hope, humanly speaking, or almost no hope, of his amendment.

. . .

65. In accordance with the norm of Canon 2236, §3, all of these penalties, inasmuch as imposed by law, cannot, once they have been applied by the judge ex officio, be remitted except by the Holy See, through the Supreme Sacred Congregation of the Holy Office.

TITLE FOUR OFFICIAL COMMUNICATIONS

66. No Ordinary is ever to omit informing the Holy Office immediately upon receiving any denunciation of the crime of solicitation. If it happens to concern a priest, whether secular or religious, having residence in another territory, he is at the same time to send (as already stated above, No. 31) to the Ordinary of the place where the denounced priest currently lives or, if this is unknown, to the Holy Office, an authentic copy of the denunciation itself with the *diligences* carried out as fully as possible, along with appropriate information and declarations.

67. Any Ordinary who has instituted a process against any soliciting priest should not fail to inform the Sacred Congregation of the Holy Office, and, if the matter concerns a religious, the priest's General Superior as well, regarding the outcome of the cause.

68. If a priest convicted of the crime of solicitation, or even merely admonished, should transfer his residence to another territory, the Ordinary *a quo* should immediately warn the Ordinary *ad quem* of the priest's record and his legal status.

69. If a priest who has been suspended in a cause of solicitation from hearing sacramental confessions, but not from sacred preaching, should go to another territory to preach, the Ordinary of that territory should be informed by his Superior, whether secular or religious, that he cannot be employed for the hearing of sacramental confessions.

70. All these official communications shall always be made *under the secret of the Holy Office*; and, since they are of the utmost importance for the common good of the Church, *the precept to make them is binding under pain of grave [sin]*.

TITLE FIVE *CRIMEN PESSIMUM*

71. The term *crimen pessimum* ['the foulest crime'] is here understood to mean any external obscene act, gravely sinful, perpetrated or attempted by a cleric in any way whatsoever with a person of his own sex.

72. Everything laid down up to this point concerning the crime of solicitation is also valid, with the change only of those things which the nature

of the matter necessarily requires, for the *crimen pessimum*, should some cleric (God forbid) happen to be accused of it before the local Ordinary, except that the obligation of denunciation [imposed] *by the positive law of the Church* [does not apply] unless perhaps it was joined with the crime of solicitation in sacramental confession. . . .

73. Equated with the *crimen pessimum,* with regard to penal effects, is any external obscene act, gravely sinful, perpetrated or attempted by a cleric in any way with pre-adolescent children [*impuberes*] of either sex or with brute animals [*bestialitas*].

FROM AN AUDIENCE WITH THE HOLY FATHER, 16 MARCH 1962

His Holiness Pope John XXIII, in an audience granted to the Most Eminent Cardinal Secretary of the Holy Office on 16 March 1962, graciously approved and confirmed this Instruction, ordering those responsible to observe it and to ensure that it is observed in every detail.

Given in Rome, from the Office of the Sacred Congregation, 16 March 1962.

L.+S. A. CARD. OTTAVIANI

Appendix C: Extracts from *Sacramentorum sanctitatus tutela*: Apostolic letter from Cardinal Ratzinger (2001)

CONGREGATION FOR THE DOCTRINE OF THE FAITH LETTER

SENT FROM THE CONGREGATION FOR THE DOCTRINE OF THE FAITH TO BISHOPS OF THE ENTIRE CATHOLIC CHURCH AND OTHER ORDINARIES AND HIERARCHS HAVING AN INTEREST

REGARDING THE MORE SERIOUS OFFENCES

RESERVED TO THE CONGREGATION FOR THE DOCTRINE OF THE FAITH

. . . the Congregation for the Doctrine of the Faith, through an ad hoc commission established, devoted itself to a diligent study of the canons on delicts both of the Code of Canon Law and the Code of Canons of the Eastern Churches in order to determine 'more grave delicts both against morals and in the celebration of the sacraments' and in order to make special procedural norms 'to declare or impose canonical sanctions,' because the instruction *Crimen Solicitationis*, issued by the supreme sacred Congregation of the Holy Office on March 16, 1962,(3) in force until now, was to be reviewed when the new canonical codes were promulgated.

. . . All these things, approved by the supreme pontiff himself, were confirmed and promulgated by the apostolic letter given motu proprio beginning with the words *Sacramentorum sanctitatis tutela*.

The more grave delicts both in the celebration of the sacraments and against morals reserved to the Congregation for the Doctrine of the Faith are:

-Delicts against the sanctity of the most august eucharistic sacrifice and the sacraments, namely:

1. Taking or retaining the consecrated species for a sacrilegious purpose or throwing them away.(4)
2. Attempting the liturgical action of the eucharistic sacrifice or simulating the same.(5)
3. Forbidden concelebration of the eucharistic sacrifice with ministers of ecclesial communities which do not have apostolic succession and do not recognize the sacramental dignity of priestly ordination.(6)
4. Consecrating for a sacrilegious purpose one matter without the other in the eucharistic celebration or even both outside a eucharistic celebration.(7)

-Delicts against the sanctity of the sacrament of penance, namely:

1. Absolution of an accomplice in sin against the Sixth Commandment of the Decalogue.(8)
2. Solicitation in the act, on the occasion or under the pretext of confession, to sin against the Sixth Commandment of the Decalogue, if it is directed to sin with the confessor himself.(9)
3. Direct violation of the sacramental seal.(10)

-A delict against morals, namely: the delict committed by a cleric against the Sixth Commandment of the Decalogue with a minor below the age of 18 years.

Only these delicts, which are indicated above with their definition, are reserved to the apostolic tribunal of the Congregation for the Doctrine of the Faith.

As often as an ordinary [i.e. bishop] or hierarch has at least probable knowledge of a reserved delict, after he has carried out the preliminary investigation he is to indicate it to the Congregation for the Doctrine of the Faith, which unless it calls the case to itself because of special circumstances of things, after transmitting appropriate norms, orders the ordinary or hierarch to proceed ahead through his own tribunal. The right of appealing against a sentence of the first instance, whether on the part of the party or the party's legal representative, or on the part of the promoter of justice, solely remains valid only to the supreme tribunal of this congregation.

It must be noted that the criminal action on delicts reserved to the Congregation for the Doctrine of the Faith is extinguished by a prescription of 10 years.(11)

The prescription runs according to the universal and common law;(12) however, in the delict perpetrated with a minor by a cleric, the prescription begins to run from the day when the minor has completed the eighteenth year of age.

In tribunals established by ordinaries or hierarchs, the functions of judge, promoter of justice, notary and legal representative can validly be performed for these cases only by priests. When the trial in the tribunal is finished in any fashion, all the acts of the case are to be transmitted ex officio as soon as possible to the Congregation for the Doctrine of the Faith.

. . .

Cases of this kind are subject to the pontifical secret.

. . .

ROME, FROM THE OFFICES OF THE CONGREGATION FOR THE DOCTRINE OF THE FAITH, MAY 18, 2001.

Cardinal Joseph Ratzinger
Prefect

Archbishop Tarcisio Bertone, SDB
Secretary

Appendix D: *de gravioribus delictis* (July 2010)

SUBSTANTIVE NORMS CONCERNING THE MOST SERIOUS CRIMES

Art. 1

§ 1. The Congregation for the Doctrine of the Faith, according to art. 52 of the Apostolic Constitution Pastor Bonus[1], judges delicts against the faith, as well as the more grave delicts committed against morals and in the celebration of the sacraments . . .

Art. 2

§ 1. The delicts against the faith referred to in art. 1 are heresy, apostasy and schism . . .

Art. 3

§ 1. The more grave delicts against the sanctity of the most Holy Sacrifice and Sacrament of the Eucharist reserved to the Congregation for the Doctrine of the Faith for judgment are:

    1. the taking or retaining for a sacrilegious purpose or the throwing away of the consecrated species[10] . . .

    2. attempting the liturgical action of the Eucharistic Sacrifice . . .

    3. the simulation of the same . . .

    4. the concelebration of the Eucharistic Sacrifice prohibited . . . with ministers of ecclesial communities which do not have apostolic succession and do not acknowledge the sacramental dignity of priestly ordination.

    . . .

Art. 4

§ 1. The more grave delicts against the sanctity of the Sacrament of Penance reserved to the Congregation for the Doctrine of the Faith are:

    1. the absolution of an accomplice in a sin against the sixth commandment of the Decalogue . . . (I.E. 'You shall not commit adultery')

    2. attempted sacramental absolution or the prohibited hearing of confession . . .

3. simulated sacramental absolution. . .

4. the *solicitation* to a sin against the sixth commandment of the Decalogue in the act, on the occasion, or under the pretext of confession . . . if it is directed to sinning with the confessor himself;

5. the direct and indirect violation of the sacramental seal . . .

§ 2. . . . also reserved to the Congregation for the Doctrine of the Faith is the more grave delict which consists in *the recording*, by whatever technical means, or in the malicious diffusion through communications media, of *what is said in sacramental confession, whether true or false, by the confessor or the penitent*. Anyone who commits such a delict is to be punished according to the gravity of the crime, not excluding, if he be a cleric, dismissal or deposition[30].

Art. 5

The more grave delict of the *attempted sacred ordination of a woman* is also reserved to the Congregation for the Doctrine of the Faith:

1. . . . both the one who attempts to confer sacred ordination on a woman, and *she who attempts to receive sacred ordination*, incur a latae sententiae excommunication reserved to the Apostolic See.

2. If the one attempting to confer sacred ordination, or the woman who attempts to receive sacred ordination, is a member of the Christian faithful subject to the Code of Canons of the Eastern Churches, . . . he or she is to be punished by major excommunication reserved to the Apostolic See.

3. If the guilty party is a cleric he may be punished by dismissal or deposition[31].

Art. 6

§ 1. The more grave delicts against morals which are reserved to the Congregation for the Doctrine of the Faith are:

1. the delict against the sixth commandment of the Decalogue *committed by a cleric with a minor below the age of eighteen years*; in this case, a person who habitually lacks the use of reason is to be considered equivalent to a minor.

2. the *acquisition, possession, or distribution by a cleric of pornographic images of minors* under the age of fourteen, for purposes of sexual gratification, by whatever means or using whatever technology;

§ 2. A cleric who commits the delicts mentioned above in § 1 is to be punished *according to the gravity of his crime*, not excluding dismissal or deposition.

Art. 7

§ 1. A criminal action for delicts reserved to the Congregation for the Doctrine of the Faith is extinguished by prescription after twenty years, with due regard to the right of the Congregation for the Doctrine of the Faith to derogate from prescription in individual cases.

. . .

PART TWO

PROCEDURAL NORMS

TITLE I   THE CONSTITUTION AND COMPETENCE OF THE TRIBUNAL

Art. 8

§ 1. The Congregation for the Doctrine of the Faith is the Supreme Apostolic Tribunal for the Latin Church as well as the Eastern Catholic Churches, for the judgment of the delicts defined in the preceding articles.

Art. 9

§ 1. The Members of the Congregation for the Doctrine of the Faith are ipso iure the judges of this Supreme Tribunal.

§ 2. The Prefect of the Congregation presides as first among equals over the college of the Members, . . .

Art. 11

To present and sustain an accusation a Promotor of Justice is to be appointed, who is to be a priest, possessing a doctorate in Canon Law, outstanding in good morals, prudence, and expertise in the law. He is to carry out his office in all grades of judgment.

Art. 13

The role of Advocate or Procurator is carried out by a priest possessing a doctorate in Canon Law. He is to be approved by the presiding judge of the college.

Art. 14

Indeed, in the other tribunals dealing with cases under these norms, only priests can validly carry out the functions of Judge, Promotor of Justice, Notary, and Patron [Procurator and Advocate].

. . .

Art. 16

Whenever the Ordinary or Hierarch receives a report of a more grave delict, which has *at least the semblance of truth*, once the preliminary investigation has been completed, *he is to communicate the matter to the Congregation for the Doctrine of the Faith* which, unless it calls the case to itself due to particular circumstances, will direct the Ordinary or Hierarch how to proceed further, with due regard, however, for the right to appeal, if the case warrants, against a sentence of the first instance only to the Supreme Tribunal of this same Congregation.
. . .

TITLE II   THE PROCEDURE TO BE FOLLOWED IN THE JUDICIAL TRIAL

Art. 21

§ 1. The more grave delicts reserved to the Congregation for the Doctrine of the Faith are to be tried in a judicial process.

§ 2. However, the Congregation for the Doctrine of the Faith may: . . .

2. present the most grave cases to the decision of the Roman Pontiff with regard to dismissal from the clerical state or deposition, together with dispensation from the law of celibacy, when it is manifestly evident that the delict was committed and after having given the guilty party the possibility of defending himself.

Art. 24
. . .

§ 2. This Tribunal must consider the particular importance of the question concerning the credibility of the accuser.

§ 3. Nevertheless, it must always be observed that any danger of violating the sacramental seal be altogether avoided.

Art. 30

§ 1. Cases of this nature are subject to the pontifical secret.

§ 2. Whoever has violated the secret, whether deliberately (ex dolo) or through grave negligence, and has caused some harm to the accused or to the witnesses, is to be punished with an appropriate penalty by the higher turns at the insistence of the injured party or even ex officio.

This text was approved by Benedict XVI on 21 May 2010 and issued as a letter to all Bishops by Cardinal Levada, Prefect of the CDF. It was not made public until 15 July 2010.

Bibliography

Books

Lord Acton (J. Rufus Fears (ed.)), *Selected Writings of Lord Acton*, Volume 3 (Liberty Fund, Indianapolis, 2000).

John L. Allen Jnr, *All the Pope's Men: The Inside Story of How the Vatican Really Thinks* (Doubleday, New York, 2004).

John L. Allen Jnr, *Pope Benedict XVI: A Biography of Joseph Ratzinger* (Continuum, London, 2005).

Anthony Aust, *Modern Treaty Law and Practice* (CUP, Cambridge, 2000).

Ann Barstow, *Married Priests and the Reforming Papacy: The 11th Century Debates (Texts and Studies in Religion)* (Edwin Mellor Press, New York, 1982).

J. P. Beal, J. A. Corinden and T. J. Green, *New Commentary on the Code of Canon Law* (Canon Law Society of America, Washington, DC, 2000).

Phillip Berryman, *Liberation Theology* (IB Taurus, London, 1987).

Tom Bingham, *The Rule of Law* (Allen Lane, London, 2010).

Ian Brownlie, *Principles of Public International Law* (6th edn, OUP, Oxford, 2003).

Ian Brownlie and Guy Goodwin-Gill, *Documents on Human Rights* (6th edn, OUP, Oxford, 2010).

Hyginus E. Cardinale, *The Holy See and the International Order* (Smythe, Bucks, 1976).

Antonio Cassesse, *International Criminal Law* (2nd edn, OUP, Oxford, 2008).

Catechism of the Catholic Church (2nd edn, English translation, St Paul's, London, 2000).

Hilary Charlesworth and Christine Chinkin, *The Boundaries of International Law: A Feminist Perspective* (Manchester University Press, Manchester, 2000).

James Corkery and Thomas Worcester (eds), *The Papacy Since 1500: From Italian Prince to Universal Pastor* (CUP, 2010).

John Cornwell, *The Pope in Winter: The Dark Face of John Paul II's Papacy* (Penguin, London, 2005).

Rupert Cornwell, *God's Banker: The Life and Death of Roberto Calvi* (Unwin, London, 1984).

James Crawford, *The Creation of States in International Law* (2nd edn, OUP, Oxford, 2006).

Christopher Duggan, *The Force of Destiny: A History of Italy Since 1796* (Allen Lane, London, 2007).

Jorri Duursma, *Fragmentation and the International Relations of Micro-states: Self-determination and Statehood* (Cambridge Studies in Comparative and International Law, Cambridge, 1996).

Carmine Galasso, *Crosses: Portraits of Clergy Abuse* (Trolley, London, 2007).

Louise Haggett, *The Bingo Report: Mandatory Celibacy and Clergy Sex Abuse* (CSRI Books, 2005).

R. K. Hanson, F. Pfafflin and M. Lutz (eds.), *Sexual Abuse in the Catholic Church: Scientific and Legal Perspectives* (Libreria Editrice Vaticana, Rome, 2003).

John Hite and Chris Henton, *Fascist Italy* (Hodder Education, London, 1998).

Patricia Knight, *Mussolini and Fascism* (Routledge, London, 2003).

Bart McDowell, *Inside the Vatican* (National Geographic Society, Washington, DC, 2008).

Phillip Morgan, *Italy 1915–1940* (Sempringham Publishing, Bedford, 1998).

John Henry Newman (Ian Ker (ed.)), *Apologia Pro Vita Sua* (Penguin Classics, London, 1994).

D. P. O'Connell, *International Law* (Stevens, London, 1970).

Hector Olasolo, *Criminal Responsibility of Senior Political and Military Leaders as Principals to International Crimes* (Hart Publishing, Oxford, 2009).

Eric Plumer, *The Catholic Church and American Culture* (University of Scranton Press, London, 2009).

E. Pollack, *The Pretender: How Martin Frankel Fooled the World* (Free Press, New York, 2002).

Steven R. Ratner, Jason S. Abrams and James L. Bischoff, *Accountability for Human Rights Atrocities in International Law* (3rd edn, OUP, Oxford, 2009).

Ivor Roberts, *Satow's Diplomatic Practice* (6th edn, OUP, Oxford, 2009).

Geoffrey Robertson QC, *Crimes Against Humanity: The Struggle for Global Justice* (3rd edn, Penguin/New Press, London/New York, 2006).

William G. Rusch (ed.), *The Pontificate of Benedict XVI: Its Promises and Premises* (Eerdmans, Michigan, 2009).

Tracey Rowland, *Ratzinger's Faith* (OUP, Oxford, 2009)

William A. Schabas, *An Introduction to the International Criminal Court* (2nd edn, CUP, Cambridge, 2004).

Malcolm Shaw, *International Law* (6th edn, CUP, Cambridge, 2008).

Gillian Triggs, *International Law: Contemporary Principles and Practices* (Butterworths/Lexis Nexis, Sydney, 2005).

Rev. John Triglio Jnr and Rev. Kenneth Brighenti, *Catholicism for Dummies* (Wiley, London, 2003).

Studies, Reports and Judicial Inquiries

The Irish Commission to Inquire into Child Abuse Public Report ('The Ryan Report'), 20 May 2009, available at http://www.childabusecommission.ie/rpt/pdfs/ (last accessed 18 July 2010).

Dublin Archdiocese Commission of Investigation Report ('The Murphy Report'), 26 November 2009, available at http://www.dacoi.ie/ (last accessed 10 July 2010).

Judge Francis D. Murphy, Helen Buckley and Larain Joyce, *Ferns Inquiry to the Minister for Health and Children* (Dublin: Government Publications, October 2005) ('The Ferns Report'), available at http://www.bishop-accountability.org/ferns/ (last accessed 22 July 2010).

John Jay College of Criminal Justice, *The Nature and Scope of the Problem of Sexual Abuse of Minors by Catholic Priests and Deacons in the United States* (2004), http://www.usccb.org/nrb/johnjstudy.

Winter Commission Report (1990), Archdiocese of St John's, Newfoundland, Canada.

Safeguarding with Confidence – Keeping Children and Vulnerable Adults Safe in the Catholic Church, The Cumberlege Commission Report (Catholic Truth Society, London 2007).

Vatican Materials

Benedict XVI, encyclical letter, *Caritas in Veritatae*, 29 June 2009.

Benedict XVI, *Pastoral Letter of the Holy Father Pope Benedict XVI to the Catholics of Ireland*, 19 March 2010, para 4, available at http://www.vatican.va/holy_father/benedict_xvi/letters/2010/documents/hf_ben-xvi_let_20100319_church-ireland_en.html (last accessed 21 July 2010).

Catechism of the Catholic Church (2nd edn, Burns & Oates, London, 1999).

Congregation of the Doctrine of Faith, *Considerations Regarding Proposals to Give Legal Recognition to Unions between Homosexual Persons*, issued by Prefect Cardinal Ratzinger, 3 June 2003, available at http://www.vatican.va/roman_curia/congregations/cfaith/documents/rc_con_cfaith_doc_20030731_homosexual-unions_en.html (last accessed 12 July 2010).

Congregation of the Doctrine of Faith, *Doctrinal Note on Some Questions Regarding the Participation of Catholics in Political Life*, issued by Cardinal Joseph Ratzinger and Tarcisio Bertone, 24 November 2002, available at http://www.vatican.va/roman_curia/congregations/cfaith/documents/rc_con_cfaith_doc_20021124_politica_en.html (last accessed 21 July 2010).

Bibliography

Msgr Leo Cushley, 'A Light to the Nations: Vatican Diplomacy and Global Politics', 2007 Habigen Lecture, available at http://www.stthomas.edu/cathstudies/programs/habiger/default.html (last accessed 20 July 2010).

Holy See, *Initial Report to the Committee on the Rights of the Child on the Optional Protocol on the Sale of Children, Child Prostitution and Child Pornography*, 14 May 2010, available at http://www2.ohchr.org/english/bodies/crc/docs/AdvanceVersions/CRC-C-OPSC-VAT-1.doc (last accessed 24 July 2010), 1, para 4(b).

Holy See, *Report to the Committee on the Rights of the Child*, 28 March 1994.

Instruction on the Manner of Proceeding in Causes involving the Crime of Solicitation (Vatican Polyglot Press, 1962), available at http://www.vatican.va/resources/resources_crimen-sollicitationis-1962_en.html (last accessed 20 July 2010).

Fr F. Lombardi, 'The Significance of the Publication of the New Norms Concerning the Most Serious Crimes', undated, available at http://www.vatican.va/resources/resources_lombardi-nota-norme_en.html (last accessed 20 July 2010).

Cardinal Joseph Ratzinger, 'Letter to the Bishops of the Catholic Church on the Pastoral Care of Homosexual Persons', 1986, available at http://www.vatican.va/roman_curia/congregations/cfaith/documents/rc_con_cfaith_doc_19861001_homosexual-persons_en.html (last accessed 15 July 2010).

Archbishop Jean-Louis Tauran, 'The Presence of the Holy See in the International Organizations', lecture at Catholic University of the Sacred Heart, Milan, 22 April 2002, available at http://www.vatican.va/roman_curia/secretariat_state/documents/rc_seg-st_doc_20020422_tauran_en.html (last accessed 20 July 2010).

Academic Articles

Yasmin Abdullah, 'The Holy See at United Nations Conferences: Church or State?' (1996), 96(7) *Colombia Law Review*, 1835.

Dina Aversano, 'Can the Pope be a Defendant in American Courts? (2006), 18 *Pace International Law Review*, 495.

Matthew N. Bathon, 'The Atypical Status of the Holy See' (2001), 34 *Vanderbilt Journal of Transnational Law*, 596.

Melanie Black, 'The Unusual Sovereign State: FSIA and Litigation against the Holy See for its Role in the Global Priest Sexual Abuse Scandal' (2009), 27(2) *Wisconsin International Law Journal*, 299.

Curtis A. Bradley and Jack L. Goldsmith, 'Foreign Sovereign Immunity, Individual Officials and Human Rights Litigation' (2009), 13 *Green Bag 2D*, 9.

James Brown-Scott, 'The Treaty Between Italy and the Vatican' (1929), 23 *American Society of International Law Proceedings*, 19.

Fr Noel Dias, 'Roman Catholic Church and International Law' (2001), 13 *Sri Lanka Law Journal*, 107.

John Finnis, 'Reason, Faith and Homosexual Acts' (2001) 62 *Catholic Social Science Review* 61.

Michael M. Gunter, 'The Problem of Mini-State Membership in the UN System: Recent Attempts towards a Solution' (1973), 12 *Columbia Journal of Transnational Law*, 464.

Gordon Ireland, 'The State of the City of the Vatican' (1933), 27 *American Journal of International Law*, 275.

Kurt Martens, 'The Position of the Holy See and Vatican City State in International Relations' (2006), 83 *University of Detroit Mercy Law Review*, 729.

Lucian C. Martinez, 'Sovereign Impunity – Does the FSIA Bar Lawsuits Against the Holy See?' (2008), 44 *Texas International Law Journal*, 123.

William Brian Mason, 'The New Call for Reform: Sex Abuse and the Foreign Sovereign Immunities Act' (2008), 33(2) *Brooklyn Journal of International Law*, 655, 679.

Daniel M. Singerman, 'Its Still God to be the King: An Argument for Maintaining the Status Quo in Foreign Head of State Immunity' (2007), 21 *Emory International Law Review*, 413.

Richard Sipe, 'Paedophiles and Celibacy', 18 March 2010, available at http://www.richardsipe.com/Miscl/vatican_connection.htm (last accessed 10 July 2010).

Alison Todd, 'Vicarious Liability for Sexual Abuse' (2002), 8 *Canterbury Law Review*, 281.

Leslie Townley, 'Conceal or Reveal? The Role of Law in Black Collar Crime' (2007), 1 *Public Space* (*The Journal of Law and Social Justice*), 30.

Jane Wangman, 'Liability for Institutional Child Sexual Assault' (2004), *Melbourne University Law Review*, 5.

Herb Wright, 'The Status of Vatican City' (1944), 38 *American Journal of International Law*, 452.

Stephen E. Young and Alison Shea, 'Separating Law From Church: A Research Guide to the Vatican City State' (2007), 99 *Law Library Journal*, 589.

Media Articles

'Africa Now Under the Spotlight Over Sex Crimes', *Legal Brief Africa*, Issue 379, 3 May 2010.

John L. Allen Jr, 'Don't be Daft – You Can't Put the Pope on Trial', *Spectator*, 14 April 2010, available at http://www.spectator.co.uk/spectator/thisweek/5879613/5911953/part_3/dont-be-daft-you-cant-put-the-pope-on-trial.thtml (last accessed 25 July 2010).

John L. Allen Jr, 'Will Ratzinger's Past Trump Benedict's Present?', *National Catholic Reporter,* 31 March 2010.

'Archbishop Dodged Apology for Abuse', *The Times*, 12 April 2010.

R. Behar, 'Washing Money in the Holy See', *Fortune*, 16 August 1999, 128–37.

'Bishops' Record in Cases of Accused Priests', *Dallas Morning News*, 12 June 2002.

'Britain's Top Catholic Protected Paedophile', *The Times*, 9 April 2010, 1.

'Cardinal Levada: We Ought to Hold Ourselves to a High Standard', *PBS Newshour*, 27 April 2010, available at http://www.pbs.org/newshour/bb/religion/jan-june10/vatican_04–27.html (last accessed 20 July 2010).

'Catholic Bishops Apologise for Terrible Crimes and Cover-ups', *Guardian*, 23 April 2010.

'CDF Official Details Response to Sex Abuse', *National Catholic Reporter*, 31 March 2010, available at http://ncronline.org/news/accountability/cdf-official-details-response-sex-abuse (last accessed 25 July 2010).

Henry Chu and Michelle Boorstein, 'US Sex Abuse Lawsuits Target Holy See', *The Age*, 29 March 2010, available at http://www.theage.com.au/world/us-sex-abuse-lawsuits-target-holy-see-20100328-r53i.html (last accessed 21 July 2010).

Andrew Cole, 'The Church's Penal Law and the Abuse of Children', *Thinking Faith*, 17 June 2010.

Bill Curry, 'Catholic Church Reluctant to Release Residential School Records', *Globe and Mail*, 6 April 2010.

Martin Daly, 'Rome Backed Sex-case Priest', *The Age*, 6 July 2002, available at http://www.theage.com.au/articles/2002/07/05/1025667059915.html (last accessed 14 July 2010).

'Gay Groups Angry at Pope Remarks', *BBC News*, 23 December 2008, available at http://news.bbc.co.uk/1/hi/7797269.stm (last accessed 10 July 2010).

Laurie Goodstein, 'Early Alarm for Church Abusers in Clergy', *The New York Times*, 2 April 2009, article and correspondence available at http://www.nytimes.com/2009/04/03/us/03church.html (last accessed 20 July 2010).

Laurie Goodstein, 'Payout is Bittersweet for Victims of Abuse', *The New York Times*, 17 July 2007, available at http://www.nytimes.com/2007/07/17/us/17abuse.html (last accessed 22 July 2010).

Alma Guillermoprieto, 'The Mission of Father Marcial', *New York Review of Books*, 24 June 2010, 28.

'He Should Have Been Watched Like a Hawk', *The Times*, 10 April 2010, 5.

'A History of Residential Schools in Canada', *CBC News*, 14 June 2010.

John Hooper, 'Former Archbishop Cormac Murphy-O'Connor to Head Papal Inquiry into Sex Abuse in Ireland', *Guardian*, 31 May 2010, available at http://www.guardian.co.uk/world/2010/may/31/cormac-murphy-o-connor-inquiry-sex-abuse-ireland (last accessed 16 July 2010).

'Insidious Challenge of Gay Marriage – the Pope Speaks', *The Times*, 14 May 2010.

'Jesuits Admit Shame Over Abuse of 200 Children', *The Times*, 28 May 2010.

'John Paul Backed Bishop for Hiding Abuse: Cardinal', *Washington Post*, 17 April 2010.

'John Paul Ignored Abuse of 2,000 Boys', *Sunday Times*, 4 April 2010.

Frank Jordans, 'UN: Vatican Child Rights Report 13 Years Overdue', *Associated Press*, 16 July 2010, available at http://www.google.com/hostednews/ap/article/.

Nick Kristof, 'The Pope and AIDS', *The New York Times*, 8 May 2005.

Sandro Magistere, 'Mission Impossible: Eject the Holy See from the UN', 21 August 2008, available at http://chiesa.espresso.repubblica.it/articolo/162301?eng=y (last accessed 22 July 2010).

Patsy McGarry, 'Cardinal Brady to Stay in Office as He Asks for Assistance', *Irish Times*, 18 May 2010, available at http://www.irishtimes.com/newspaper/frontpage/2010/0518/1224270601322.html (last accessed 20 July 2010).

Nick McKenzie and Rafael Epstein, '300 Abuse Cases, One Defrocking', *The Age*, 22 April 2010, available at http://www.theage.com.au/victoria/300-abuse-cases-one-defrocking-20100421-szz6.html (last accessed 23 July 2010).

Richard N. Ostling, 'Sex and the Single Priest', *Time Magazine*, 5 July 1993.

'Papal Diplomacy: God's Ambassadors', *Economist*, 21 July 2007.

'Pope Accused of Stoking Homophobia After He Equates Homosexuality to Climate Change', *The Times*, 23 December 2008, available at www.timesonline.co.uk/tol/comment/faith/article5387858.ece (last accessed 10 July 2010).

'Pope Calls for Church Repentance Over Sins', *Guardian*, 16 April 2010.

'Pope Engineered Cover-up of Child Sex Abuses Says Theologian', *Irish Times*, 16 April 2010.

'Pope Expresses "Sorrow" for Abuse at Residential Schools', *CBC News*, 29 April 2009.

'Pope Weeps as He Meets Abuse Victims for First Time', *The Times*, 17 April 2010; 19 April 2010.

'Pope's Message to the World Ignores Sex Scandal', *The Times*, 5 April 2010, 14.

'Pope's Top Advisor Blames Gays as Rome Seeks Scapegoats for Sex Abuse Scandals', *The Times*, 14 April 2010.

Peter Popham, 'Made in His Own Image: The Catholic Church Faces Another Scandal', *Independent*, 28 June 2010.

'Priest Used Worker Like Prostitute, Court Told', *The Age*, 24 October 2002, available at http://www.theage.com.au/articles/2002/10/23/1034561548990.html (last accessed 15 July 2010).

Sarah Shenker, 'Legacy of Canada's Residential Schools', *BBC News*, 11 June 2008.

'Signature on Letter Implicates Pope in Abuse Cover-up', *The Times*, 10 April 2010.

Richard Sipe, 'Facts, Truth, Trust and Numbers', 23 January 2007, available at http://www.richardsipe.com/Dialogue/Dialogue-05-2007-01-23.html (last accessed 25 July 2010).

Richard Sipe and K. K. Murray, 'International Traffic of Priests Who Abuse', *SNAP* (US), 17 April 2007, available at http://www.bishop-accountability.org/news2007/03_04/2007_04_17_Sipe_InternationalTraffic.htm (last accessed 22 July 2010).

Farrah Tomazin, 'Priest's Return Worries Parents', *The Age*, 13 May 2004, available at http://www.theage.com.au/articles/2004/05/12/1084289749587.html (last accessed 20 July 2010).

'Top Cardinal Made Plea for Pinochet', *Sunday Times*, 11 February 1999, 24.

'Vatican Rebukes Austrian Cardinal', *The New York Times*, 29 June 2010.

'Victims of Sex Abuse to Sue Vatican', *Sunday Times*, 28 March 2010.

'What the Bishop Knew', *Guardian*, 3 April 2010, 27.

Gary Wills, 'Forgive Not', *New Republic*, 18 May 2010.

Richard Wilson, 'The Catholic Church Acts as a Law Unto Itself', *New Humanist*, Volume 125, Issue 3, May/June 2010, 13.

Jonathan Wynne-Jones, 'Vatican Allowed Paedophile Living in Britain to Remain as a Priest', *Sunday Telegraph*, 11 April 2010.

Cases

Accordance with International Law of the Unilateral Declaration of Independence in Respect of Kosovo, International Court of Justice, 22 July 2010.

Al-Adsani v The United Kingdom, Application No. 35763/97, European Court of Human Rights, 21 November 2001.

Alamieyeseigha v CPS [2005] EWHC 2104.

Alperin v Vatican Bank (2005) 410 F. 3d 532 (US).

Baxter v Attorney-General of Canada, 2006 CanLII 41673, Ontario Superior Court, 15 December 2006.

Bazley v Curry (1999) 174 DLR (4th) 45 (Supreme Court of Canada).

Case Concerning the Arrest Warrant of 11 April 2000 (Democratic Republic of the Congo v Belgium) (2002) ICJ Rep 2.

Christian v R [2007] 2 AC 400 (PC).

Decision Pursuant to Article 15 of the Rome Statute on the Authorization of an Investigation into the Situation in the Republic of Kenya, ICC-01/09, International Criminal Court (ICC), 31 March 2010.

Doe v Holy See 434 F Supp 2d (US).

In re E (a child) (AP) (Appellant) (Northern Ireland) [2008] UKHL 66.

Ellis v Pell [2006] NSWSC 109.

Gillfillan v R (1980) 637 F 2b 924.

Holy See (Petitioner) v John V Doe, United States Supreme Court Case No. 09–1.

Lautsi v Italy, App No. 30814/06, European Court of Human Rights, 3 November 2009 (referred to Grand Chamber).

Lister v Hesley Hall [2002] 1 AC 215 (UK House of Lords).

Maga v Trustees of Birmingham Catholic Archdiocese [2010] EWCA Civ 256.

Menesheva v Russia (2006) ECHR Application No. 59261/00, 9 March 2006.

NSW v Lepore (2003) 195 ALR 412 (High Court of Australia).

O'Bryan v Holy See 471 at Supp 2d (US).

Pelligrino v Italy, App No. 30882/96, European Court of Human Rights, 20 July 2001.

Prosecutor v Akayesu, Case No ICTR-96-4-T, September 1998.

Prosecutor v Brima, Kamara and Kanu (AFRC Appeal Judgment), Special Court for Sierra Leone, 22 February 2008.

Prosecutor v Kunarac, IT-96-23/I-A, 12 June 2002.

Prosecutor v Tadic Decision on Defence Motion, IT-94-1-AR72-2, October 1994.

Prosecutor v Vasiljevic IT-98-32T, 29 November 2002.

R v Rafique [1993] QB 843.

Raquel Martí de Mejía v Perú, Case 10.970, Report No. 5/96, Inter-Am.C.H.R., OEA/Ser.L/V/II.91 Doc. 7 at 157 (1996).

Reverend James O'Callaghan v Reverend Charles O'Sullivan (1925) Irish Reports 90.

Right Reverend Jonathan Blake v Associated Newspapers [2003] EWHC 1960 (QB).

Roman Catholic Diocese of Galvarston–Houston 408 F Supp 2d at 276.

Thome Guadaloupe v Assoc Italiana di St Cecelia (1937) 8 ILR 151.

Trustees of the Roman Catholic Church v Ellis (2007) NSWCA 117.

United States v Ohlendorf (Case 9) (1946–7) IV Trials of War Criminals before Nuremberg Military Tribunals.

Wilkins v Jennings and Pope John Paul II (1985) ATR 68–754.

Notes

1. SUFFER THE LITTLE CHILDREN

1. John Henry Newman (Ian Ker (ed.)), *Apologia Pro Vita Sua* (Penguin Classics, London, 1994), 241.

2. Universal Declaration of Human Rights, Article 18.

3. See Tom Bingham, *The Rule of Law* (Allen Lane, London, 2010), 4.

4. Carmine Galasso, *Crosses: Portraits of Clergy Abuse* (Trolley, London, 2007). Father Doyle is cited in *Power and Glory*, Yallop, Chapter 2 note 12, pp 466–7.

5. *Christian v The Queen* [2007] 2 AC 400 (PC) at 419, [48].

6. Richard Sipe, 'Facts, Truth, Trust and Numbers', 23 January 2007, available at http://www.richardsipe.com/Dialogue/Dialogue-05-2007-01-23.html (last accessed 25 July 2010). See also 'What the Church could learn from Freud', *National Catholic Reporter*, August 10 2010, where figures as high as 9–10 per cent are supported.

7. Richard Sipe, 'Paedophiles and Celibacy', 18 March 2010, http://www.richardsipe.com/Miscl/vatican_connection.htm (last accessed 10 July 2010).

8. Gary Wills, 'Forgive Not', *New Republic*, 18 May 2010. And See Laurie Taylor, 'Suffer the Little Children', *New Humanist*, Jan/Feb 2010, 16. The incidence of clerical sex abuse some estimate as high and 9 per cent. See chapter 1, note 6.

9. Richard Sipe and K. K. Murray, 'International Traffic of Priests Who Abuse', *SNAP* (US), 17 April 2007, available at http://www.bishop-accountability.org/news2007/03_04/2007_04_17_Sipe_International Traffic.htm (last accessed 22 July 2010).

10. See, for example, 'Gay Groups Angry at Pope Remarks', *BBC News*, 23 December 2008, available at http://news.bbc.co.uk/1/hi/7797269.stm (last accessed 10 July 2010), and 'Pope Accused of Stoking Homophobia After He Equates Homosexuality to Climate Change', *The Times*, 23 December 2008, available at http://www.timesonline.co.uk/tol/comment/faith/article5387858.ece (last accessed 10 July 2010). See also Congregation for the Doctrine of the Faith (CDF), *Considerations Regarding Proposals to Give Legal Recognition to Unions between Homosexual Persons*, issued by Prefect Cardinal Ratzinger, 31 July 2003, available at http://www.vatican.va/roman_curia/congregations/cfaith/documents/rc_con_cfaith_doc_20030731_homosexual-unions_en.html (last accessed 12 July 2010), and Cardinal Joseph Ratzinger, 'Letter to the Bishops of the Catholic Church on the Pastoral Care of Homosexual Persons', 1986, available at http://www.

vatican.va/roman_curia/congregations/cfaith/documents/rc_con_cfaith_
doc_19861001_homosexual-persons_en.html (last accessed 15 July 2010).

11. See Vatican website, 'State Departments', available at http://www.vaticanstate.
va/EN/State_and_Government/State/StateDepartments/index.htm (last accessed
22 July 2010).

12. See Fr Noel Dias, 'Roman Catholic Church and International Law' (2001) 13 *Sri
Lanka Law Journal*, 107.

2. SINS OF THE FATHERS

1. See Charles Scicluna, 'Description of the Problem from the Church Perspective'
in Hanson, Pfafflin and Lutz (eds.), *Sexual Abuse in the Catholic Church: Scientific
and Legal Perspectives* (Libreria Editrice Vaticana, Rome, 2003). *The Book of Gom-
orrah* published *c.* 1051 by St Peter Damian, urged the Pope to take action against
the sodomy said to be rife among priests.

2. Letter from Reverend Gerald Fitzgerald to Bishop Durick, 10 September 1964 –
see Laurie Goodstein, 'Early Alarm for Church Abusers in Clergy', *The New
York Times*, 2 April 2009, article and correspondence available at http://www.
nytimes.com/2009/04/03/us/03church.html (last accessed 20 July 2010). See also
Letter from Matthew Brady, Bishop of Manchester (New Hampshire) to Reverend Gerald Fitzgerald, 23 September 1967 and Letter from Reverend Gerald
Fitzgerald to Bishop of Reno, 12 September 1952. This correspondence was
obtained on discovery in a US legal action. By 1957, Fitzgerald determined to
refuse sanctuary to paedophile priests, and castigated bishops who permitted
'the blasphemy' of allowing them to offer communion.

3. 'What the Bishop Knew', *Guardian*, 3 April 2010, 27; see Laurie Goodstein, 'Payout
is Bittersweet for Victims of Abuse', *The New York Times*, 17 July 2007, available at
http://www.nytimes.com/2007/07/17/us/17abuse.html (last accessed 22 July 2010).

4. See William Brian Mason, 'The New Call for Reform: Sex Abuse and the Foreign
Sovereign Immunities Act' (2008), 33(2) *Brooklyn Journal of International Law*, 655.

5. See 'Bishops' Record in Cases of Accused Priests', *Dallas Morning News*, 12 June
2002. The cases and quotations in paragraphs 21 and 22 are all reported in this
lengthy round-up of US abuse cases.

6. These quotes are from John L. Allen Jnr, *All the Pope's Men: The Inside Story of
How the Vatican Really Thinks* (Doubleday, New York, 2004), 242–272.

7. Ibid, 279.

8. John Jay College of Criminal Justice, *The Nature and Scope of the Problem of Sexual
Abuse of Minors by Catholic Priests and Deacons in the United States* (2004), http://
www.usccb.org/nrb/johnjstudy ('John Jay study'). The incidence of clerical sex
abuse some estimate as high as 9 per cent. See chapter 1, note 6.

9. John Jay study, 6–7.

10. Bishop Imola, quoted in Ann Barstow, *Married Priests and the Reforming Papacy:*

The 11th Century Debates (Texts and Studies in Religion) (Edwin Mellor Press, New York, 1982), 112.

11. John Jay study, 60.

12. David Yallop, *The Power and the Glory* (Constable, London, 2007), 452.

13. See 'Signature on Letter Implicates Pope in Abuse Cover-up', *The Times*, 10 April 2010, 4.

14. See Richard N. Ostling, 'Sex and the Single Priest', *Time Magazine*, 5 July 1993.

15. Vatican spokesman, quoted in Henry Chu and Michelle Boorstein, 'US Sex Abuse Lawsuits Target Holy See', *The Age*, 29 March 2010, available at http://www.theage.com.au/world/us-sex-abuse-lawsuits-target-holy-see-20100328-r53i.html (last accessed 21 July 2010).

16. Interviewed by Margaret Warner for PBS *Newshour* on 27 April 2010. See transcript: 'Cardinal Levada: We Ought to Hold Ourselves to a High Standard', *PBS Newshour,* 27 April 2010, available at http://www.pbs.org/newshour/bb/religion/jan-june10/vatican_04-27.html (last accessed 20 July 2010).

17. Judge Francis D. Murphy, Helen Buckley and Larain Joyce, *Ferns Inquiry to the Minister for Health and Children* (Dublin: Government Publications, October 2005) ('The Ferns Report'), Executive Summary, available at http://www.bishop-accountability.org/ferns/ (last accessed 22 July 2010).

18. See the Commission to Inquire into Child Abuse, CICA *Public Report* ('The Ryan Report'), 20 May 2009, Executive Summary, paras 18–20, available at http://www.childabusecommission.ie/rpt/execsummary.php (last accessed 18 July 2010).

19. Ibid, para 21.

20. Ibid, paras 29–30.

21. See Patsy McGarry, 'Cardinal Brady to Stay in Office as He Asks for Assistance', *Irish Times*, 18 May 2010, available at http://www.irishtimes.com/newspaper/frontpage/2010/0518/1224270601322.html (last accessed 20 July 2010). See also 'Pope Retains Bishops', *Irish Times*, 12 August 2010, which reports that the Pope's decision to refuse the resignations will 'shock many people. It sends the most contradictory of messages'.

22. *Dublin Archdiocese Commission of Investigation Report* ('Murphy Report'), 26 November 2009, Chapter 1.15; 1.113 (Conclusion), available at http://www.dacoi.ie/ (last accessed 10 July 2010).

23. See Murphy Report, Chapter 1, para 113.

24. Ibid, para 1.35.

25. Ibid, Chapter 4, para 90.

26. 'Jesuits Admit Shame Over Abuse of 200 Children', *The Times*, 28 May 2010.

27. 'Victims of Sex Abuse to Sue Vatican', *Sunday Times*, 28 March 2010. This priest, Father Peter Hullermann, was finally convicted in a German court in 1986 of offences that would probably not have been committed if Bishop Ratzinger had reported him to the police in 1979. The Pope's defenders say that although

Ratzinger was in overall charge, the See was large and an assistant dealt with the case.

28. 'Africa Now Under the Spotlight Over Sex Crimes', *Legal Brief Africa*, Issue No. 379, 3 May 2010.

29. See 'John Paul Ignored Abuse of 2,000 Boys', *Sunday Times*, 4 April 2010, 19.

30. 'Pope Weeps as He Meets Abuse Victims for First Time', *The Times,* 17 April 2010, 41; 19 April 2010, 29.

31. See Nick McKenzie and Rafael Epstein, '300 Abuse Cases, One Defrocking', *The Age*, 22 April 2010, available at http://www.theage.com.au/victoria/300-abuse-cases-one-defrocking-20100421-szz6.html (last accessed 23 July 2010).

32. See Martin Daly, 'Rome Backed Sex-case Priest', *The Age*, 6 July 2002, available at http://www.theage.com.au/articles/2002/07/05/1025667059915.html (last accessed 14 July 2010), and 'Priest Used Worker Like Prostitute, Court Told', *The Age*, 24 October 2002, available at http://www.theage.com.au/articles/2002/10/23/1034561548990.html (last accessed 15 July 2010).

33. See 'In Memory of Father Maurie Crocker, a Brave Priest who Exposed Child Abuse in Australia', available at http://brokenrites.alphalink.com.au/nletter/page14.html (last accessed 25 July 2010).

34. *Winter Commission Report* (1990), Archdiocese of St John's, Newfoundland, Canada.

35. 'A History of Residential Schools in Canada', *Canadian Broadcasting Corporation News*, 14 June 2010; Sarah Shenker, 'Legacy of Canada's Residential Schools', BBC *News*, 11 June 2008.

36. *Baxter v Attorney-General of Canada*, 2006, CanLII 41673, Ontario Superior Court, 15 December 2006.

37. 'Pope Expresses "Sorrow" for Abuse at Residential Schools', *CBC News*, 29 April 2009.

38. Bill Curry, 'Catholic Church Reluctant to Release Residential School Records', *Globe and Mail*, 6 April 2010.

39. *Safeguarding with Confidence – Keeping Children and Vulnerable Adults Safe in the Catholic Church*, The Cumberlege Commission Report (Catholic Truth Society, London, 2007) 4, 21, 57, 89, 90. The recommendation was for a special territorial law applying to England and Wales which would give juridical authority to the church's most important safeguarding rules for children and vulnerable adults and also secure a right of recourse to the Holy See if any person or congregation failed to fulfil their obligations to safeguard children (Recommendation 72).

40. John Hooper, 'Former Archbishop Cormac Murphy-O'Connor to Head Papal Inquiry into Sex Abuse in Ireland', *Guardian*, 31 May 2010, available at http://www.guardian.co.uk/world/2010/may/31/cormac-murphy-o-connor-inquiry-sex-abuse-ireland (last accessed 16 July 2010).

41. 'He Should Have Been Watched Like a Hawk', *The Times*, 10 April 2010, 5; 'Britain's Top Catholic Protected Paedophile', *The Times*, 9 April 2010, 1;

'Archbishop Dodged Apology for Abuse', *The Times*, 12 April 2010; 'QC to Lead Abuse Inquiry at Catholic School', *The Times*, 6 August 2010. 'Abuse Scandal to hang over Papal visit', *The Times*, 18 August 2010.

42. See Jonathan Wynne-Jones, 'Vatican Allowed Paedophile Living in Britain to Remain as a Priest', *Sunday Telegraph*, 11 April 2010.

43. National Catholic Safeguarding Committee, *Safeguarding Procedures Manual*, http://www.csas.uk.net. See Sections 2.5.6 (Disagreements), 3.1 (Information Sharing) and 4.1 (Sacrament of Reconciliation).

44. 'Catholic Bishops Apologise for Terrible Crimes and Cover-ups', *Guardian*, 23 April 2010.

45. *Pastoral Letter of the Holy Father Pope Benedict XVI to the Catholics of Ireland*, 19 March 2010, para 4, available at http://www.vatican.va/holy_father/benedict_xvi/letters/2010/documents/hf_ben-xvi_let_20100319_church-ireland_en.html (last accessed 21 July 2010).

46. Ibid, para 11.

47. See 'Pope's Message to the World Ignores Sex Scandal', *The Times*, 5 April 2010, 14.

48. 'Vatican Rebukes Austrian Cardinal', *New York Times*, 29 June 2010.

49. 'Pope's Top Advisor Blames Gays as Rome Seeks Scapegoats for Sex Abuse Scandals', *The Times,* 14 April 2010.

50. 'Pope Calls for Church Repentance Over Sins', *Guardian*, 16 April 2010.

51. *Caritas in Veritate* encyclical 29 June 2009, para 34.

52. 'Insidious Challenge of Gay Marriage – the Pope Speaks', *The Times*, 14 May 2010.

3 . CANON LAW

1. 'John Paul Backed Bishop for Hiding Abuse: Cardinal', *Washington Post*, 17 April 2010; Peter Popham, 'Made in His Own Image: The Catholic Church Faces Another Scandal', *Independent*, 28 June 2010.

2. See Ladislas M. Orsy, SJ, 'Theology and Canon Law', in J. P. Beal, J. A. Corinden and T. J. Green, *New Commentary on the Code of Canon Law* (Canon Law Society of America, Washington, DC, 2000), 1.

3. See *New Commentary on the Code of Canon Law*, 1371–3.

4. Ibid, 1529 (Thomas J. Green).

5. Ibid, 1532.

6. Ibid, 1600.

7. Murphy Report, Chapter 4, para 11.

8. 1983 Code Canon 1395(2).

9. See Murphy Report, Chapter 4, paras 59–61.

10. *Instruction on the Manner of Proceeding in Causes involving the Crime of Solicitation* (Vatican Polyglot Press, 1962), available at http://www.vatican.va/resources/resources_crimen-sollicitationis-1962_en.html (last accessed 20 July 2010), para 73. See extracts in Appendix B.

11. Ibid, para 42.
12. Ibid, para 42c.
13. Ibid, para 52.
14. Allen, *All the Pope's Men,* 300–301.
15. See Geoffrey Robertson and Andrew Nicol, *Media Law* (3rd edn, Penguin, London, 2006), 462–3.
16. See Eric Plumer, *The Catholic Church and American Culture* (University of Scranton Press, London, 2009), 51.
17. *Crimen Sollicitationis,* Appendix B, para 11.
18. Ibid, para 65.
19. Ibid, para 52.
20. Defendant's memorandum in support of second motion to dismiss for subject matter jurisdiction, 16–17.
21. Murphy Report, Chapter 4, para 82.
22. Murphy Report, Chapter 4, para 24.
23. Excerpt from *Codicis Iuris Canonici Fontes,* 20 February 1866, para 14.
24. 2002 Letter. See US Conference of Catholic Bishops, *Essential Norms,* approved 8 December 2002, note 7.
25. The *Guide* is available at the Vatican website: http://www.vatican.va/resources/resources_guide-CDF-procedures_en.html (last accessed 20 July 2010).
26. Andrew Cole, 'The Church's Penal Law and the Abuse of Children', *Thinking Faith,* 17 June 2010, 2. Father Cole has assumed the website 'Guidance' reflects Canon Law, but it has now been overruled by *de gravioribus delictus.*
27. Fr F. Lombardi, 'The Significance of the Publication of the New Norms Concerning the Most Serious Crimes', undated, available at http://www.vatican.va/resources/resources_lombardi-nota-norme_en.html (last accessed 20 July 2010).

4. THE LATERAN TREATY

1. Lord Acton, letter to Mandell Creighton, 5 April 1887.
2. D. P. O'Connell, *International Law* (Stevens, London, 1970), 289.
3. *Thome Guadaloupe v Assoc Italiana di St Cecelia* (1937) 8 ILR 151.
4. 'The Presence of the Holy See in the International Organizations', lecture by Archbishop Jean-Louis Tauran, 22 April 2002, available at http://www.vatican.va/roman_curia/secretariat_state/documents/rc_seg-st_doc_20020422_tauran_en.html.
5. Ibid, 6.
6. CDF, *Doctrinal Note on Some Questions Regarding the Participation of Catholics in Political Life,* issued by Cardinal Joseph Ratzinger and Tarcisio Bertone, 24 November 2002, available at http://www.vatican.va/roman_curia/congregations/cfaith/documents/rc_con_cfaith_doc_20021124_politica_en.html (last accessed 21 July 2010). On the prohibition of sexual intercourse within marriage if it is only for

pleasure, see John Finnis, 'Reason, Faith and Homosexual Acts' (2001) 62 *Catholic Social Science Review* 61.

7. CDF, *Considerations Regarding Proposals to Give Legal Recognition to Unions between Homosexual Persons*, issued by Cardinal Ratzinger, 3 June 2003, para 4.

8. See the statement of sovereignty given by the Holy See to the UN Committee on the Rights of the Child, in Holy See, *Initial Report to the Committee on the Rights of the Child on the Optional Protocol on the Sale of Children, Child Prostitution and Child Pornography*, 14 May 2010, available at http://www2.ohchr.org/english/bodies/crc/docs/AdvanceVersions/CRC-C-OPSC-VAT-1.doc (last accessed 24 July 2010), 1, para 4(b).

9. See, for example, Philip Morgan, *Italy 1915–1940* (Sempringham Publishing, Bedford, 1998), 6–9, 25, 50–52, and Patricia Knight, *Mussolini and Fascism* (Routledge, London, 2003), 478.

10. Lord Acton (J. Rufus Fears (ed.)), *Selected Writings of Lord Acton*, Volume 3 (Liberty Fund, Indianapolis, 2000), 340.

11. See John Hite and Chris Henton, *Fascist Italy* (Hodder Education, London, 1998) 75, quoting letter from Pius XI to French Ambassador Beyens.

12. See Christopher Duggan, *The Force of Destiny: A History of Italy since 1796* (Allen Lane, London, 2007), 478.

13. David Yallop, *In God's Name* (Corgi, London, 1985), 146–7. In this period, the Vatican Bank also acquired ownership of a company that manufactured condoms.

14. *Vienna Convention on the Law of Treaties* (1969), Article 2. Article 3 mentions that 'the present Convention does not apply to agreements concluded between states and other subjects of international law' – other subjects like, I suggest, the Holy See.

15. Gary Wills, 'Forgive Not', *New Republic*, 18 May 2010.

16. See James Brown-Scott, 'The Treaty Between Italy and the Vatican', (1929), 23 *American Society of International Law Proceedings*, 19.

17. Ibid.

18. See 'Papal Diplomacy: God's Ambassadors', *Economist*, 21 July 2007.

19. 'Britain's Human Rights Policies Violate National Law, Pope Says', *The Times*, 2 February 2010.

20. Letter from FCO to Jennifer Robinson, 19 July 2010.

21. Letter from FCO to Jennifer Robinson, 10 August 2010.

22. 'Britain Sparks Row with Vatican Over Proposal to Close Embassy', *The Times*, 9 January 2006.

23. Letter from FCO to Jennifer Robinson, 4 August 2010.

5. THE STATEHOOD TEST

1. The 'declaratory theory' of recognition of states whereby statehood depends on satisfying formal criteria has replaced the constitutive theory. See, for example, James Crawford, *The Creation of States in International Law* (2nd edn,

OUP, Oxford, 2006); Ian Brownlie, *Principles of Public International Law* (6th edn, OUP, Oxford, 2003), 86–8; Gillian Triggs, *International Law: Contemporary Principles and Practices* (Butterworths/Lexis Nexis, Sydney, 2005), 93.

2. Bart McDowell, *Inside the Vatican* (National Geographic Society, Washington, DC, 2008), 15. Recent FCO travel advice (April 2010) counts the Vatican population as numbering 466, with 333 diplomats working abroad.

3. See Yasmin Abdullah, 'The Holy See at United Nations Conferences: Church or State?', (1996), 96(7) *Columbia Law Review*, 1835.

4. See Hyginus E. Cardinale, *The Holy See and the International Order* (Smythe, Bucks, 1976).

5. See Herb Wright, 'The Status of Vatican City' (1944), 38 *American Journal of International Law*, 452.

6. *Inside the Vatican,* produced by Gruppe S Filmproduktion for ZDF, Episode I, 'An Easter Lamb'.

7. Ian Brownlie, *Principles of Public International Law* (6th edn, OUP, Oxford, 2003), 71.

8. Cardinale, *The Holy See and the International Order*, 32.

9. Abdullah, 'The Holy See at United Nations Conferences', 1865.

10. See Stephen E. Young and Alison Shea, 'Separating Law from Church: A Research Guide to the Vatican City State' (2007), 99 *Law Library Journal*, 589, 595.

11. *Vienna Convention on Consular Relations* (1963), Article 5, 'Consular Functions'.

12. See Young and Shea, 'Separating Law from Church', note 10 above, 595.

13. The most cynical of such appointments come from Australia, where Labour governments have exploited the attraction of the post (until 2009, coupled with Ireland), for Catholic politicians: hence the appointment of Vince Gair (an opposition senator whose seat was coveted), Brian Burke (a reward for a corrupt crony) and Tim Fischer (leader of an opposition party).

14. Sandro Magistere, 'Mission Impossible: Eject the Holy See from the UN', 21 August 2008, available at http://chiesa.espresso.repubblica.it/articolo/162301?eng=y (last accessed 22 July 2010).

15. See Young and Shea, 'Separating Law from Church', 605–6.

16. Crawford, *The Creation of States in International Law*, 221–5.

17. Triggs, *International Law*, 188

18. Crawford, citing Jorri Duursma, *Fragmentation and the International Relations of Micro-states: Self-determination and Statehood* (Cambridge Studies in Comparative and International Law, Cambridge, 1996), 386–7.

19. D. P. O'Connell, *International Law* (Stevens, London, 1970), 290.

20. Brownlie, *Principles of Public International Law*, 64.

21. The best treatment is Abdullah, 'The Holy See at United Nations Conferences'. *Satow's Diplomatic Practice*, which recognizes the Holy See as a state.

22. Rupert Cornwell, *God's Banker: The Life and Death of Roberto Calvi* (Unwin, London, 1984). The Vatican refused to take delivery of Italian court summonses on

Marcinkus on the ground that since it was a sovereign state they had to be presented through the Italian Foreign Ministry and the Italian Embassy to the Holy See: see 225.

23. David Yallop, *In God's Name* (Corgi, 1985).

24. Rev. John Triglio Jnr and Rev. Kenneth Brighenti, Catholicism for Dummies (Wiley, London, 2003), 384.

25. See *Alperin v Vatican Bank* (2005) 410 F. 3d 532; R. Behar, 'Washing Money in the Holy See', *Fortune*, 16 August 1999, 128–37; and E. Pollack, *The Pretender: How Martin Frankel Fooled the World* (Free Press, New York, 2002).

26. Young and Shea, 'Separating Law from Church', 599.

27. Msgr Leo Cushley, 'A Light to the Nations: Vatican Diplomacy and Global Politics', 2007 Habigen Lecture, available at http://www.stthomas.edu/cathstudies/programs/habiger/default.html (last accessed 20 July 2010), 7–8.

6. THE HOLY SEE AND THE UNITED NATIONS

1. See Cardinale, *The Holy See and the International Order*, 256.

2. André Hellegers, quoted in Yallop, *In God's Name*, 59. The Commission were 64:4 in favour of contraception.

3. 'Papal Diplomacy: God's Ambassadors', *Economist*, 21 July 2007.

4. ECOSOC Resolution 1296 (XLIV), *Arrangements for Consultation with Non-Governmental Organizations*, 23 May 1968, para 12.

5. Christian Koenig, *International Review of the Red Cross*, 280 (28 February 1991), 37–48.

6. Hilary Charlesworth and Christine Chinkin, *The Boundaries of International Law: A Feminist Perspective* (Manchester University Press, Manchester, 2000), 135.

7. See 'U.S. Catholic Bishops Conference Says Pro-Abortion Politicians Should be Shunned', *LifeSite News*, 21 September 2004, and 27 September 2004.

8. The best account is found in Yasmin Abdullah, 'The Holy See at UN Conferences – Church or State?' (1996), 96(7) *Colombia Law Review*, 1835.

9. Ibid, 1851, note 126.

10. Ibid, 1853. Also Charlesworth and Chinkin, *The Boundaries of International Law*, 134–6.

11. Paola Totaro, 'The Enforcer with a Gentle Manner', *Sydney Morning Herald*, 15 April 2010.

12. Nick Kristof, 'The Pope and AIDS', *The New York Times*, 8 May 2005.

13. Kathy Lette, 'Ovarian Roulette', in *Because I Am a Girl* (Vintage, London, 2010), 69.

14. Vatican's Archbishop Burke, 'No Communion for Catholic Politicians Who Support Abortion', *Lifestyle News*, 2 May 2009.

15. Charlesworth and Chinkin, *The Boundaries of International Law*, 134.

16. Allen, *All the Pope's Men*, 375–6.

17. Geoffrey Robertson, *Crimes Against Humanity* (Penguin, London, 2006) 340, 424, 433–4.

18. 'Top Cardinal Made Plea for Pinochet', *Sunday Times*, 11 February 1999, 24.

19. See Carla del Ponte, *'Madame Prosecutor: Confrontations with the Culture of Impunity'* (Other Press, 2008), 189–91; 267–9.

20. See Richard Wilson, 'The Catholic Church Acts as a Law Unto Itself', *New Humanist*, Volume 125, Issue 3, May/June 2010, 13.

21. *Prosecutor v Akayesu*, Case No. ICTR-96–4-T, September 1998, para 597.

22. *Raquel Martí de Mejía v Perú*, Case 10.970, Report No. 5/96, Inter-Am.C.H.R., OEA/Ser.L/V/II.91 Doc. 7 at 157 (1996).

23. See *Menesheva v Russia* (2006) ECHR Application No. 59261/00, 9 March 2006.

24. *In re E (a child) (AP) (Appellant) (Northern Ireland)* [2008] UKHL 66.

25. See Cherie Booth's contribution in Peter Stanford (ed) 'Why I am Still a Catholic' (Continuum Publishing, 2005) 25.

26. This internal war began with 'The Ratzinger Letter', which condemned the liberation theology movement on the basis that its Marxist influences and class-based critiques were contrary to church teachings and might lead to socialist dictatorships: 'Those who make themselves accomplices of similar enslavements betray the very poor they mean to help.' Concerned in the 1980s about guerrilla priests and not paedophile priests, Ratzinger expelled Leonardo Boff and other intellectual leaders who urged the church to radical action in taking up the cause of the peasants and the unemployed: see Phillip Berryman, *Liberation Theology* (IB Taurus, London, 1987), 185–200 ('The Ratzinger Letter').

27. Ian Linden, *Global Catholicism* (Hurst, London, 2009), 148.

28. John Cornwall, *The Pope in Winter* (Penguin, London, 2005), 255.

29. Ibid, 276–7.

30. John L. Allen Jnr, *Pope Benedict XVI* (Continuum, London, 2005). 17 (amnesia); 27–30 (whitewashing); 152 *et seq* (liberation theology); 177 (women); 189 (IVF); 205 (condoms); 206 (gays); 213 (beatings of gays).

7. THE CONVENTION ON THE RIGHTS OF THE CHILD

1. Holy See, *Report to the Committee on the Rights of the Child*, 28 March 1994. Article 2(d) of the Vienna Convention on the Law of Treaties defines a reservation as 'a unilateral statement ... made by a state, whereby it purports to exclude or modify the legal effect of certain provisions of the treaties in their application to that state'. Article 19 insists that a reservation 'must not be inconsistent with the object and purpose of the treaty'.

2. Committee on the Rights of the Child, *Concluding Observations of the Committee on the Rights of the Child: Holy See*, 27 November 1995, CRC/C/15/Add.46.

3. See recent criticism of the Holy See's failure to report: Frank Jordans, 'UN: Vatican Child Rights Report 13 Years Overdue', *Associated Press*, 16 July 2010, available at http://www.google.com/hostednews/ap/article/ALeqM5iVXpIdqtw NCWrNHwSiMtY3LCMNxAD9GVICLOo (last accessed 22 July 2010).

4. See Articles 2(d) and 19 of the Convention.

5. Holy See, *Initial Report to the Committee on the Rights of the Child on the Optional Protocol on the Sale of Children, Child Prostitution and Child Pornography*, 14 May 2010, CRC/C/3/Add 27, para 57.

6. CRC/C/3/Add.27, para. 16 (b).

7. Cumberledge Report, *Safeguarding with Confidence* (2007), 5.21

8. CRC/C/3/Add.27, para 23 (a).

8. A CASE TO ANSWER?

1. 'Pope Engineered Cover-up of Child Sex Abuses Says Theologian', *Irish Times*, 16 April 2010.

2. Alan Dershowitz, 'Thou Shalt Not Stereotype', http://www.huffingtonpost.com/alan-dershowitz.

3. Gary Wills, 'Forgive Not', *New Republic*, 18 May 2010.

4. See the *Convention on the Non-Applicability of Statutory Limitations to War Crimes & Crimes Against Humanity* (1968) and Geoffrey Robertson, *Crimes Against Humanity* (Penguin, London, 2006) Chapter 7.

5. Rev. John Triglio and Rev. Kenneth Brighenti, 'Catholicism for Dummies' (Wiley), 129.

6. *W v Edgell* [1990] 1 All ER 835, and *Tarasoff v Regents of University of California* (1976) 17 Cal 3d 425.

7. John L. Allen Jr, 'Don't be Daft – You Can't Put the Pope on Trial', *Spectator*, 14 April 2010, available at http://www.spectator.co.uk/spectator/thisweek/5879613/5911953/part_3/dont-be-daft-you-cant-put-the-pope-on-trial.thtml (last accessed 25 July 2010).

8. *Crimen*, paras 66–8.

9. Ibid, para 70.

10. See Alma Guillermoprieto, 'The Mission of Father Marcial', *New York Review of Books*, 24 June 2010, 28.

11. 'Pope, in Sermon, Says He Won't be Intimidated', *The New York Times*, 28 March 2010, available at http://www.nytimes.com/2010/03/29/world/europe/29pope.html (last accessed 25 July 2010).

12. 'CDF Official Details Response to Sex Abuse', *National Catholic Reporter*, 31 March 2010, available at http://ncronline.org/news/accountability/cdf-official-details-response-sex-abuse (last accessed 25 July 2010).

13. Leslie Townley, 'Conceal or Reveal? The Role of Law in Black Collar Crime' (2007), 1 *Public Space* (*The Journal of Law and Social Justice*), 30. And see, for Pope John Paul II's rejection of the 'zero tolerance' option as contrary to Canon Law, David Yallop, *The Power and the Glory* (Constable, London, 2007) 449. Pope Benedict has, for the US but not for the rest of the world, accepted that a watered-down version of 'one strike and you are out' can be applied by US

bishops to the extent that one act of sexual abuse should disqualify a priest from 'continuing in active ministry': see 'Something Missing', *National Catholic Reporter* 9 August 2010.

9. CRIMES AGAINST HUMANITY

1. *United States v Ohlendorf (Case 9)* (1946–7) IV Trials of War Criminals before Nuremberg Military Tribunals, 408.
2. The Regensburg District Authority has issued a press release confirming that Benedict, born in the village of Pentling in the district of Regensburg, has not renounced his German citizenship or applied for its cancellation. German law allows dual citizenship and Benedict remains entitled to vote in German elections.
3. *Prosecutor v Tadic* Decision on Defence Motion, IT-94–1-AR72–2, October 1994, para 141.
4. *United Nations Diplomatic Conference of Plenipotentiaries on the Establishment of an International Criminal Court*, Rome, 15–17 July 1998, Official Records, Volume II, 150–52.
5. *Decision Pursuant to Article 15 of the Rome Statute on the Authorization of an Investigation into the Situation in the Republic of Kenya*, ICC-01/09, International Criminal Court (ICC), 31 March 2010, available at: http://www.unhcr.org/refworld/docid/4bc2fe372.html (accessed 26 July 2010).
6. Article 7(1)(g) Rome Statute.
7. Article 7(1)(k) Rome Statute.
8. *Prosecutor v Brima, Kamara and Kanu (AFRC Appeal Judgment)*, Special Court for Sierra Leone, 22 February 2008, paras 197–202.
9. *Prosecutor v Vasiljevic* IT-98–32T, 29 November 2002, para 29.
10. *Yamashita v US* (1946) 327 US.1.
11. Antonio Cassese, *International Criminal Law* (2nd edn, OUP, Oxford, 2008), 245–6, and see paras 11.4.2 to 11.4.4.
12. See Hector Olasolo, *Criminal Responsibility of Senior Political and Military Leaders as Principals to International Crimes* (Hart Publishing, Oxford, 2009), 103 and n. 120 therein.
13. International Court Assembly of State Parties, *Elements of Crimes*, ICC-ASP/1/3 (part II(b)) adopted 9 September 2002.
14. Ibid.
15. See Rome Statute, Article 21, and William A. Schabas, *An Introduction to the International Criminal Court* (2nd edn, CUP, Cambridge, 2004), 356.
16. This was the ruling of the ICTY Appeal Chamber in *Prosecutor v Kunarac*, IT-96–23/I-A, 12 June 2002, para 98: 'A Policy component is no part of customary law, so long as the crimes against humanity are more than "isolated or random acts".' Others have suggested that the inconsistency may not be as stark as I fear. Thus Darryll Robinson argues that it simply reasserts the principle that a

'policy' cannot be inferred from the mere fact of inaction, but if the state was awar of the crimes, and had the means to punish or report them but did not do so, an inference could still be drawn that it intended to encourage them. See Roy S. Lee (ed.), *The ICC: Elements of Crime and Rules of Procedure and Evidence* (2001), 76.

17. See Cassesse, *International Criminal Law*, 93.

18. *Case Concerning the Arrest Warrant of 11 April 2000 (Democratic Republic of the Congo v Belgium)* (2002) ICJ Rep 2.

19. See, for example, *Al-Adsani v The United Kingdom*, App No. 35763/97, Council of Europe: European Court of Human Rights, 21 November 2001.

20. See 'Police Seize Cardinal's Computer in Sex Abuse Enquiry', *The Times*, 25 June 2010, 43, and 'Police Raids in Sex Abuse Cases Focus on Belgium's Catholic Hierarchy', *Guardian,* 25 June 2010, 20.

21. *Lautsi v Italy*, App No. 30814/06, European Court of Human Rights, 3 November 2009 (referred to Grand Chamber).

22. *Pelligrino v Italy*, App No. 30882/96, European Court of Human Rights, 20 July 2001.

23. *Reverend James O'Callaghan v Reverend Charles O'Sullivan* (1925) Irish Reports 90.

24. *Gillfillan v R* (1980) 637 F 2b 924.

25. Justice Secretary Kenneth Clarke has now announced that the UK's universal jurisdiction law will be further shackled by a requirement that no warrant can be obtained without the DPP's consent.

26. *R v Rafique* [1993] QB 843.

10. CAN THE POPE BE SUED?

1. See *Bazley v Curry* (1999) 174 DLR (4th) 45 (Supreme Court of Canada); *Lister v Hesley Hall* [2002] 1 AC 215 (UK House of Lords) and *NSW v Lepore* (2003) 195 ALR 412 (High Court of Australia), discussed in Simon Deakin, Angus Johnson and Basil Markesinis, *Tort Law* (5th edn, OUP, Oxford, 2003), 593–5. In *Maga v Trustees of Birmingham Catholic Archdiocese* [2010] EWCA Civ 256, the English Court of Appeal gave broad scope to the requirement of a 'connection' between a priest and the church that is necessary to support a child sex abuse claim.

2. See *Trustees of the Roman Catholic Church v Ellis* (2007) NSWCA 117, where a body representing members of the Catholic Church could not be made liable for actions by an assistant parish priest. This was a bad case where the victim had complained to the priest's superior who, without his knowledge, arranged for him to be confronted by his abuser to 'work things out'. 'It is rather chilling to contemplate', said the judge, that the superior might have been another sex abuser. See first instance decision *Ellis v Pell* [2006] NSWSC 109, para 90.

3. Lucian C. Martinez, 'Sovereign Impunity: Does the Foreign Sovereign Immunity Act Bar Lawsuits Against the Holy See in Clerical Sexual abuse Cases?' (2008), 44 *Texas International Law Journal*, 123, 144.